Protestants First
Orangeism in Nineteenth Century Scotland

Protestants First
Orangeism in Nineteenth Century Scotland

E. W. McFarland

EDINBURGH UNIVERSITY PRESS

© Elaine McFarland 1990

Edinburgh University Press
22 George Square, Edinburgh

Distributed in North America
by Columbia University Press
New York

Set in Linotron Plantin
by Koinonia Ltd, Bury and
Printed in Great Britain by
The Alden Press,
Oxford

British Library Cataloguing
   in Publication Data
McFarland, Elaine
   Protestants first: orangeism in
   nineteenth century Scotland.
   1. Scotland. Protestantism,
   history
   I. Title
   280.409411

ISBN 0 7486 0202 X

Contents

Key to Abbreviations

DGM	Deputy Grand Master.
DS	District Secretary
GC	Glasgow Courier.
GCA	Glasgow Conservative Association
GCOA	Glasgow Conservative Operatives Association.
GH	Glasgow Herald.
GN	Glasgow News.
GS	Grand Secretary
GT	Greenock Telegraph.
GWMEA	Glasgow Working Men's Evangelistic Association.
HDGM	Honorary Deputy Grand Master.
HSGM	Honorary Substitute Grand Master.
INL	Irish National League.
LOI	Loyal Orange Institution.
LOL	Loyal Orange Lodge.
LU	Liberal Unionist.
MWCGM	Most Worshipful County Grand Master.
MWGM	Most Worshipful Grand Master.
NBDM	North British Daily Mail.
OAS	Orange Association of Scotland.
OI of GB	Orange Institution of Great Britain.
OPWA	Orange and Protestant Workers Association.
PCA	Paisley Conservative Association.
RBP	Royal Black Preceptory.
SPA	Scottish Protestant Alliance.
SRA	Strathclyde Regional Archives.
SRO	Scottish Records Office.
SRS	Scottish Reformation Society.
WDC	Western Divisional Council.
WPGM	Worshipful Past Grand Master.
WSPA	West of Scotland Protestant Association.

Preface

Orangeism is a major form of working class organisation in Low-lands Scotland, and estimates of its current membership range from 50,000 to 80,000. Yet, despite its high profile on Scotland's streets during the summer marching season, the Loyal Orange Institution (LOI) remains for most a shadowy and perplexing body. Much has been assumed about the movement, and it has proved fertile ground for myths, anecdotes and general hysteria.

This book examines the LOI's formative period of development in the nineteenth century, using actual manuscript and archival material. It is not a polemic against, and even less an apology for Orangeism. Adequate supplies of both already exist. I have instead tried to understand the movement from a sociological standpoint.

The opening chapters deal with the organisational structure and belief system of Orangeism. Previous theoretical approaches to the movement are critically assessed, and its relevance to debates on the nature of class domination and working class sectionalism under-lined. This is followed by an overview of the Order's development outside Scotland.

A central aim of chapters four to ten is to explain why the ideological power of Orangeism was not fully mobilised as a mass social force in nineteenth century Scotland. For this we analyse the internal characteristics which lay behind its numerical strength, such as a high Ulster Protestant membership and rank and file tensions, and consider how these interacted with certain unique features of Scottish society and politics. Orange relations with the Scottish Churches and the Conservative Party are featured in detail.

Finally, the present role of Orangeism in modern Scotland is examined, identifying potential lines of development, particularly in terms of political involvement.

The book began life as a doctoral thesis at Glasgow University and thanks are due to my supervisors Bridget Fowler and H. F. Moore-house, and also to John Foster, Henry Patterson, Jim Whiston, John

McFarland and Miss Ann C. Hay of the Conservative and Unionist Association, Edinburgh. I am particularly grateful to those LOI members who gave me their time and assistance. Most are identified by their initials. Thanks to Margaret Bright and Gemma McLaughlin for typing .

1
What is Orangeism?

This is a very basic question, yet a precise definition is necessary given the diffuse body of militant Protestant and anti-Catholic sentiment to which an 'Orange' epithet is often confusingly applied.

Much to the dismay of conspiracy theorists, one point which should be clarified at the outset is the relation between Orangeism and Freemasonry. This has often been misconceived in anecdotal accounts. Freemasonry does represent one of the most important precursors of Orangeism in terms of organisation and symbolism. 'Borrowings' from the older body, as the Orange historian Sibbet indicates, were notably employed in the LOI's formative years.[1] This seems particularly probable in Scotland with the strength of Masonry here in the eighteenth century.[2] There is, however, *no* evidence of an organisational link between the two bodies in Scotland, nor of an overlap of personnel in the period of study.

Instead a more fruitful point of reference with the Masonic Society is the hierarchical system of lodges which characterised the Scottish LOI for most of the nineteenth century and beyond. There were, for example, four types of Orange Lodge: the Local, sometimes referred to as the Private or Primary Lodge; the District, covering an area such as Bridgeton or Paisley; the County Grand Lodge, such as Ayrshire; and the Grand Orange Lodge of Scotland.[3]

Again like Freemasonry a certain democratic input was present in this structure. Thus every Orangeman joined firstly his local lodge whose officebearers were open to annual election. In turn the members of the District Lodge were drawn from the Private Lodges in the area, and the Grand Lodge consisted of officers drawn from the Districts and Counties. Meeting twice yearly, this latter body provided policy direction for the movement, organised and co-ordinated the major 12th of July demonstration and November *soirée* each year, and acted as a final court of appeal on disciplinary matters. As in the local lodges its officers, including that of Most Worshipful Grand Master (MWGM) were open to annual election, though often this could become a formality.[4]

In the local lodges, each with an average of 30-40 members, the majority of business seems to have been dominated by Scripture readings, routine administrative work, and the applications of new members. Indeed, three accounts from very different stages of Orange history describe meetings which follow this familiar format.[5]

As well as its fairly straightforward organisational structure, a further similarity with the Masonic Order was the LOI's structure of 'degrees' of knowledge and initiation, which played a further vital part in the regular lodge meeting. Through this mechanism the new entrant was first initiated into the ritual of the 'Orange' degree and the scriptural knowledge and biblical allegory and symbolism associated with this rank. After six months good conduct he would move into the 'Purple Marksman's' degree, having been initiated into the meaning of another set of signs and allegories. This 'inner circle' was originally introduced around the 1798 Rebellion in Ireland when the persecution of the republican United Irishmen drove many former members and associates into the Orange Order for protection, and it functioned as a means of excluding those of dubious political affiliations from further infiltration into the Order.

Based on 'Gideon's Chosen Few' from the Old Testament, the initiation rituals associated with these degrees, though possibly involving some test of courage in the past, were more usually pedestrian versions of original Masonic degrees.[6]

These were the basic structural characteristics of the nineteenth century LOI. However, before moving on to an analysis of the movement's belief system it is worth noting a parallel body which, unlike Freemasonry, *has* been decisively linked by membership and ideology. This is the splendidly named 'Imperial Black Chapter of the British Commonwealth', or 'Royal Black Preceptory'.

Known colloquially as 'the sedate order' as opposed to the 'rag-tag' rank and file Orange Institution, the RBP appealed to a more discerning interest in ceremony and ritual rather than public procession. For although sharing the same roots as the Purple degree, it displayed much more of an esoteric and allegorical emphasis described as a 'system of Byzantine splendour'. Though technically a separate body with its headquarters in Belfast, one could not become a member of a Black Preceptory (ie lodge) without first being an Orangeman. Again this organisation included a complex degree and rank system, and on joining every member was able to go through a series of ten degrees based on an elaborate interpretation of the Scriptures.

IDEOLOGY

Orangeism's organisational features were complemented by a distinctive ideology.

No single authoritative source exists for the Orange world view and as well as Orange public utterances of the period, four key texts have been employed: *Popery, the Man of Sin and the Son of Iniquity* (1853) by Orange Chaplain Rev. Robert Gault; *The Burning of Santiago, but an Accident in the Mariolatry of the Church of Rome* (1864) by Grand Secretary Thomas Macklin; *The Protestant Magazine* (1873/4) by H. A. Long; and *A Catechism of the Principles of Protestantism* (1879) by Grand Master Chalmers I. Paton. These texts were available to the average Orangeman. Familiarity with the 'Catechism', in fact, became a prerequisite for passing to the Purple degree.

One useful way to approach a clearer codification of the material contained here is to assess in turn the positive and negative moments in the LOI's ideology, militant Protestantism and anti-Catholicism.

As regards the former, the traditional Reformation concepts of Biblical authority and the sole mediatorship of Christ were central, with particular importance being attached to a fundamentalist interpretation of the Scriptures. Thus, reasoned Paton, Protestantism is:

> Pure Scriptural Christianity... the very religion brought by Our Lord Jesus Christ and by His Apostles... The Bible alone is the Protestant rule of faith from which nothing can be taken away and nothing added. Absolute and supreme authority belongs to the Bible because it is the Word of God. The whole Word of God is contained in the Scriptures... which are the very Word of God and nothing else and we have no other revelation of the Truth or the Word of God.[7]

Co-existing with these traditional evangelical sentiments was also an awareness of the liberating potential of Protestantism. The point was given particular emphasis by Paton:

> Protestants hold that every man is entitled – nay bound – to think for himself in matters of religion, to enquire for himself into the meaning of scriptures, the doctrines to be believed.[8]

Although at this point there may seem little to distinguish Orangeism from wider evangelical tendencies, in fact as Roberts notes, the LOI's framework of belief contains a unique mixture of both Lutheran and Calvinist strains, emphasising respectively faith, the Scriptures and an Apostolic church, and individual acceptance of the work ethic and salvation by divine grace.[9] Crucially this in turn gave the Order a basis for claiming a superior ecumenical stance. As

Grand Master George McLeod explained, 'we have in our ranks episcopalians and presbyterians of various denominations and we never allow the little schisms between these parties to be an obstacle in our way'.[10]

Whereas in the contemporary Order, as Bruce notes, this 'ecumenicalism' has produced a highly generalised and non-controversial position on ecclesiastical issues, in the nineteenth century it was accompanied by very definite views on church government and the church and state relationship, with the Order holding that:

> the establishment of the Church of Scotland was consistent with the National religion of God and the Church of God and the religion taught in the Holy Scriptures and that its disestablishment would be a great national sin and national calamity.[11]

In addition the ability to appeal to *all* Protestants set the LOI, it believed, above the various competing denominations with its own members 'adoring the Gospel, walking by faith, fighting the good fight of faith and rejoicing in hope: not mere controversialists but humble and devout followers of Christ'.[12] In contrast with the supineness of 'nominal protestants' and assaults from within the fortress of evangelical Christianity, indicted by Gault, the Order was quite simply '*the* foremost organisation for Protestantism' or 'Protestantism in action'.[13] Indeed the language and symbolism of Orangeism here were frequently drawn from the Old Testament books of Exodus, the Prophets and Ruth and were quite coherent with casting the Orangemen in the role of 'the Chosen Few' and 'the Children of Israel'.[14] Such strident claims were bound to affect relations with the Scottish churches.

The religious and ecclesiastical principles of Orangeism also brought it into the political arena, for the primary safeguards for 'the Protestant Religion' in Britain were seen as lying precisely in 'the Protestant Crown and Constitution', as established in the Revolutionary settlement of 1689. In practice, in the nineteenth century this promoted Orange support for the Conservative Party as the best guardians of these institutions. 'They go in for a national church, national creed... as well as individual Christianity... '[15] Again it is important to note that in this alliance the LOI was viewed by its members as the *superior* organisation, for its 'true Christianity' set it above political as well as ecclesiastical party.

We will examine in detail later how 'loyal' support for the Conservatives was also basically *conditional* on the party retaining its 'Protestant' reputation in Orange eyes. At this point though, the subversive potential of the 'Protestantism First' principle is best illustrated by the rather surprising instance of Orange monarchism.

Thus, although the monarch received extremes of veneration and loyalty, this was largely dependent on his or her retaining the 'true faith' and a proper respect for Civil and Religious Liberty. For implicit here, as Roberts suggests, was Huguenot belief inspired by the neo-Calvinist Beza, and propagated in sixteenth century Scotland by Andrew Melville, that there is a right of necessary and lawful resistance to injustice and tyranny.[16] It was such a position, as Roberts again suggests, that provided the specific justification for UVF involvement before 1914 but was also most strongly voiced in the nineteenth century by H. A. Long against no less a figure than Queen Victoria.

> We have been often grieved to see our Queen travelling on the Sabbath. Should Her Majesty so far forget herself as to do so again, we may see a blessed strike – men refusing to toil unnecessarily on the Lord's day. A lesson of this sort from the million to the ten would be the proper thing. Our operatives have often struck against capital; let them strike against sin in high places.[17]

The same sense of 'absolute values' can also be identified in Orangeism's anti-Catholicism. Though in keeping with the Grand Lodge's quest for a respectable status for the LOI. as a religious organisation rather than a fighting society, it was on Roman Catholicism as a system not on its individual practitioners that the official Orange attack was concentrated. Again C I Paton emphasised the position when he used the term 'deadly foe', 'he did not speak of papists but of Popery. We ought to have no unkindly feelings towards the poor benighted members of the Church of Rome, but we cannot reject popery with too intense detestation'.[18]

In essence this official ideology stated that Popery differed from Protestantism in its rule of faith, which was basically unscriptural. 'Instead the tradition of the Church is granted equal authority with the Holy Scriptures in all that relates to faith and religious practice'.[19] From this element of human invention, substituted for the spirit and truth of God's worship, were seen to flow three evil consequences: first, it resulted in theological errors such as papal supremacy and infallibility and various sacramental practices; secondly, it produced superstition, exemplified in saint worship and the adoration of relics; finally, it engendered cruelty as demonstrated historically by the Church's intolerant and persecuting spirit and its great wealth as contrasted with its exploitation of poor Roman Catholics. Again a certain democratic element enters the critique here.

In turn, these elements of error, superstition and cruelty pro-

duced among believers another three-fold harvest not only of immorality and disloyalty but of pauperism. At this point indeed the
Orange world view approaches a 'sociology' of religious affiliation,
with some resemblance to an extremely crude version of Weber's
thesis on Protestantism and the rise of capitalism.[20] Paton voices the
point particularly well and is worth quoting at length:

> These differences [between the private judgement of Protes-
> tantism and Roman Catholic spiritual authoritarianism] have
> great effects not only on the whole religious life of those who
> receive them, but extending beyond it and appearing even in
> the intellectual development of those subject to their influ-
> ences; Protestant communities being characterised by general
> intelligence, pursuit of knowledge, activity, industry and enter-
> prise, Popery by apathy, indolence and supineness, so that
> while Protestant communities are generally flourishing, the
> condition of Popish communities is generally the reverse. The
> Protestant doctrine of the right of personal judgement facili-
> tates the mind to activity, whilst the Popish doctrine lays an
> arrest on the very exercise of the intellectual faculties and
> reduces man to a state where something of a mental torpor
> locks securely chains which bind the soul.[21]

The geographical evidence provided here was plentiful, including
the economic contrasts between Holland and Spain, or New England and Mexico. For Rev. Gault, however, it was above all Ireland
which 'affords a lamentable illustration of the baneful effects of
Popery... where it was fatal to temperance and prosperity... a weight
which hinders the progress of all to whom it is allowed'.[22]

There is less in Orangeism's 'No Popery' than in the Order's
'positive Protestantism' to distinguish it from other anti-Catholic
groups of the nineteenth century, such as the West of Scotland
Protestant Association, but it is particularly remarkable for the
extremely formulaic and stylised nature of its rhetoric. This feature
indeed leads itself to presentation in diagrammatic form (see Fig. 1).

Here it must be emphasised that it is not possible to reconstruct
with any degree of accuracy how the mass of such material was
understood and articulated by ordinary rank and file Orangemen
(particularly the more arcane fulminations on the Waldensian and
Albigensian martyrs). Nevertheless, the official Orange ideology
does appear vital for the repertoire of images and explanations
ordinary members could draw on in their relations with Roman
Catholics in the community and the workplace; although in its
reproduction here 'No Popery' did tend to be reduced to hostility
towards 'the individual erring Roman Catholic', a fact much bemoaned

Fig 1: Summary of Orange Charges against Catholicism

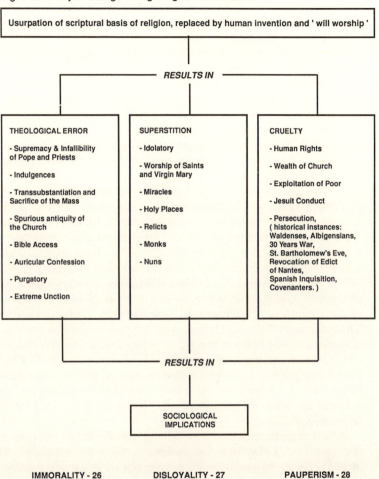

Usurpation of scriptural basis of religion, replaced by human invention and ' will worship '

RESULTS IN

THEOLOGICAL ERROR

- Supremacy & Infallibility of Pope and Priests
- Indulgences
- Transsubstantiation and Sacrifice of the Mass
- Spurious antiquity of the Church
- Bible Access
- Auricular Confession
- Purgatory
- Extreme Unction

SUPERSTITION

- Idolatory
- Worship of Saints and Virgin Mary
- Miracles
- Holy Places
- Relicts
- Monks
- Nuns

CRUELTY

- Human Rights
- Wealth of Church
- Exploitation of Poor
- Jesuit Conduct
- Persecution, (historical instances: Waldenses, Albigensians, 30 Years War, St. Bartholomew's Eve, Revocation of Edict of Nantes, Spanish Inquisition, Covenanters.)

RESULTS IN

SOCIOLOGICAL IMPLICATIONS

IMMORALITY - 26   DISLOYALITY - 27   PAUPERISM - 28 by leading Orangemen such as Robert Stewart. 'I am sorry to say the principles of a good many Orangemen consist of blind hatred to Roman Catholics. This should not be, Roman Catholics are still our brothers, the principles which bind them are the enemy'.[29]

Several other features of the Grand Lodge's 'No Popery' platform also promoted its successful transmission among the Orange rank and file. First, while there is a certain constant quality about elements of the ideology, this does not mean that it was wholly static and unchallenged by actual experience. For particularly significant is the way in which interpretations of the 'Papal threat' which animated 'No Popery' decisively shifted around mid-century from a millennial to a conspiracy emphasis, in accordance with political and ecclesiastical developments in the United Kingdom and on the Continent.

As Best points out, until Biblical criticism freed them in the late nineteenth century, Christians had to make something out of the Biblical prophetic books, since it was orthodox belief that the whole of the Word was spiritually meaningful. One point which seemed clear to many of them was that the downfall of the Pope was prophesied and therefore was a necessary overture to Christ's second coming.[30]

Not surprisingly this was a view enthusiastically embraced in early Orangeism. Gault, for example, writing in the early 1850's was in no doubt. Rome was Babylon and the Pope 'the man of sin… ' of Second Thessalonians ii 3 (hence his book's title). Popery's rise was predicted in Daniel xxii 24-6 but its ruin was decreed by Paul's epistle to Timothy iv 1-3 and in the Book of Revelation. 'The fall of Babylon', Gault confidently predicted, 'will be… the termination of the long night of Romish error, superstition and crime, and will be the dawning of the millenial day when the earth shall enjoy a grand and universal jubilee (Revelations xx, 1-4)'.[31]

A further example of this train of thought is offered in a most bizarre tract from H. A. Long, *Mene: the Numeration of Babylon Mystical* written in 1865. By an extremely obscure computation of Biblical numbers Long predicted the fall of the papacy in 1866. 'Strictly speaking', he explained, 'the Pope is merely a torso, a subsection, a mere hinder part of the Antichrist destined soon to be swept off his pedestal. His toe will go when the ten toes go…'. He continued in strains reminiscent of Blake:

> The mighty eagle will soon uplift the symbolic millstone and cast it into the Tyrian sea. The rising tidal cry will o'ertop the Cottian Alps… on will roll the swelling sound across plains baptized with the blood of the gentle Albigensian maids and brave Hugenot men. Give cheer ye sons of Hamilton! Each man sworn to a life of war against Rome. Ye Orangemen shout

aloud! For Erin Victrix lifts her shamrock from the dust of ages and now embraces , her twin sisters Anglia and Scotia![32]

Although such auguries seem to have been most strongly represented among the educated Victorian bourgeoisie (Long explained that a former tract on 'transubstantiation' was intended for 'the working man' while the *Mene* tract was 'for thinking men only'), it is interesting to speculate here whether this rhetoric contains an echo of Thompson's 'chiliasm of the hopeless'.[33] For such emotional apocalyptic optimism may also have appealed to the average lodge member of the early nineteenth century, many of whom were agricultural workers only recently uprooted from their native province of Ulster and brought to a rapidly industrialising West of Scotland.

At any rate, with greater certainty one can trace the impact of real historical developments upon this millenialism. Initially events in Italy mid-century, with the nationalist uprisings and curbing of Pope Pius IX's temporal powers, seemed to confirm that the fulfilment of Gault and Long's prophecies was imminent. A silver collection was raised for Garibaldi at a *soirée* addressed by the former.[34] However, the driving of the Pontiff from the Papal States did not, of course, produce the Roman Catholic Church's demise and as 1866 passed without the apocalypse such views must have appeared increasingly suspect.

From the late 1860s, though, as the Papacy actually entered a more aggressive 'Ultramontane' phase with the promulgation of the Syllabus of Errors and the Doctrine of Papal Infallibility, millennialism became supplanted in the Orange ideology by conspiracy theory. Basically it stated that Popery was again on the march with a proud and usurping spirit. Emanating from the Pope in Rome but under the particular direction of the Jesuits, a plan had been forged to destroy Protestantism in Britain by undermining it in Crown and Constitution. To this end Gladstone and the Liberal Party, Secularists, Unitarians and Voluntaryists (those opposed to links between church and state) were being actively employed. At a Grand Lodge meeting in 1877, for example, it was resolved that:

> While the government and the mass of professing Protestants in this country seem utterly blind to this [Popery on the offensive], the attempt being made to disestablish churches in the destruction of the acts of parliament which established the Reformation and the Glorious Revolution... may justly excite attention insomuch as such a movement... will pave the way for the complete trump of Popery.... The late increase of Popery in influential quarters [Lord Beaconsfield had recently attended the

Duke of Norfolk's wedding at Brompton Oratory] mean proof
that the dangers in question are far from visionary.[35]

In particular, in Scotland these dangers were threatened by the
restoration of the Roman Catholic hierarchy in the late 1870s, which
the Rev. Robert Thompson explained was 'merely the working
engine, with the Pope and Cardinals for the propagation of their
ends, the wirepullers were the Jesuits, and they work the world'.[36]

Thus, while apocalyptic fervour may have assisted the first Orangemen, this all-embracing theory of Jesuitical conspiracy proved
more appropriate to later generations, many of whom were now
arriving from Ulster in less straitened circumstances, already experienced in industrial work, in textiles and shipbuilding. For them it
provided a 'total' world view – complemented, by the lodges' 'total'
material provisions. As such it was able to encompass not only inter-
communal conflict but major religio-political developments such as
the Disestablishment of the Church of Ireland, Scottish Disestablishment agitation and, above all, threats of Irish Home Rule.

As a final point in analysing the reproduction of the Orange
ideology among the mass of members, it should also be noted that
Grand Lodge figures communicated this not only by Scriptural
exegesis but by ridicule and an emphasis on items of a salacious and
pathological interest in Roman Catholicism. At such level, again in
the attack, the distinction between Catholicism as a system and
individual Roman Catholics often became blurred.

An excellent example here is Macklin's tract on mariolatry (undue
veneration of the Virgin Mary). This work was occasioned by a
disastrous fire in a Chapel in Santiago in Spain, at the height of a
Mass for the festival of the Virgin attended by thousands of female
worshippers. The author eagerly invokes, 'the charred remains and
human cinders... of more than 2500 devotees, suffering in the
worship of the Queen of Mercy. Rome... reeking with the blood of
the human holocaust, the whole burnt offering of maiden innocence
and blooming life'.[37]

Of even greater fascination, though, was the role of the of the
priesthood and convents in Roman Catholicism. The sexual morals
of the celibate priest were particularly suspect, Protestants prefer-
ring, as Best suggests, 'that the clergy face and tower triumphant over
the lusts of the flesh... rather than simply be unconscious of them'.[38]
Thus from auricular confession not only moral corruption but
physical seduction might result – a point which C. I. Paton unfortunately could not bring himself to dwell upon, for the sake of decency.
Frequently underlying such sentiments, again suggests Best, was a
danger perceived towards fathers, husbands and Protestant women,

with the priest seen as embodying a 'particularly Latin form of wickedness' or as Irish and particularly 'virile'. Since the ideal Victorian woman was considered weak, pliable and submissive, she was easy prey.[39]

The latter stress is also present in Orange attitudes towards nuns; as Gault comments, 'women bring all the softness and grace of the female character to win victories for the anti-Christ and his vanguard'. There was, moreover, no scriptural basis for nunneries. 'Christ enjoined on his followers self denial but he never enjoined them to sacrifice their purest and best affections'. Besides, Gault hinted darkly, 'immorality may be no stranger among the inmates'.[40]

The vogue for 'anti conventualism' in the wider militant Protestant movement, when it peaked in the 1840s to 1860s, indeed produced a vast amount of literature ranging from *The Captive Life...* by 'A Clergyman's Widow' to *Geralda, the Demon Nun* and other penny dreadfuls displaying a sadistic interest in 'nun punishments'.[41] The LOI did not apparently enter this market but glancing back at the material above, and particularly at the work of Gault and Long, it is difficult to avoid the suggestion that a semiological reading of some nineteenth century texts would be extremely rewarding. Consistently in *The Man of Sin...*, for example, the former identifies with Protestantism 'truth', 'faith', 'light' and 'liberty'; and with Popery 'the harlot', 'the scarlet woman', 'the holy serpent', 'the viper', 'degeneracy', 'darkness', and the sensuality of worship 'seducing' Protestants into 'Popish places of worship'.[42]

Some of the 'poetry' published in 'The Protestant' too resembles some of the more unpleasant imagery of Wesleyan hymns identified by Thompson.

> A church that's soaked in martyrs' blood,
> Raised many a burning pyre,
> Is surely of Satanic mould,
> Impure, Unholy, Vile.[42]

or witness an example quoted by Cleary:

> Scarlet church of all uncleanness,
> Sink thou to the deep abyss,
> To the orgies of obsceneness,
> Where the hell-bound furies hiss.
> Where thy father Satan's eye,
> May hail thee blood-stained Papacy.
>
> Harlot, cause the midnight rambles,
> Prowling for the life of saints,

Henceforth sit in hellish shambles,
When the scent of murder taints.
Every gust that passeth by -
Ogre, ghoul of Papacy.[44]

Such then were the essentials of the 'True Protestant' and 'No Popery' categories available to the nineteenth century Orangeman. Indeed a large measure of continuity is evident in the present day, though as Bruce suggests the focus of anti-Catholicism has shifted from accusations of sexual depravity to more mundane constitutional issues.[45]

Having dealt with Orangeism's structure and ideology in a fairly descriptive fashion, the remainder of this chapter will briefly examine how the movement can be typified, using approaches from the sociology of religion. The issue here is not only a conceptual one, for this exercise also underlines Orangeism's ideological complexity and potential for internal conflict.

TYPOLOGIES

Many typologies of religious organisations have been presented with various degrees of detail, but most focus on the 'sect'/'church' distinction – the former defined as a non-hierarchical and voluntary association of persons qualified by their religion, the latter a formal and compulsory association for the administration of grace. The difficulty, however, in finding an acceptable 'fit' for Orangeism within any of these typologies is firstly, as noted above, that it had an interdenominational character and membership. Secondly, as subsequent chapters indicate, it has also assumed a number of different roles and emphases in accordance with different historical exigencies. These too continued to co-exist frequently within it as contradictory and ambiguous tendencies in practice and doctrine. In this way, as Roberts suggests, many of the characteristics and attributes of the various points of any typology can appear together.[46]

Let us take as an example one of the main distinguishing features between church and sect, that of qualifications of membership. Those of the LOI mentioned in the Laws and Ordinances are officially rigorous and sect-like, notably in their emphasis on exclusivity. However, as Roberts again indicates, there were times especially in the 1886-1920 period of the Home Rule crisis when membership was open to almost any Protestant, a practical test of membership being whether the candidate was a communicant of one of the Protestant churches. Since those churches' own member-ship qualifications were not always of a sectarian type, then logically neither could the Order's be and in fact there has always been a strong familial and generational motivation to join.

Nor does the movement's ideology provide a definite categorisation. For while on the one hand its backing for state support of the churches and enthusiasm for the Establishment principle as the bulwark of 'National religion' leaned towards the church paradigm, its anti-Catholicism was grounded in more sectarian types, particularly in the juxtaposition of Protestants' private judgement with the authoritarian and compulsory element of Roman Catholicism.

In fact, Orangeism would seem to exhibit a specific combination of both church and sect attributes. Indeed its odd balance of these opposing tendencies may assist in understanding some of its dynamics and successes, for if the church type dominates compromise can lead to rigidity, whereas if the sect type is dominant, initial drive is burned out in a struggle against superior forces.

Nor is it possible in the absence of a crisp and well-defined answer here to simply label the movement a 'secret society'. As regards its system of oaths, its symbolism and practices of concealment, this attribution satisfies Cleary who proceeds to rank Orangeism with other diverse secret societies such as '...the Illuminati, the Sons of Satan, the Know-Nothings, the Communists, the International, the Nihilists and last but not least, 'the bomb-throwing Anarchists, poisonous fungi and wood leeches hugging the deep shade of the lonely forest'.[47]

Cleary's picturesque rhetoric aside, however, one must be mindful above all of the sociologist Simmel's injunction that the protection of a secret society is absolute but temporary.[48] The problem here is that while Orangeism displays in abundance the more superficial of Simmel's criteria, such as degrees of initiation and signs of recognition, in the movement towards expansion and elaboration these elements tended to become more marginal to the Order's everyday functioning.[49] It is perhaps then more correct to speak of Orangeism, for the largest part of its history, as a semi-secret society rather than a formal oath-bound body, though this was its original form.

In short, these points suggest a number of potential sources of tension within Orangeism which in turn militate against a historically monolithic structure. The first stems from its admixture of church and sectarian elements, for despite its positive contribution, noted above, this may also produce friction between the former's hierarchical and sacerdotal tendencies and the latter's ideals of open mobility and equality, which can entail a certain ethos of democracy. The second, though, lies within the movement's ideology, focusing around those conservative and radical elements of theology, between Lutheran piety and respect for authority and the neo-Calvinist conception of lawful resistance to tyranny. Finally, one should also note the more basic potential for disjuncture *between* Orangeism's structure and ideology. If, for example, in any particular period Orangeism had organisationally assumed a markedly hierarchical and authoritarian form, this is no reason to rule out *a priori* the existence of an ideology capable even of a measure of militant populism. This was actually the case in Belfast in the early twentieth century, and is a point neglected in Gibbon's inference that the lodges, 'because of their partly Masonic character... and their ideological fusion with church and chapel structure, their politics and values were in no sense open to democratic contestation.'[50]

NOTES

1. R Sibbet, *Orangeism in Ireland and Throughout the Empire* (1939), Chapter xxiv.
2. See Knoop and Jones, *A Short History of Freemasonry* (1940).
3. See *Glasgow News* (GN), 20/12/1873; 23/9/75; 18/12/75; 22/12/77 for some examples of the latter's meetings. The September 1875 meeting was to commemorate the battle of the Diamond, 21st September, 1795.
4. George McLeod was MWGM for five years and C. I. Paton served from 1874 till his death in 1889.
5. For a very early example see *The Orange Institution, A Slight Sketch*, a promotional pamphlet of 1813 – actually containing recruitment advertisements. It describes the order of business: 1. Lodge to open with a prayer (members standing). 2. General Rules to be read. 3. Members proposed 4. Representations from committee. 5. Names of members called over. 6. Members balloted for. 7. Members made. 8. Lodge closed with prayer (members standing).

   This can be compared with the *Glasgow News'* description of an ordinary lodge meeting in the 1870s, Campsie LOL No. 105 at the Tontine Hall, Glasgow, 'The lodge was opened in due form, a portion of scripture read, minutes of the last meeting read and approved by the secretary. The roll was called and well responded to, 3 new members initiated into the First Order and 3 admitted by certificate. Other business was gone through and the lodge closed in the usual manner', GN, 6/11/73.

   T Gray in *The Orange Order* (1976) also cites the more elaborate breakdown in procedure set out in the 1897 'Laws and Ordinances' which he suggests remains substantially similar today.
   1. The Chair is taken. 2. The Deputy chair taken. 3. A Tyler (doorman) is appointed. 4. A steward is appointed. 5. Opening prayer is read (brethren standing). 6. Scripture reading. 7. Minutes. *8. General Qualifications read. 9. Preliminary correspondence. 10. Dues. 11. Appeals relating to elections. 12. Election of officers (where applicable). 13. Other correspondence. 14. Business arising. *15. Election of candidates. 16. Admission of candidates. †17. Appeals. †18. Reports from inferior lodges. 19. General Business. †20. Names of candidates for next meeting. 21. Closing prayer.

* At local lodges only; † at higher lodges.

6. Father Cleary in *The Orange Society* (1897) suggests examples of bizarre rituals and offers the case of Joseph Rankine of Airbles initiation to the purple degree of Motherwell Lodge when he was blindfolded and tossed in a blanket so violently he broke his neck. However, the actual texts of the rituals offered by Cleary himself seem much nearer the truth. These were confirmed as largely accurate in conversations with contemporary Orangemen, though apparently kneeling does not take place in the Scottish ceremonial.

7. *Catechism of the principles of Protestantism* (1879), pp. 1-2.

8. *Ibid.*

9. D Roberts, 'The Orange Order in Ireland: a Religious Institution?' *British Journal of Sociology* XXII, 1971, pp. 269-283.

10. GN, 13/7/1874.

11. S Bruce, *No Pope of Rome* (1985), see Chapter 6, p 151. Petition signed by Grand Lodge and sent to Lord Beaconsfield, GN 10/5/82.

12. GN, 19/12/1874.

13. Gault, *The Man of Sin and the Son of Iniquity* (1853), Introduction, p. 7.

14. GN 14/11/1874.

15. George McLeod letter, GN 28/7/1874.

16. Roberts, *op. cit.* (1971), p. 276. For Melville, see T McCrie, *Life of Andrew Melville: containing illustrations of the ecclesiastical and a literary history of Scotland in latter part of 16th century and beginning of 17th century* (1824).

17. *The Protestant*, 16/12/1873. See Cleary *op. cit.* (1898) for an 'expose' of conditional loyalty. Bruce (1985) suggests interesting continuities with the present movement p. 229.

18. GN, 29/11/1881.

19. GN, 23/9/1875.

20. M Weber, *The Protestant Ethic and the Spirit of Capitalism* (1976).

21. C I Paton, *op. cit.* (1879), p. l.

22. Gault, *op. cit.* (1853), pp. 370ff.

23. For examples in the text, *The Pope*, etc, Gault, p. 326, p. 305, The Protestant, p. 121; *Indulgences*, Gault, p. 301; *Mass*, Macklin passim; Gault, Chapter VI, p. 261; Long, Transubstantiation tract, first of Glasgow Green Tracts (1864), *Antiquity*, Gault, pp. 11-13, pp. 29.204; *Bible*, The Protestant, p. 377; Gault, p. 223; *Confession*, Gault, p. 338, The Protestant, 16/12/73, p. 12; *Purgatory*, Gault, p. 280.

24. *Idolatry*, Gault, p. 242; *Saints*, Gault, p. 286; *Virgin Mary*, Macklin passim; The Protestant, p. 137; Gault, p. 299; *Miracles*, The Protestant, pp. 9.17; *Monks and Nuns*, Gault, pp. 334-6, 'A Monastery in Mayo'.

25. *Human Rights*, Gault, vi-vii; *Wealth*, Macklin, The Protestant, p. 129 (vestments); *Jesuits, Historical examples*, for example, Gault, p. 370-1, Ciocci – Prisoner of the Jesuits; Popery 'the work of Satan to recover lost ground', pp. 29-204, a very comprehensive treatment ranging from medieval period to Covenanters and 17th and 18th century massacres of Protestants in Ireland.

26. *Immorality*, The Protestant, p. 329; Gault, p. 82-4 (evil Popes and flagellants).

27. *Disloyalty*, The Protestant, p. 105.

28. *Pauperism*, Gault, p. 371, p. 376; The Protestant, p. 265. For geographical evidence of above see Gault, p. 370ff and his history of popery cited above, Part IV and Part V 'The present State of Popery'

which presents a statistical account i) Ireland; ii) Great Britain; iii) France; iv) Iberian Peninsula; v) Holland; vi) Italy; vii) Germany; viii) Russia and Turkey; ix) Asia; x) Africa; xi) America; xii) Australia.

29. GN, 29/11/81.
30. G. F. A. Best, 'Popular Protestantism', in *Ideas and Institutions of Victorian Britain*, R Robson (ed.), (1967), p. 119.
31. Gault, *op. cit.* (1853), Preface.
32. H A Long, *Mene: The numeration of Babylon Mystical* (1865), 'Therefore I will number to you the sword'.
33. E P Thompson, *Making of the English Working Class* (1968), Chapter 11, p. 411ff. There is though less of an emphasis on material promise for the future in the Orange case.
34. *Glasgow Herald* (GH), 2/11/1864.
35. GN, 24/11/1877. As a politically expedient convert to Anglicanism, Disraeli (Beaconsfield) was most unlikely to become a Roman Catholic.
36. GH, 24/12/1872.
37. Macklin, *op. cit.* (1864), p. 308. See *The Sentinel* 6/2/64 for details of the fire at Santiago. The church was lit with candles and liquid gas which ignited round the altar. The Jesuit priest grabbed the chalice and vestments and blocked the sacristy door, the only escape route.
38. Best, *op. cit.* (1967).
39. Ibid. For attitudes towards Irish, see L P Curtis, *Apes and Angels: The Irishman in Victorian Caricature* (1971).
40. Gault, *op. cit.* (1853), pp. 334-6.
41. Best, *op. cit.* (1967), pp. 125-37. For further examples see Louis James, *Fiction for the Working Man*, Chapter 5, 'The Tale of Terror'. On anti-conventualism, see W. Arnstein, *Protestant versus Catholic in mid-Victorian England : Mr Newdegate and the Nuns* (1984).
42. Gault, *op. cit.* (1853), p. 362. He uses the example of Nottingham Cathedral.
43. *The Protestant* carries many such examples, see issues 1-6. E P Thompson, *op. cit.* (1968) Chapter 11.
44. Cleary, *op. cit.* (1897), p. 153.
45. Bruce, *op. cit.* (1985), see Chapter 5.
46. Roberts, *op. cit.* (1971), p. 280.
47. Cleary, *op. cit.* (1897), p. 103.
48. Wolff (ed) (1950), *The Sociology of George Simmel*, pp. 330-75.
49. It might be argued though that they remain more central in the RBP which has more of a 'masonic' character. This body seems to have been motivated more than the LOI by Simmels 'aristocratic motive' of honorific self-conscious separation.
50. p. Gibbon, 'The Dialectic of Religion and Class in Ulster', *New Left Review* 55, (1969), p. 26.

2
Theoretical Approaches

Moving on to discuss some of the theoretical issues raised by Orangeism, it quickly becomes necessary to look beyond the sociology of religion. For while this can help in initial conceptualisation, as in Roberts' isolation of the Order's sociologically hybrid nature, essentially the limited range of such analyses fail to confront a central point in the LOI's historical development in Scotland, namely that it was a basically working class movement.[1] This implies that a more profitable strategy to explain Orangeism's impact is to engage with debates on working class sectionalism and 'contradictory' class allegiances, rather than the intricacies of classification and typology.

Yet, this brings its own difficulties, an initial imperative being to cut through what may be termed the 'mythology' of Orangeism and the working class. Here much of the imagery is of the LOI as a skilled workers' movement 'naturally' allied to the Tory party, where explanatory attributions of 'bigotry' and 'sectarianism', or at best the 'marginal privilege', of Protestant workers over Catholics usually suffice. In advance of thorough-going empirical work this is actually rooted in the wealth of anecdotal material which not surprisingly surrounds so emotive a subject.[2] Significantly though, some of the anecdotal commonplaces seem also to have crept into the academic literature.

There is a great lack of secondary sources on Scottish Orangeism, but basically the relevant texts are of two types: first, those dealing with the movement itself, which are largely concerned with its manifestations in Ireland; and secondly, those dealing with class relations, particularly in Scotland, which may cover the LOI, although their major focus of interest lies elsewhere.

ORANGEISM IN IRELAND: TRADITIONAL MARXIST APPROACHES

As regards the first category, this again subdivides into two major schools of thought. In the first of these, the traditional Marxist position, the phenomenon of Orangeism is associated with the issue of Ulster's 'profoundly awkward class' – working class loyalists. It employs as analytic tools a series of variations on the theme of false consciousness and master-class strategy. The corollary here is an overwhelming focus on the politically integrative function of Orangeism, often standing in place of its actual political and ideological content.

Now, while to cite such rather anachronistic theories on almost any other aspect of nineteenth century labour history could be dismissed as the setting up of a 'straw man' for easy demolition, in this particular instance it is vital to stress that they have been the prevailing orthodoxy and still have considerable currency. Testament indeed to the marginalisation of Orangeism and related developments in much historiography, it is possible in fact to trace an important line of continuity, stretching from James Connolly to the more recent interventions of Michael Farrell and Liam de Paor.

Perceiving real differences in the material conditions of the Protestant and Roman Catholic working class in Ulster, Connolly, for example, still attributed the main responsibility for the conservative ideology and political practice dominant among the former to the Protestant ruling class, 'The fault lies not with the generation of toilers but with those pastors and masters who deceived it and enslaved it in the past'.[3] The LOI here represents a prime mechanism through which the ruling class manipulated religious divisions to prevent the development of a strong labour movement.

In this diagnosis the main ideological currents among Protestant workers are further defined *a priori* as problems and obstacles, in Connolly's formulation 'atavistic survivals' impeding the development of a 'correct' working class consciousness. Consequently the actual complexities of forces within the Protestant community are reduced to a series of devices to protect and legitimise bourgeois power. Although in his later work he is more sensitive to the Ulster bourgeoisie's progressive cross-sectarian role in the United Irishmen's movement in the 1798 Rebellion, and to the historical basis and independent strength of Protestant ideology, this sits uneasily with the more basic notion of bourgeois manipulation which has tended to guide subsequent analyses.

In this way, in his account of the origins of 'the Troubles' De Paor writes:

> In Ulster where industrialisation was more advanced than in any other part of the country a development of social revolutionary movements might have been expected... but the working class of Ulster was divided and the division was fostered and maintained by the middle and upper classes. Especially after the revival of Orangeism, the workers tended to organise in Orange lodges or in the opposing clubs of the corresponding Catholic organisation.[4]

Similarly in Farrell's account of the 44 hour strike in 1919 and criticism of the reformism of the General Strike Committee, a further consequence of this approach is amplified.[5] Here as a result of his tendency to treat the ideology of Orangeism as a simple instrument to divert the attention of workers from their real interests, compounded by his conception of too close a correspondence between economics and politics, every economic conflict seems to hold out the possibility of workers 'seeing through' the ideology in question and becoming involved in a conflict with more far reaching political and social implications. Such a view can in fact be convincingly refuted by the real history of late nineteenth century Labour Unionism – with the fusing of class antagonism and militant loyalism in Protestant labour movement ideology and practice.[6]

The pervasiveness of the traditional position is further emphasised in the ease with which it has been applied to Orangeism's development in Scotland. Thus, Young suggests that the early Orange lodges here in the 1820s and 30s were employed by Tory aristocratic figures as a divisive political force to 'dish the working class radicals and split the nascent working class movement for reform...', so that the institution assisted the authorities in maintaining the status quo 'whether out of conviction or bribery'. This might be dismissed as in keeping with Young's rather idiosyncratic account of 'the rousing of the Scottish working class', but his views on Orangeism as a creature of aristocratic patronage are cited in Clarke and Dickson's thorough and detailed account of class relations and class consciousness in Paisley from 1770 to 1850.[7]

ORANGEISM IN IRELAND: NEO-MARXIST APPROACHES

In reconsidering traditional Marxist views, Patterson's work on inter-Protestant conflicts and independent Orangeism in Belfast in the late nineteenth and early twentieth centuries offers a considerable theoretical and empirical advance.[8]

Patterson rejects the conspiratorial position that Orangeism is the product of the ideological domination of a ruling class, or more correctly ruling class bloc, and instead draws on Poulantzas' analysis of the relatively independent role of political and ideological factors, in this case creating a working class fractionalised along religious lines.[9] At the same time, his empirical examinations of successive splits within the Unionist, Protestant bloc and the account of the fluctuating relations between Independent Orangeism and labour ideologies permit him to reinterpret the conventional wisdom on the Belfast working class to show it less than fully pliable in the hands of Unionist politicians.

Orangeism, Patterson claims for instance, worked precisely because it was 'rooted in the conditions of existence of the Protestant working class... therefore was simply not "on tap" for the bourgeoisie'.[10] In these conditions Orange ideology could even provide a means by which 'certain limited forms of class conflict could be expressed', albeit assuming a specifically sectarian form, often over the assertion of the Orangemen's right to demonstrate and exert a measure of local control.

A useful emphasis is placed firstly here on the theoretical concept of 'practical adequacy'. In other words, Orangemen were far from passive receptacles for manipulative ideas. The ideological provisions of Orangeism had to be adequate in offering intelligible explanations of real world situations. Secondly instructive is Patterson's interrogation of the concept of 'sectarianism' – itself often posited in commonsense accounts as an 'explanation' for Orangeism – and the reinterpretation of the relationship between this and sectionalism. In the case of Belfast, Patterson argues the rapid expansion of a highly concentrated industrial proletariat in shipyards, engineering works and linen mills actually produced new and durable channels for the transmission of a sectarian ideology. Discrimination was certainly systematic in Belfast but the traditional explanation of its causes must be inverted. Skilled workers tended to be Orangemen but sectarianism was also highly dependent on their prior status as craft workers. In this way sectional and sectarian consciousness complemented and fed on each other, defensive control of recruitment and wage differentials proving the ideal bearers of discriminatory practices.

Yet this is not to suggest that Patterson's stress on 'relative autonomy' should replace the social control model as a new universal orthodoxy for the study of Orangeism. For indeed this analysis raises some difficulties in its own right.

These operate at various levels. There is, for example, in Patterson's work a retention of the labour aristocracy concept, inherited from the traditional Marxist problematic. Problems with this are discussed in detail in Chapter 5, in a consideration of Scottish Orangeism's class basis. Secondly, while political dissent within Orangeism is now well documented for Belfast, there is also a temptation to pursue a potentially fruitless search for similar behaviour, indicative of political and ideological autonomy, to bring Scotland into this general analysis. Again, prior assumptions can be dangerously distorting. Thirdly, there is also a worrying tendency in the neo-Marxist type of approach, that in avoiding attributions of conspiracy we almost completely erase instances of social control which can arise from the inequality of power in capitalism, in turn the result of economic inequalities and control of the state apparatus. Here even Gramsci's 'pivotal and commanding' concept of hegemony which is usually invoked as an alternative on these occasions becomes something of an incantation to edge round problems of control.[11]

At this point there are two possible responses. First, one course strongly suggested by the empirical material is simply to use the concepts like hegemony in a more realistic and pragmatic way to denote shifting combinations of force and consent. Hegemony then is made to refer to certain periods under study in the nineteenth century when diverse and often potentially 'subversive' political practices were subordinated and controlled; the point being to enlarge the whole notion of class domination and not to set coercion and consent in hermetically sealed compartments.

Although in most cases, for instance, 'control' is not appropriate to analyse the activities of the LOI. as a whole, particularly as regards its political practice, one should also stress that most Orangemen belonged to the industrial working class and in that capacity forms of social control could have been applied through, for example, the provision of company housing or company education for their children.

Attempts at giving the following chapters theoretical direction could quite conceivably end here with the 'toughening up' of the relative autonomy position. The second option here and a rather more candid one is, however, to give reign to some further serious and 'heterodox' doubts arising from this case study.

For it becomes apparent that a classic or 'Manifesto' Marxist approach simply does not square with the history of Orangeism. The application of this problematic, as indicated in Farrell's treatment of the involvement of Protestant workers in industrial action, in fact displays elements of economism and teleology and would lead to the portrayal of the Institution as of monolithic and unchanging manipulative significance, when the extent of its function of political integration has actually been historically variable, with a compelling reciprocity of control and consent.

However, when one attempts to bring a more sophisticated Marxist analysis, as sketched above, to bear on Orangeism's actual political and ideological content, again a dilemma arises. For if this is a better 'fit', is it in its rejection of the basic unity of the proletariat in favour of heterogeneity and endemic fractionalisation abandoning, albeit unconsciously, the distinctive features of Marxist class analysis?

This is, despite of course its lingering insistence on principal definition by location in the productive process and 'the lonely hour of the last instance', or protestations that Marxism 'is about changing realities and there can be no eternal truths'. In such a guise indeed there seems little to distinguish Marxism from Weberian sociology. Some accounts of hegemony and social structure are indeed remarkable for their single-minded attempt to rid the former concept of any class dimension.[12] This point is acknowledged by Bloomfield, though her comments clearly fail to confront the challenge, '...the recognition of phenomena to which Weber drew attention does not imply commitment to his conceptualisation of them – they could combine to a more complex and flexible understanding of Marxist concepts of class struggle'.[13]

CLASS RELATIONS STUDIES: IMPLICATIONS FOR ORANGEISM

Nor are these difficulties resolved in turning to a second group of texts, those relevant to Orangeism, albeit with a broader class analysis. In fact, the general situation above is mirrored in this material, a point illustrated in the strongly contrasting contributions of Joan Smith and Roger Penn.

The object of Smith's thesis, for example, is a study of the development of class consciousness in Glasgow and Liverpool, using Gramsci's concepts of 'social organism' and 'commonsense thought'. Gramsci, she argues, is particularly fruitful here since he adds an understanding of the relation between social being and consciousness, base and superstructure as an 'organic totality' rather than Lukacs' 'essential totality' or Althusser's 'unitary totality'.[14]

Smith then applies the organic totality approach to the cities' different social structures, with respect to 'natural social organisms' including, for example, industrial structures; 'voluntary social organisms' among which she situates the LOI ; and the commonsense thought held by Glasgow and Liverpool working men. As regards the latter, while in Liverpool, Smith suggests, the 'commonsense' was Tory democrat and militant Protestant in a casual workers' city, where right-wing Labourism and revolutionary syndicalism developed; in Glasgow, the skilled workers' city, the commonsense was a Liberal one, with militant Protestantism and Orangeism marginalised and a radical Independent Labour Party (ILP) and societies of revolutionary socialism prominent.

Despite this theoretical basis, in practice Smith's analysis displays some elements more commonly associated with the 'Manifesto' Marxist position, most notably again the retention of the labour aristocracy concept.

A similar emphasis is also present when she deals specifically with Orangeism. Various reasons are cited as to the limitations on the movement in Glasgow, including the failure of an Orange/Tory caucus to develop.[15] There was, for example, the 'overwhelming Liberal commonsense for whom the enemy was the landlord and the despot not the Irish'; consequently the predominant societies of the working class were Friendly Societies, Co-operatives and Trade Unions dominated by labour aristocrats, leaving little room for Orange mobilisation; thirdly, the city's economy was based on a skilled workforce, whose ticket to employment was their individual apprenticeships, and who could see themselves as tradesmen first and Protestants second; finally, the city's economy was expanding from the 1880s onwards.

Unfortunately, difficulties arise with this analysis once it is put to a detailed empirical test by the case of Orangeism, which is, of course, beyond the mandate of Smith's research. First, on a substantive level, while the general stress on Orangeism's relative weakness in Scotland is correct, Smith is rather dismissive on its absolute strength, and in particular underestimates the real extent of Orangeism's involvement with the West of Scotland Conservatives. Secondly, and more seriously, in her consideration of the role of the 'Liberal commonsense', is the positing of an unproductive Labour movement/Orange dichotomy. This neglects the real complexity of the relationship which instead appears as a unilinear process whereby the innate progress of the former wins over, or at least neutralises, potential supporters from the latter. Despite her explicit Gramscian starting point, Smith's approach here again seems close to the more orthodox view of a working class possessed of universal and almost 'pre-given' characteristics of solidarity and internationalism in the face of capitalist relations, confusing, perhaps, structural potential with the facts of working class history.

In particular this view overlooks the fact that the motive forces of class and sectarianism have not always been totally opposed to each other in practice. This is strongly suggested, for example, in Patterson's identification, noted above, of a certain partial or limited class consciousness, precisely among those who were still stalwart Orangemen. Though one must also indicate the likely extent to which Orangeism could itself influence labour movement sentiments, either directly through Orange membership in key Trade Unions and Trades Councils, or indirectly by fear of an Orange backlash in some electoral districts.

Following on from this, one may also conjecture whether it was always the attraction of the 'liberal beehive' which held Scottish skilled and supervisory workers aloof from Orangeism; their self definition as tradesmen first, suggested by Smith, may also have meant that Freemasonry and the Volunteer Movement were more socially congenial than the populist LOI.

Finally, however, there is a tendency with Smith's general account of the LOI's relative weakness to rest too firmly on 'economic' factors. The West of Scotland's industrial prosperity may indeed have circumscribed its agitational role, particularly in the workplace, but such broad factors seem insufficient in themselves to explain the precise nature of Orangeism's limited impact on Scotland's political structure or its religious institutions, compared with its other major concentrations in Ulster, Canada and Liverpool. For this, it will be suggested, an important dimension should be a sensitivity to Scotland's cultural and political peculiarities.

It is precisely towards the practical problems raised by traditional Marxist emphases that Penn's analysis addresses itself.[16] In considering the internal division of the manual working class in Britain around the axis of skill, and its possible translation into equivalent 'social boundaries' in the non-economic sphere, his initial assumptions on the validity of the labour aristocracy concept and a naturally united proletariat were repeatedly challenged by the reality of market and work relations and their social manifestations in the test case of Rochdale.

At the heart of the Marxist model of class, Penn argues, is the question of why capitalism has not been overthrown. This is because of the 'teleological' assumptions within Marx's works, that modern social development necessarily follows a progressive movement towards socialism through the agency of the industrial proletariat, which embodies the fundamental contradiction within the capitalist system between capital and labour. In particular, the main implication here, he suggests, is a focus on the obstacles to revolutionary class consciousness and the construction of a second level of theory as a safety net, introducing historical contingencies such as the development of a labour aristocracy which are said to block the more basic and organic line of development.

For Penn the central objection here is that such analyses 'put the cart before the horse' assuming that the working class existed in some positive fashion without empirical investigation. The solution here involves a move into Weberian sociology drawing on Giddens' concept of class structuration.

In this Giddens emphasises the role of relative mobility chances in the structuration or boundedness of class divisions, focused in the market place and in the division of labour. In this way a class structure becomes more rigid, thereby exhibiting a high degree of classness to the extent that mobility across and within generations is restricted.

The central image of a class system with a set of economic divisions that may or may not be translated into social boundaries, as Penn points out, derives from Weber's comments that an economic class may or may not be translated into class conflict and class consciousness in a Marxist sense, and that social structuration is often associated with value systems distinct from the economic class structure of capitalism and which are embodied in status groups. In short, the important point in this tradition, argues Penn, is that '...it makes many issues in class investigation the object of empirical and therefore scientific study'.[17]

Although Penn does not deal with Orangeism directly, in the first place his detailed historical material does offer two substantive insights. In pointing out, for example, that the central feature of skilled manual work is some form of social exclusion, he argues that, despite appearances, this does not refer to those exclusive devices which are intended to restrict entry into an occupation by means of particularistic ascriptive criteria. Historically these have been features of skilled work in the cases of printing and metalwork which were investigated by Penn; however, 'simply restricting entry into occupations to men of the same family or religion cannot suffice to maintain skill'.[18] More crucial to maintaining this were, in fact, exclusive controls over the operation and utilisation of machinery.

These would again seem to corroborate Patterson's view that Orangemen's discriminatory practice was most frequently dependent on their prior status as skilled workers in trades with rules such as those indicated by Penn for the Rochdale Association of Powerloom Overlookers, in this case excluding other workers from manning automatic weaving equipment. Here Orange-inspired anti-Catholicism could determine the specific language of craft control but could not, by itself, sustain it.

Penn is also valuable in his reconsideration of labour aristocracy theory. He argues not only that the evidence of the persistence of a skilled divide in the cotton and engineering industries does not follow the cadences of 'homogenisation' and 'sectionalisation' suggested in the theory, but also that the rhythms of marital endogamy do not reflect the underlying economic class structure. At least then, as measured for the available data for Rochdale, 'the clear bifurcation of the working class in the economic sphere has not been translated into a parallel or isomorphic set of social boundaries'.[19]

In this way Penn challenges the view that images and identities from the workplace must necessarily be translated into the community, unchallenged by the wider self-definitions possible here, and renders the question of sectional self-identification a subject for further empirical investigation. This becomes particularly important in examining internal politics and the rough/respectable differentiation in Orangeism. The latter, it will be suggested, actually cut across workplace hierarchies and indeed the Order itself, or more commonly the 'sedate' Black preceptories could themselves be used to build an alternative identity to that determined by skill and pay.

Ultimately, however, Penn's commitment to a Weberian perspective must be confronted. This might seem a valid strategy for the present study, given the dilemma sketched above in Marxist theory between, on the one hand, traditional accounts where Orangeism is seen as a dependent variable and product of false consciousness, operating a diversion from the real material struggles of the working class; and, on the other, more sophisticated approaches which eschew 'the naive assumption of working class unity as normality', and view Orangeism within the context of the totality of the social formation in question, determined only in the last instance by the mode of production. Whereas the former, as suggested, does not bear sustained empirical scrutiny, the latter seems already shading towards a quasi-Weberianism despite retaining a Marxist vocabulary.

Yet accepting a full Weberian position raises decisive difficulties. The nature of the Weberian causal regress means the heterogeneity of the proletariat, its 'contradictory' class allegiances are simply not a problem here. Now while this might seem a relief given some of the tortuous debates on these subjects, one must also question whether this more restricted problematic is really equipped to deal adequately with the phenomenon of Orangeism, since this does seem to require asking questions about the dynamics of Orange allegiance. How, for example, is one to make sense of the support of many working class Orangemen for that version of the dominant ideology embodied in the Conservative party? If such questions are suppressed it does not seem a great advance from the sociology of religion perspectives whose limited range was criticised at the outset of this chapter.

Given, therefore, the problems with existing Marxist approaches and doubts over an easy escape route with Weber, if the analysis is not to retreat to a completely relativistic position, obviously there is a need to build some new theoretical approach to internal structural and ideological divisions within the working class.

One can suggest that this might retain a Marxist or at least 'Marxian' basis. For while Penn rigidly counterposes Weber's emphasis on the 'indeterminate and empirical' against Marxism's 'determinism and teleology' this is not supported by all interpretations of the latter's method.

Essentially what is being introduced here is a conception of Marxism which is basically opposed to that underpinning the traditional economistic thesis and its Althusserian variants. Rather than a body of substantive theory this views the distinctiveness of Marx's contribution in terms of the methodology implicit in his analysis, which is above all 'open exploratory and empirical'.[20] In this way one may employ his classic analytical conceptions of the endemic structural inequality of capitalism, its central conflicts between capital and labour and the competition between capitals, the interaction of which renders the system dynamic. One may also introduce the hypothesis that behind the 'heterogeneity' and 'complexity' that result from the variety of experiences in the capitalist order there *is* a proletariat. In accordance with Marx's method this hypothesis itself must be empirically testable, and in fact there are historical cases where sectionalism has been prevented from completely eroding class-based movements, as E P Thompson suggests in his analysis of British Jacobinism and Chartism.[21]

In conclusion, this is not the place to make any detailed attempt at a new theory of sectionalism – indeed one of the major lessons from much of the preceding discussion is precisely the need for concrete historical work rather than another grand overarching theory. The subject of Orangeism in Scotland, however, raises a number of major themes for further theoretical consumption, some of which were introduced above.

First, for example, one should re-emphasise that the false consciousness, social control problematic is not as appropriate for Orangeism as is often assumed in secondary sources. For most of the movement's history it is more fruitful to employ a model grounded in concepts such as practical adequacy and an extended notion of class power and domination, using the hegemony concept. Yet in avoiding generalised conspiracy notions one must still remain sensitive to the attempts at coercion and control which have impinged at certain points – usually unsuccessfully – in the progress of Scottish Orangeism.

Secondly, it becomes necessary to rethink the relation between sectarianism and sectionalism in the workplace, important in commonsense perceptions of the Order. Related to this must also be a reconsideration of the relevance of the labour aristocracy concept and the explanatory value of marginal privilege in connection with Orangeism.

Thirdly, the absolute strength of the Orangeism will be examined
and also its relative weakness in comparison with Ulster and other
major Orange importations in Canada and Liverpool. Not only are
these important historical points, but the latter also lays stress on the
unfortunate interaction between certain intrinsic characteristics of
the LOI as an 'Ulster body', with the cultural and political, as well as
major economic features of Scottish society.

Finally, and perhaps most important, for any new approach to
working class sectionalism, one must concur with Penn on the need
for 'a phenomenological input into class analysis'.[22] Penn has in
mind here the battle for skill in the workshop, but sensitivity to
meanings and self perceptions seems also indispensable in understanding both the attraction of the Institution to the average Orangeman and the internal tensions which beset it, with its attempts to
achieve 'respectable' status in Scotland.

NOTES

1. Roberts, *op. cit.* (1971), pp. 269-283.
2. N Belton, 'Ireland – Unravelling the Knot', *Bulletin of Scottish Politics*,
   No. 2 (1981), for example, points to the 'utopian function' Ireland has
   performed for the British left – the Irish threatening 'an apocalyptic
   alternative: insurgent republicans attacking the heart of the physical
   power of the British state on the one hand; ugly, overtly reactionary
   Protestants led by a seemingly mad demagogue on the other', p. 188.
3. 'North East Ulster' in *Ireland on the Dissecting Table, Connolly on Ulster*,
   Cork Workers Club (1975). For a later Connolly approach, 'Forward',
   3/5/1913.
4. L de Paor, *Divided Ulster*, (1971), p. 61.
5. M Farrel, *The Orange State*, (1976), p. 81.
6. H Patterson, *Class Conflict and Sectarianism* (1981). For a succinct
   account of the phenomenon, see also Belton's review in *Bulletin of Scottish
   Politics*, No. 2, 1981, pp. 188-192.
7. *The Rousing of the Scottish Working Class* (1979), p. 80, *Capital and Class
   in Scotland* (1982), p. 25.
8. Patterson, *op. cit.* (1981).
9. See N Poulantzas, *Political Power and Social Classes* (1973).
10. Patterson, *op. cit.* (1981), p. 85.
11. For hegemony, see S Hall, 'Culture, Media and the Ideological Effect',
    in *Mass Communications on Society*, J Curran (ed.) (1977), pp. 331-6.
12. E Laclau and C Mouffe, *Hegemony and Socialist Strategy: Towards a
    Radical Democratic Strategy* (1985).
13. *Marxism Today*, October 1978, Judith Bloomfield 'A Discussion of
    Marxist Writing on Class', pp. 328-332.
14. *Commonsense and Working Class Consciousness: Some Aspects of Glasgow
    and Liverpool Labour Movements in the early years of the 20th century*, Ph.D.
    thesis, University of Edinburgh 1984.
15. *Ibid.* p. 183.
16. R Penn, *Skilled Workers in the Class Structure* (1985).
17. *Ibid.* See particularly Chapter 8.
18. *Ibid.* p. 129.

19. *Ibid.* p. 186. Penn particularly tends to oversimplify Foster's position on endogamy, which does not reduce class to relations of production. J Foster, *Class Struggle in the Industrial Revolution* (1974).

20. See D Sayer, 'Method and Dogma in Historical Materialism', *Sociological Review* (1975) and *Marx's Method* (1979), particularly Chapters 1, 5, 9.

21. Thompson, *op. cit.* (1968).

22. R Penn, *op. cit.* (1985), p. 187.

3
Historical Overview: 'The Lodge of Diamond in Armagh'

This chapter examines Orangeism's main course of development outside Scotland. 'A concrete analysis of a concrete situation',[1] it again illustrates the inappropriateness of a single static model of class relations to understand the movement's history.

Some practical difficulties can also be met in the account. First, an overview is important for the sake of clarity, since despite its stable and enduring elements, for an appreciable period of its history Orangeism displayed a protean character. In other words, it has met the obstructions raised by attempts at proscription by confusingly changing form and title, albeit choosing from a rather unimaginative repertoire: 'Royal Orange Institution', 'Loyal and Benevolent Orange Institution', 'Loyal Orange Association' and 'Brunswick Clubs'.

Secondly, the LOI's own interpretation of its history also obscures the real chronology of the movement. This official interpretation often takes the form of an obsessive and exclusive focus on the 'Glorious, Pious and Immortal Memory of William, Prince of Orange'. It is, as Cleary suggests, as if the clock of time stopped short at 1690.[2] More commonly in more sophisticated accounts the intention is rather to couple this fascination with noble forebears to more recent events. Thus at all costs continuity is stressed in Orange practice and ideology stemming from what is recognised as the Order's 'fons et origo' in the 'Glorious Revolution and the Dawn of Civil and Religious Liberty'.[3] An alternative periodisation of Orangeism's origin and stages of development serves as a useful corrective.

PRECEDENTS AND RISE 1688-1795

There is, of course, a sense in which the rather opaque official account of Orange history is not totally spurious. For obviously without the events of 1688-90 there would have been no 'Orange' precedents to build the movement around. Yet this does not mean that the Orange Institution in its present form can be traced directly and unproblematically from the battle of the Boyne. For above all the problem with official histories is their conflation of two distinct facets of Orangeism; on the one hand, a diffuse 'Orange tradition' dating from the late seventeenth century, and on the other the objective circumstances surrounding its rise in the late eighteenth century. It was the latter circumstances which in fact determined how the tradition was drawn upon, with elements of the older ideology being appropriated selectively often to give a meaning to actions in the present.

To pursue this distinction between the two inputs, the Orange tradition found concrete expression in various clubs established in early eighteenth century Ireland to propagate and celebrate the Protestant Ascendancy. Prominent examples were the 'Royal Boyne Society', the 'Aldermen of Skinner's Alley' and the 'Apprentice Boys of Derry', like many clubs of the period often displaying an interclass mix and a certain democratic or fraternal spirit. Similarly, some Masonic lodges in Belfast and Londonderry bore the prefix 'Orange' and there existed, too, in the British army's Forth Regiment of Foot 'the Society of the Blue and Orange', founded in 1727 and in operation till its absorption into the Orange Institution in 1822. In all these cases 'Orange' denotes 'merely a formal Protestant patriotism',[4] which was also widespread in many less institutionalised ways, or as Brown expresses it in rather sentimental terms, 'In most places where Protestants were found Orange lilies and Sweet William grew side by side in their gardens. It all symbolised pride of ancestry and religion and a certain unity of heart and mind'.[5]

Such strong antecedent conditions may assist in understanding the comparative ease of Orangeism's reception in Ireland, but they are by no means sufficient to explain the actual inception of the Order. Indeed, the Orange tradition had become set in a perceptible decline in the middle decades of the eighteenth century and by the 1790s stood in need of a revival.

Instead one must turn to the second major input, namely the agrarian conflicts between Protestant and Roman Catholic peasants in the border counties of Ulster. Basic to these was a land-population ratio which resulted in chronic land hunger and a system of land tenure inhospitable to improvement.[6] In the 1760s and 70s these conditions promoted profound economic rivalries which found expression in agrarian secret societies, usually regional and non-political such as the 'Oakboys' and 'Whiteboys'.

Although directed primarily against landlords and despite the special efforts of bourgeois radicals and dissenting clergymen, these were a potential source of sectarian conflict. This potential was fully realised in Armagh in the 1790s, largely through Catholic involve-

ment in the Volunteer movement which left them illegally in possession of arms, and also through the extension of the franchise in the
Relief Acts which equalised land rights and appeared to threaten
Protestant living standards. To maintain their status, in Senior's
words, as a 'plebeian aristocracy', the latter group undertook day-
break raids to disarm Catholic peasants (hence the 'Peep o' Day
Boys' soubriquet they assumed). In the face of superior Protestant
strength the Catholic bands of 'Defenders' grew into a more formally organised federated society. The subsequent history of both
groups, as Cleary notes, was 'a hopeless tangle of provocation,
outrage and retaliation'.[7]

Against this background the decisive conflict came on 21st
September 1795 at the Diamond hamlet in County Armagh, the day
being known afterwards in the district as 'running' Monday.[8] Immediately after this battle in which Protestants repulsed a Defender
force greatly superior in numbers, the first embryonic Orange lodge
was founded. A fairly elaborate ritual and system of secret signs and
passwords, based loosely on Freemasonry and the models of earlier
Protestant defensive associations, was devised the same day at the
Loughgall Inn of James Sloan, who became the movement's first
titular head, responsible for the issue of warrants to establish other
lodges. Despite the high cost of one or possibly two Irish guineas,
these were eagerly sought in the aftermath of victory, particularly in
Armagh, Antrim and the Lagan valley. The new movement, while
appealing to the Orange tradition appeared also to offer the possibility of greater stability and more thorough organisation than its
immediate precursor, James Wilson's 'Orange Boys' founded in
1793. Around such basic facts of what even the Protestant historian,
Killen, terms as Orangeism's 'ominous beginning'[9] much intense,
and esoteric, debate has arisen over issues such as the numbering of
warrants, and links with the Peep o' Day Boys.[10] Penetrating the
elaborate layer of official Orange mythology, though, two major
points must be made on the Orange 'Hegira', as Cleary describes the
Diamond episode.[11]

First, the initial organisation of Orangeism was a spontaneous
popular phenomenon accomplished with virtually no aid from the
gentry – the exception being a few notable families such as the
Verners and Blackers. While *Chambers Encyclopedia's* description of
the Institution as being the product of 'a rude and illiterate mob'[12] is
rather overstating the point, its founders do seem to have been small
to medium tenant proprietors in fear of their livelihood. The issue of
gentry control indeed proved a divisive one from the outset. One
faction among the original lodges represented by James Wilson drew

on the presbyterian ideology of independent action and wished to restrict this to a minimum. Another, which tended to dominate, did wish formal gentry leadership and links with the established Church of Ireland. At this stage though, as Senior suggests, the gentry reserved judgement, some hoping at least to obstruct the anti-landlord tendencies of the Peep o' Day Boys, with other elements hoping more positively that Orangeism might prove useful if made 'respectable' enough to allow co-operation.

Secondly, it is important to emphasise that when set against the general tide of religious toleration and penetration of Enlightenment ideas in the eighteenth century Orangeism was something of an anachronism even at its moment of birth. Given such a paradox the rapid growth and energy of this movement of the 'lower orders' – by 1796 the Orangemen numbered several thousand organised in at least ninety lodges – must have appeared puzzling to bourgeois radicals in the North, supporters of the Rights of Man and 'a brotherhood of affection' between Protestant and Roman Catholic.

EARLY DEVELOPMENT IN IRELAND 1795-1825

This is an instance in Orange history when classical Marxist concepts are particularly useful in aiding analysis. For, the early success of the Order is best understood in the context of changes in the process of capital accumulation and mode of production in the north of Ireland.

The origins of Orangeism among the Protestant peasantry were noted above, but its ranks were also swelled subsequently by a new class of journeyman weavers who owed their emergence precisely to developments in productive forces and relations. By the second half of the eighteenth century linen manufacture had become almost universal in South and Mid Ulster, and particularly in Armagh this was accompanied by a rapid slump in small scale rural commodity production.[13] This process led in turn to the virtual eradication of independent weavers, artisans, and small farmers, and the growth of a new class of weaver employees in the linen mills. Yet the declining status and loss of autonomy felt by this emergent class did not produce a situation of class conflict for, as Gibbon indicates, 'the pace of local industrial and peasant differentiation was sufficiently rapid in removing most sources of social and political independence from the countryside, while at the same time it was sufficiently slow to prevent the new classes of employees assuming strategic positions'.[14]

Instead the new Protestant proletariat expressed their resentment of this decline through a renewed determination to defend their status within the Protestant Ascendancy, demanding the preservation of traditional barriers to Roman Catholic social mobility in the labour market. Here the organised Orange lodges were able to assume a vital function in the intimidation of Catholic weavers. During the period 1795-6 large numbers of Roman Catholic families were driven out of Armagh and mill owners or linen manufacturers who employed them were also attacked.[15]

The development of the new mode of production, in fact, as Gibbon again points out, reinforced the hegemony of the landlord class in these areas:

> It ensured that landlords who stood largely outside the linen trade would find themselves cast in the role of tribune, of potential champions and courts of appeal to a population suffering for the first time the vicissitudes of submission to free market relations. This tendency was supported by the structural difficulties standing in the way of new proletarians developing their own leadership, constituted by the fragmentation of centres of production.[16]

This general situation was clearly very favourable for patrician involvement in a populist movement such as Orangeism and, in fact, its opening years, perhaps more than any other time, lend themselves to the orthodox Marxist approach of James Connolly. Initially, as indicated, the gentry did hold aloof, alienated perhaps by the early anti-landlord taint of the lodges and their involvement in the violent outbreaks in Armagh. As Sibbet elliptically expresses it, 'some forgetful of the dignity and genius acknowledged by the Divine Head of the Church when he selected the poor fishermen to be heads of his kingdom – affected to look down on a system which had such lowly origin'.[17]

Quite rapidly, such prejudices were overtaken by expediency as the ability of the Protestant ruling class to hold its huge tracts of land and extract the maximum rent from it, appeared threatened by the revolutionary republicanism of the United Irishmen, the underground militia force organised by Protestants and Catholics, influenced by the example of the French Revolution.

In these circumstances the lodges gained increasing recognition from the gentry as useful channels for directing the energies of the Protestant peasantry and nascent proletariat, and as a means of keeping them under some measure of control. As early as 12th July 1797 a directing body, The Grand Lodge of Ulster, had been established at Portadown. This and the creation of a gentlemen's lodge in Dublin, to which many of the Southern landowners were admitted, greatly enhanced Orangeism's prestige. Subsequently, its gentlemen leaders thought it advisable to bring activities more into the open and regulate the rapidly growing membership by moving the Grand Lodge to Dublin, thus establishing a real national organisation on 8th March 1798.

This move was vindicated by the United Irishmen's revolt in the same year, when under pressure the government actually entered into a 'de facto' alliance with the lodges by arming bands of Orangemen and making no attempt to suppress Orange societies in the armed forces. In the revolt they indeed played a vital role as the predominant influence in the yeomanry and militia, in effect turning these corps into a useful counter-revolutionary force, and acting as loyal irregular auxiliaries in the standing army.[18]

However, the example of 1798 gentry manipulation of Orangeism as a popular instrument against radical insurgency cannot be effectively extended to cover subsequent decades. Direct gentry involvement and Orange influence in government circles generally prospered with national conflict and unrest, but when these were not in evidence decline, schisms and attempts at reorganisation by the plebeian lodges rapidly ensued.[19]

Senior deals with these years in detail but to be brief, in 1802 with the relaxation of the revolution threat the Orangemen's favoured position in Irish politics began to be eroded, and the lodges shifted in emphasis from fighting societies to social and benefit clubs. This decline was not arrested till a further rebellion led by Robert Emmet and the renewal of the war with France, which again enabled Orangeism to be an 'energetic goad' in Ireland until 1815.[19]

Similarly after 1817 as famine dampened the seditious tendencies of the Roman Catholic peasantry, the lodges were left without active opposition and became involved in internal disputes, notably over the appropriateness of extra 'degrees' of initiation.[20]

With such wrangling the movement remained dormant for several years until some recovery was stimulated by a renewal of agrarian disturbances, a controversial Viceregal administration, and the resurgence of Daniel O'Connell's Catholic Emancipation movement. Yet crucially the intimacy with ruling class and government circles of ten years earlier could not be recaptured.

Two fundamental facts underpinned this decline. First, the ordinary Orangemen could never be completely incorporated into the gentry leadership's strategies, for they had their own unique social practices and definitions and indeed their own objective location in the structure of production relations. This ensured, for example, that even their definitions of the Protestant Ascendancy were quite distinct. For the gentry it meant the defence of their own political power and property rights, while for the rank and file the emphasis was on traditional No Popery. The latter in practice meant keeping down local Roman Catholics, and here the regular triumphalist processions by the lodges were felt essential.

Secondly important were developments in the state apparatus, in particular the creation of a new constabulary force and the introduction of stipendiary magistrates, which combined to weaken Orange influence. Restrictive legislation also threatened in the shape of the Unlawful Oaths Act 1823, the Unlawful Associations Act 1825 and repeated bans on Party processions. The loyal militancy of the Orangemen was now much less at a premium as attempts were made increasingly by the government to conciliate rather than coerce the mass of the Irish population.

In these circumstances, the average Orangemen began to lose confidence in the powers of leading members of the Order to offer legal protection via the lodges. This view was reinforced by the dissolution of the Grand Lodge of Ireland in the wake of the 1825 Act, thus bringing the first major stage of Orange history to a close.

GREAT BRITAIN 1795-1825

Orangeism did, however, enjoy one other major growth point up until 1825, namely in England.

The principal means by which the Order became established here was military, through the exchange of Irish and English militia units in 1798 and the founding of lodges in British regiments in Ireland. It was very much an NCO's movement with the first lodges little more than ex-servicemen's clubs. Though gradually they came to include civilians, unlike Ireland they continued to function mainly as Protestant friendly societies initially with very little active part in politics.[21]

The first instance of an authorised lodge travelling to England was in 1798 when Col Stanley of the first regiment of Lancashire militia carried warrant No. 220 to Manchester, where a civilian lodge was subsequently founded. In 1799 Silvester's Salford Volunteers returned with warrant No. 1128 and after that various regiments brought warrants to Oldham, Bury, Rochdale and Wigan. Liverpool also became a stronghold, though Manchester remained the main centre with the Grand Lodge of Great Britain being established there in 1808.[22]

Although well rooted in the northern industrial areas by the mid 1820s, the number of lodges at no time, however, exceeded 300, 30 of which were military. Since the maximum meeting under a warrant was seldom more than 30 it is unlikely, as Senior suggests, that there were more than six thousand members in the 270 civilian lodges; by this calculation there could only have been around 500 members in 15 lodges in London, for example. Hence contemporary estimates of 15,000 accepted by Cleary seem a great exaggeration.

Important factors lie behind this very weak condition. It becomes clear, for example, that Orangeism in this period could simply not thrive in Britain except where large Irish Protestant populations existed. Senior suggests that, in fact, the largest party of men joining the early English lodges were from this group, those who had enlisted in English militia regiments or had come to England for work. Constituting a minority within a minority they wished to distance themselves from the Catholic Irish by forming societies in which the co-religionist indigenous population might join. Also vital was a rough equivalent of the sort of economic competition which had prevailed in Armagh in the 1790s – this was found, for example, in Liverpool, a commercial and distributive centre where casual labour predominated.[23]

In the absence of these material conditions, however, in other areas such as London and the south the Order appeared an alien and exotic import. Furthermore, despite Orangemen's involvement in measures against real or imagined conspiracies such as the 1812 Luddite agitation, there was nothing on the scale of the United Irishmen worthy of political exploitation nor was there Orange influence in the yeomanry. On a more practical level the Order could not confer the same benefits in the form of patronage and immunity from the law as it had in late eighteenth century Ireland.

'CONSPIRACY' 1825-36

In Orangeism's next major phase it is once more advisable to treat the Irish and British movements together, as they were closely intertwined in practice.

The dissolution of the Irish Grand Lodge in 1825 broke the dynamic link between the militant Protestantism of the Ulster peasantry and weavers and the politically expedient anti-Catholicism of the upper classes, and for the next three years despite O'Connell's revival of the Catholic Associations its development was much curtailed.

Instead, experiments in compromise and attempts to avoid proscription were pioneered in the form of a benevolent society but the 'Loyal and Benevolent Orange Institution of Ireland' or the more politically orientated 'Brunswick Clubs' proved uninspiring and raised limited support from the average Orangeman. In 1828, though, the Grand Lodge of Ireland was again reconstituted and the movement received something of a reviving stimulus from the twin threats of Catholic Emancipation and Church Disestablishment in the 1830s.

The British organisation's fortunes also saw an improvement and here again attempts were made to employ the lodges as a means of social control. For despite the Orangemen's lack of numbers on the mainland, their potential – already proved in Ireland – for forming a broad-based popular movement sympathetic to the causes of entrenched conservatism, opposition to parliamentary reform and Catholic emancipation, attracted the Ultra-Tory faction including the Dukes of York and Cumberland.

On entering the 1830s events in the British lodges became even more dramatic, as the role of 'travelling organiser' was entrusted to an eccentric half-pay officer, William Blenerhasset Fairman, who in 1832 and 1833 embarked on extensive tours of the Midlands, northern England and Scotland. The basic intention here was to reorganise the rank and file lodges on more disciplined and dignified lines, as befitted the nucleus for a new right-wing party, and also to rally substantial support from the gentry and Conservative bourgeoisie for the British Order, as sections of the Irish gentry had rallied to Orangeism in 1798.

The full reproduction of this classic control model, however, was again confronted by practical obstacles. The British landed classes, for example, were still not threatened by anything like the Defender movement and had no equivalent of Armagh peasantry to press Orange leadership upon them. Even if rural lodges of tenants had been established their effectiveness against a parliamentary reform movement which was urban based is doubtful. The existing strength of Orangeism was in the Northern cities, but here its rank and file had no interest in opposing reform and indeed many, as Cassirer suggests, were probably strongly in favour, for, as already indicated, their No Popery was not without a certain 'democratic' element, particularly in its critique of 'Papal Monarchism' and defence of private judgement.[24]

Once again the ordinary Orangemen were not malleable material for their leadership's political aspirations. Not surprisingly then Fairman's tour met with indifferent success, his only solid achievement being the creation of two gentlemen's lodges in Yorkshire and Glasgow.

Much greater reversals were impending. The new Whig administration was not itself prepared to make Orangeism a political issue but the absence of an absolute parliamentary majority made it sensitive to radical and Irish pressure and forced its hand. When the radical MPs Hume and Finn again raised the question of a parliamentary investigation the demand was therefore granted in the spring of 1835, and a select committee was established. This subsequently submitted four huge reports on the Irish and British movements.

The material in the Irish reports established the already common knowledge that Orangemen controlled the yeomanry and had lodges in the army, enjoyed a measure of legal immunity and were frequently involved in civil disturbances. The British report under Hume's personal direction presented a summary suggesting that the lodges, whose strength it greatly over-estimated, were involved in a dangerous conspiracy to stage a *coup d'état*. In fact, as Senior suggests, this threat had little substance outside Fairman's flamboyant oratory and vivid imagination, but the very fact that a Royal Duke was head of a society with illegal military lodges was sufficient to ensure parliament could not let it subside. In these circumstances, Cumberland dissolved the British Grand Lodge in February 1836, the Irish version following suit in April. The second major phase of Orange history was thus brought to a close.

EBB TIDE AND RECOVERY 1836-1885

Cleary's typically florid assertion that the movement 'fell like another temple of Dagon' requires considerable qualification.[25] For although the Grand Lodge edifice did collapse, the plebeian lodges showed remarkable resilience and continued to meet and parade without the leadership's direction, the *Northern Whig* reporting that County Antrim on 12th July 1836 'even in the heyday of Orangeism seldom if ever exhibited a stronger muster of the degraded faction'.

Besides, the Order was positively prospering in the colonies where the modes of introduction had again been military and the membership largely Protestant Irish immigrants. Canada, where the first lodge was founded in 1825, proved the most active and energetic colonial offshoot under the tuition of the Irishman, Ogle R Gowan. By 1851 the Institution had become so popular that they were invited to be present at the turning of the first sod of the Northern Railroad, and on the 12th of July the following year the largest procession ever seen in Toronto took place with over 10,000 Orangemen.[26]

There were similar developments though to a lesser extent in the USA, New Zealand and Australia where the first lodge was established in 1833. In these cases Orangeism again succeeded as an active irritant in party quarrels, particularly around the 12th of July.[27]

By the 1850s and 60s indeed, Orangeism was again in an expansionary phase both in the North of England and in Ulster. In the

English case, Orangeism flourished in the general climate of sectarian violence which, Joyce suggests, followed the pattern of the arrival and dispersal of the Irish poor in the Northern textile towns from the late 1840s.[28] Ethnic tensions were intensified in the 1860s with economic depression and the Fenian scare, although the Orange attack could be directed at Nonconformists, as well as Irish Catholics.

The lodges seem by this time to have outgrown their military antecedents in the North of England, though it is impossible to determine to what extent Ulster migrants were still dominant in their membership. More certainly they remained a proletarian movement, and one highly susceptible to Tory populism.[29]

Turning to Ulster, the Orders impressive mid-century progress can again be viewed against developments in the mode of production, with the industrialisation of the North East.

Only in Ulster did free trade with Britain lead to industrial expansion and prosperity. It was the introduction of the textiles industry to Ireland that first caused Belfast to develop into an industrial city, and during the first half of the nineteenth century its population increased five-fold reaching 100,000 by 1850. Also in the 1850s it acquired its second major industry, iron shipbuilding, and on the basis of its success a host of smaller industrial concerns. Now local capital was reinvested, supplemented by Scottish and English capital, and as Gibbon notes its concentration and centralisation became a dominant feature in the late nineteenth century.[30]

Many members of the new industrial labour force were migrants from the agricultural counties and the Orange lodges provided a familiar rallying point for them in unfamiliar surroundings. Also since the process of industrialisation in Ulster had little impact in the other provinces, many Roman Catholics were compelled to come to Belfast to find employment as an alternative to emigration. This resulted in an extremely volatile situation of inter-communal competition for housing and jobs and there were severe outbreaks of sectarian violence particularly in the 1860s. Though Bell has noted that, by World War I Belfast was one of the most prosperous cities in Britain, where wages were keeping pace with mainland cities and there was little unemployment.[31]

And yet at this point the Orange Institution did not reach its full potential in growth. For although the movement was a vital means by which the effective dominance of the Conservative ruling class was constructed in Belfast, the traditional ideology of Protestant ascendancy which it imported into areas like the Shankhill and Sandy Row still, as Patterson details, had different meanings for different classes in the Protestant-Unionist bloc.[32]

While for the upper classes this remained the defence of the Protestant Constitution and property rights, for the working class it now involved a more 'practical' No Popery advocating the domination of Protestants in the composition of the town council and local work forces.

There were two implications here. In the first place, vital in maintaining the ascendancy for the average Orangeman were regular marches and confrontations, yet the reputation thus gained by the Institution for provoking violence and disorder led it into disrepute and crucially alienated middle and upper class support. Secondly, attempts by Belfast Conservatives to enforce the Party Processions Act to curb this disorder and the willingness of the LOI's gentry leadership to comply provoked not only a renewal of internal Orange conflict, but provoked a major appearance of class divisions in the Protestant community in the 1868-85 period.

The most prominent dissident Orange group in the 1860s and 70s was the Orange and Protestant Workers' Association led by William Johnstone of Ballykillbeg, the main critic of the Grand Lodge's acceptance of the Party Processions Act, and by a small committee, mostly of small businessmen and skilled workers. The OPWA made contact with Belfast Whigs and Liberals, but its main strategy to secure Johnstone's election to parliament was to concentrate on the newly enfranchised working class. Though, as Patterson notes, 'the degree of positive identification with working class interests was slight'.[33] Johnstone already had a reputation as a radical because he supported Irish land reform, and now what he did was to emphasise upper class 'manipulation' and 'betrayal' of the 'true blue' rank and file of the Order.

Johnstone was actually victorious in 1868 over his official Conservative opponent, an industrialist perceived as a timeserver and opportunist by the OPWA and working class Orangemen, but this campaign also indicates the restrictions on the form of class consciousness expressed here. It was, for example, a mobilisation from above and attempts at a class analysis in the OPWA, though significant, were subordinated to a political and ideological preoccupation with Protestant Ascendancy – typically contrasting the Tory ruling class and patrician Orange leadership's timid defence of this with the Orange rank and file's robust and physical emphasis. In short, class conflict, or class resentment, was employed by 'democratic' Orangemen like Johnstone as a weapon to gain more favourable terms from the Conservatives for the delivery of Orange support, the main bargaining counter being the increased working class electorate.

Johnstone left the OPWA in 1878, astutely he had never personally cut himself off from the traditional Orange and Tory leaders. Subsequently the organisation shrunk to a minority status in Belfast Orangeism, drawing on Tory democrat notions of 'the just claims of labour'. Reorganisation of the city's Conservative Association in 1872 also removed some of the OPWA's grievances, for a closer relationship with the LOI ensued with lodges represented on ward committees. Leading Tories also gave individual lodges increasing financial support.

Such developments tended generally to undermine the LOI's potential for independent action, but tension and conflict within the Protestant bloc were still by no means precluded.

HALCYON DAYS AGAIN 1886-1905

The pattern of uneven economic development in Ireland also promoted Ulster's isolation from the mainstream of Irish political life, which now revolved around the resurgence of Irish nationalism. In 1882 the Home Rule League had come under the inspired leadership of C S Parnell and, skilfully utilising the newly extended franchise, winning over the Roman Catholic hierarchy in the South, and taking advantage of the Land League and the Irish population in Britain, he united most Irish Roman Catholics in a demand for the repeal of the Union. A Bill to accomplish this was imminent following the winter election that brought the Liberals to power in 1885.

In the same election this party failed to win a single seat in Ulster and control of the Unionist cause was placed firmly in the hands of the Conservatives. Severe unrest in the South and West with the Land League's campaign drove many Liberals into the Tory camp, though particularly crucial in assisting the strength and cohesion of the Unionism was the active intervention of the Orange Institution. This used its influence, for example, in sponsoring huge meetings and demonstrations such as that at the Ulster Hall in February 1886, which was addressed by Randolph Churchill.[34]

Above all, this was now a revitalised order, at last transcending its earlier weaknesses and becoming a highly respectable politico-religious mass movement. It retained its proletarian base but was also attracting more applicants from the professional and commercial bourgeoisie, who were joining up just as the gentry had in the 1790s. This group was indeed aware of the significance of the lodges' intervention in the United Irishmen's revolt, and now perceived in them the basis of a powerful political and ideological apparatus.[35]

Yet despite analyses to the contrary, Orangeism here was not simply absorbed into Unionism to be manipulated by the Ulster Tories or indeed by the Order's own Grand Lodge. First, the

Protestant working class who formed the Orange rank and file had their own clear material interest in upholding the Union, particularly the more skilled elements who at the beginning of this century were earning wages well above their Dublin counterparts. Conservative leaders in the 1880s had to focus on this interest and develop an ideology of classic social imperialism as a cornerstone of a united Unionist movement. Moreover, as Buckland indicates, the Home Rule crises of the 1880s and the 1920s coincided with economic crises which curtailed the working class's independence and further prompted it to accept the leadership of Conservative employers.[36] Secondly, just as class and economic rivalries between landlords and tenant farmers had marked the foundation of the LOI, now conflicts between capitalists and Protestant industrial workers were liable to undermine the modern movement.

The most significant instance of class conflict within the LOI, and the Unionist bloc generally, was the Independent Orange Order (IOO). The beginning appeared inauspicious. At a 12th July demonstration in 1902 the County Grand Master of Belfast Col. Saunderson was heckled by Bro. Thomas Sloan, a member of the Belfast Protestant Association, the complaint being that he had voted against the inspection of convent laundries. Sloan was suspended from the LOI, and in June 1903 formed the breakaway IOO with the journalist Lindsay Crawford as its Grand Master.

In the next few years the IOO enjoyed a steady growth based probably on inter-lodge and district loyalties; its 12th July parade in 1904 attracted 6,000.[37] During these years Crawford used his paper *The Irish Protestant* to encourage a complete break with the Orange tradition. He shared Sloan's populism attacking the 'bloated plutocrats' of the Unionist establishment and supporting the women's suffrage campaign. In an even more radical fashion he moved towards Home Rule, issuing at Magheramorne in July 1905 a new manifesto which berated clericalism, called for compulsory land purchases and demanded a review of Irish finances. There was even a brief alliance with the Belfast Labour Party and the Ancient Order of Hibernians.

Some caution is necessary, to avoid overstating the radical implications of the IOO phenomenon, like Boyle, for example, who interprets the emergence of the Order as the product of class struggle in a very simple and uncomplicated sense.[38] One problem in this analysis, as Patterson suggests, is that it conflates the ideology of the IOO with the progressiveness of its Grand Master Crawford, who was indeed eventually expelled from the Order for his Home Rule sympathies. The former ideology finds a more correct resonance with the fusion of limited class consciousness and traditional sectarian combativity, that characterised early examples of dissident Orangeism such as the OPWA.

Thus the 100 did not represent a *single* upward trajectory against bourgeois and gentry dominance, for its origins were also rooted in opposition to the policy of 'constructive Unionism', as practised by the Conservative administration at Dublin Castle. This involved a more conciliatory attitude towards Irish Roman Catholics as regards education and land holding. The 'convent laundry' incident then should be placed in the context of a general critique of compromising upper class politicians whose docility and Romanising proclivities, the 100 believed, resulted from their social integration into the Westminster and Dublin governing oligarchies and rendered them less able for the defence of Irish Protestantism against party machinations and Papal assaults. This critique was accompanied by a strong 'regionalist consciousness' again drawing on the Orangemen's experience of underdevelopment, which counterposed the industrial North East to the backwardness and, in particular, clerical domination of the South. In fact Patterson indicates 'a similarity of the diagnosis of Irish ills, if not the proposed remedy to that put forward in Sir Horace Plunkett's *Ireland in the New Century*.[39]

Despite the juxtaposition of positive and negative emphasis in the 100, however, one must finally concur when even an official Orange historian comments '...it had a vision of large scale dimensions in a small screen world'.[40] It had at least created favourable conditions for local labour campaigns and its decline from 1905, following a resolution of the crisis of Unionist politics and the renewal of the Home Rule threat, was an important factor in an increasingly hostile environment for progressive politics in Ulster.

In summing up, the 100 should not be treated as an uncharacteristic episode in an undifferentiated history of 'manipulation' and 'reaction', for in itself it displays some of Orangeism's most enduring themes. Thus neither was the parent movement in Ireland the simple product of an ideological onslaught from the ruling class nor was it only significant for its integrative function. At various points, notably during the political crises of the late eighteenth century and early nineteenth century the LOI, did prove an effective weapon retarding the development of class unity, and gained recognition as such from the Irish gentry. Yet at other times, as in the 1860s and 70s and early twentieth century the very zeal and militancy of the proletarian lodges, in pursuing their own variant of the Orange ideology with a literal definition of Protestant Ascendancy, could bring conflict with the state agencies and disrupt ruling class strategies.

NOTES

1. Advocated by Poulantzas, *op. cit.* (1975), pp.11-33.
2. Cleary, *op. cit.* (1897), p.5.
3. In Sibbet's *Orangeism in Ireland and throughout the Empire* (1939) no less than the first 14 chapters of the first volume are taken up with an extremely detailed narrative of the Williamite campaigns. Similarly in a more recent official history, M W Dewar et al, *Orangeism: a New Historical Appreciation* (1967) the first 80 pages cover the same topic. 'Remember 1690', states the prologue, 'is not the motto of a historical cult but reminds Ulster Protestants of present threats to their security'.
4. H Senior, *Orangeism in Ireland in Britain 1795-1836* (1966).
5. In Dewar, et al *op. cit.* (1967), p.101.
6. See R Miles, *Racism and Migrant Labour* (1982), Chapter 6 for a useful summary.
7. Cleary, *op. cit.* (1897), p.52.
8. The event is celebrated in the usual Orange literary style,

   'There Blacker, Sloan and Aitken's sons stood true unto the core,
   With Sinclair and Dan Winter too, and Verner evermore,
   These were the sons that led the van and did true valour show,
   At the Battle of the Diamond, boys, a hundred years ago'.

   In Dewar, *op. cit.* (1967), p.85.
9. Killen, *Ecclesiastical History of Ireland*, vol. ii, p.359.
10. Cleary wishes to use Peep o' Day Boys and Orangemen interchangably. Sibbet's disclaimer of any link is modified even in Dewar, and some overlapping membership seems logical.
11. Cleary, *op. cit.* (1897), p.36.
12. *Chambers Encyclopedia* Ed. 1865, 'Orangeism' article.
13. B Probert, *Beyond Orange and Green* (1978), p.26.
14. P. Gibbon, *The Origins of Ulster Unionism* (1976), p.32.
15. Probert, *op. cit.* (1978), p.36.
16. Gibbon, *op. cit.* (1976), p.32.
17. Sibbet, *op. cit.*, vol. 2 (1939), p.289.
18. The '98 victory is again celebrated in song.

    'Poor croppies ye knew that your sentence was come,
    When you heard the dread sound of the Protestant drum.
    In memory of William we hoisted our flag,
    And so,on the bright Orange put down the green rag.
    Down, down, croppies, lie down.'

    Dewar, et al *op. cit.* (1967), p.111.
19. Senior, *op. cit.* (1966), Chapter 5.
20. *Ibid*, for a detailed account. Scarlet and Black degrees had been added as further 'inner circles'. The gentry could not see their relevance.
21. *Ibid*, Chapter 7.
22. For Liverpool Orangeism's early history, see Waller, *Democracy and Sectarianism: a Political and Social History of Liverpool 1868-1939* (1981).
23. *Ibid*, Chapter 1.
24. For the early history of the English Lodges, see Cassirer, *The Irish Influence on the Liberal Movement in England 1798-1832*, Ph.D., London, 1938.
25. Cleary, *op. cit.* (1897), p.4.
26. H Senior, *Orangeism: the Canadian Phase*, nd.

27. For Australia, see Cleary, *op. cit.* (1897), pp.6-10, a very partisan account.

28. P Joyce, *Work, Society and Politics. The Culture of the Factory in Later Victorian England* (1980), p. 251. There are doubts about extending the immigration/reaction argument to Scotland, however, see Chapter 6.

29. Joyce, *op. cit.* (1980), pp.256-8. See also N Kirk, 'Ethnicity Class and Popular Toryism, 1850-1870', in *Hosts, Immigrants and Minorities*, K Lunn (Ed.) (1980).

30. Gibbon, *op. cit.* (1976), p.16.

31. G Bell, *The Protestants of Ulster* (1976), pp.17-23.

32. H Patterson, Class, Conflict and Sectarianism, Chapter 2 (1981) and 'Independent Orangeism and Class Conflict in Edwardian Belfast', *Proceedings of Royal Irish Academy*, Vol. 80, C. No. 1 (1980), pp.11-12.

33. *Ibid.*

34. For an account of Churchill's tour, see *Illustrated News*, January-June 1886.

35. The LOI's network of local lodges also provided a ready made framework for recruiting and training the UVF in 1912.

36. P Buckland, 'The unity of Ulster Unionism 1886-1929', in *History*. 60 (1972), p.214.

37. Patterson, *op. cit.* (1980), p.16.

38. J W Boyle, 'The Belfast Protestant Association and the Independent Orange Order' in *Irish Historical Studies*, Vol. xiii (1962), pp.117-52.

39. Patterson, *op. cit.* (1980), pp.18-19.

40. Dewar, et al, *op. cit.* (1967), p.154.

4

The early History of Orangeism in Scotland 1799–1865

Unlike the case of the Irish movement, sources for the early period of Scottish Orangeism are extremely limited. What follows is a general social history of these opening decades, with some tentative analysis of the Order's relatively weak political impact in Scotland.

Orangemen as bearers of a distinct tradition have always perceived themselves as participating in a continuous historical process. While in part relevant to an understanding of the survival and periodic revivals of the Institution, in general application, as already noted, this official view obscures more than it clarifies.

This indeed holds true for Scotland. The claim of Lilburn, for example, that Orangeism here is 'as old as the Glorious Revolution' is fairly modest when set beside the contemporary Orange view that the Institution's forebears were no less than the seventeenth century martyrs of the Covenant.[1]

In the Scottish case the line must be drawn for accuracy's sake not only between the actual institutional genesis of the LOI, and the rather vague and eclectic 'Orange tradition', as in Ireland, but also between these and an indigenous tradition of emotional opposition to 'Popish machinations'.

Although the *Orange Gazette*, a daily intelligence of Glorious Revolution events 'with extraordinary news both at home and abroad', made its appearance in Edinburgh in 1689,[2] the Orange tradition, drawing on the Revolution and subsequent Williamite campaigns, was much less prominent and relevant in Scotland than in Ireland – the actual site of 'Derry, Aughrim, Enniskillen and the Boyne', where the tradition had had huge symbolic value for the embattled settler community.[3]

Far more powerful, however, was a much older, undifferentiated form of militant Protestantism which it could be argued owed as much to the course of the Scottish Reformation as it did to the events of 1688-90.[4] Representative of this indigenous ideology was the Protestant Association, an 'ill-defined amalgam of extra-religious and extra parliamentary forces' with the simple, negative aim of repealing the Roman Catholic Relief Act of 1778 in England, and withstanding the attempt to extend its provisions to Scotland.[5]

Its first public meetings in Edinburgh in December 1778 resolved to petition parliament and form a committee of correspondence, a subordinate committee being established in the West of Scotland within three weeks. By the following year the Association had blossomed into 85 societies with 12,000 members issuing a mass of pamphlets and broadsides. By means of these it helped provoke large scale riots in Edinburgh and Glasgow in July and February 1779. Above all, it was successful, suggests Black, because it acted on the traditional anti-Catholic prejudices of the Scottish people, efficiently mobilising this literate public into direct action. Indeed the first Relief Act was not passed in Scotland till 1793. Being a single issue movement, though, once its aim was achieved 'it vanished as Prospero's phantoms into thin air'.[6]

Such early developments are significant. Above all they emphasise the need for sensitivity towards Scotland's unique cultural and ideological identity, in particular underlining the strength of militant Protestant sentiments, which despite similar themes and rhetoric were articulated quite independently of Orangeism.

Indeed, it is vital not to confuse the two. The Protestant Association, for example, preceded the foundation of the LOI in Scotland by over twenty years and displayed the characteristics of a modern political pressure group rather than a fighting or convivial society. It is extremely unlikely, moreover, that there was any significant overlap in membership between the two bodies. The Association was broadly based throughout Scotland with branches in Selkirk, Nairn, Jedburgh and the East Coast and attracted a fairly sizeable bourgeois membership, particularly in Glasgow where it represented 'groups of substantial social interests and prestige';[7] the Orange lodges, however, as to be detailed below, were concentrated in the West and were strongly proletarian in character.

Nevertheless two more direct institutional precedents for the Order did emerge in the eighteenth century, both drawing on what little of the 'Orange Tradition' there was in Scotland. The first, analogous to the Irish 'Apprentice Boys' and 'Royal Boyne Society', was the Old Revolution Club, a vaguely political society pledged to the defence of Protestant patriotism. The certificate presented on the occasion of the admission to membership of Sir Andrew Agnew in 1747, for example, ran as follows:

> Compared to Sir Andrew Agnew and humbly desired to be admitted to be a member of the Old Revolution Club and having declared the grateful sense he has of the deliverance of the

Kingdom from Popery and Slavery by King William and Queen Mary of Glorious Memory and of the further security of our religion by the settlement of the Crown on the illustrious House of Hanover...we do admit him as a member of the said club.

Besides its basic political orientation, the club also seems to have been given to some rather esoteric flourishes, the seal to the certificate being attached by a blue and buff ribbon and 'sundry mysterious-looking emblems' engraved with the legends 'Tandem bona causa triumphant' and 'mente manuque'.[9]

This mild degree of mysticism, however, pales in comparison with Orangeism's second precursor in Scotland, the 'Imperial Grand Black Lodge of Malta and Parent Black Lodge of the Universe' – also known as 'the Grand Black Lodge of Scotland of the Most Ancient, Illustrious and Knightly Order of the Knights Hospitaller of St. John of Jerusalem'.

Founded in Scotland apparently around the middle of the eighteenth century and claiming to be based on the famous chivalric order, its emphasis was on ritual rather than constitutional defence. As regards its class basis, it seems to have had a strong representation from craftsmen and artisans, often 'hedge masons' who had found orthodox Freemasonry too pedestrian or had been refused admission to an official lodge.[10] Despite its peculiarities, though, it had an even greater relevance to the general progress of Orangeism. Spreading to Ireland in the late eighteenth century, a Grand Black Lodge of Ireland was established in 1802. This developed into the directing body of the Royal Black Preceptory, the sister organisation of the LOI.[11]

Such interesting antecedents, though, should not be permitted to obscure the real beginnings of Scottish Orangeism, for this was, in fact, a quite unplanned offshoot from the Irish body formed in Armagh in 1795. The Institution took at least four years to reach Scotland, the means of transition being the same as for England – the militia regiments who had served in Ireland during the '98 Rebellion and its aftermath.

Senior, following Sibbet, suggests the movement was introduced by the Argyle Fencibles, who had served with distinction at the battle of Ballynahinch.[12] Since the first lodge was at Maybole in South Ayrshire this is implausible.[13] It is more likely that the Ayrshire and Wigtownshire Militia (a company of which under the title of the Loyal Carrick Volunteers had been formed in Maybole in February 1797)[14] brought back an Orange Warrant of authority from the Irish Grand Lodge sometime in 1799, when returning from service in Ireland.[15]

No official records are extant for this very early period. The class composition of the pioneer lodge then is impossible to specify with any degree of certainty. The lack of records itself may indicate the participants' limitations of literacy, but on the other hand comprehensive minute books, and membership records of the type observed by McClelland for Ireland may simply have been lost or destroyed.[16]

A rather better indicator is provided by the economic and occupational basis of the early centres of Orangeism. Thus Maybole and towns like Wigtown and Tarbolton were involved mainly in small manufacturing, with the large majority of the former's male population engaged in weaving and shoe-making.[17] One may infer from this that the bulk of the membership of the early Scottish lodges was drawn from the same proletarian class as their Irish contemporaries, though with more emphasis on the artisan and craftsman elements than the peasant proprietor who was already a rarer species in Scotland.

Indeed, it is extremely probable that many of the first Orangemen in Scotland were themselves Protestant Irish migrants, notably represented being that strata of weavers whose independence and prosperity had been undermined by the emergence of the new mode of production in the North East of Ireland.[18] Immigration to Maybole, for example, began precisely in the 1795-1800 period, the settlers being exclusively working class and employed in the traditional trades noted above.[19]

Ulstermen do seem to have been instrumental in setting up lodges in Airdrie, Beith, Kilbirnie, Ardrossan and Port Glasgow – and also in Glasgow according to the Roman Catholic Bishop, Dr. Scott, in 1836.[20]

The advent of Orangeism in Scotland was much less dramatic and auspicious than in Ireland, with no equivalent of the battle of the Diamond and its associated folklore. The Scottish Institution seems to have arrived without eliciting significant comment from any quarter for, as in the North of England, the original lodges seem to have functioned mainly as private ex-servicemen's clubs, with an additional role as benefit societies. The latter were extremely prolific in Scotland in this period. It was probably members of the early Glasgow lodges, for example, at a meeting in King William's Tavern on 6th September 1834, who resolved to establish a financial society. The result was the Glasgow Orange Union Funeral Society, originally based around the Calton and Mile End area.[21]

Like the English example the early growth of the lodges in the 1800-20 period was not prodigious, one large contributory factor here again being the absence of revolutionary threats similar to those occurring in Ireland from 1798 to 1817. And yet a definite diffusion of Orangeism did take place in these early years. The movement first spread South and West, the next lodges being founded in Tarbolton, Wigtown, Girvan and Stranraer.[22] By 1807 a lodge was also in existence in Argyle. The Order then moved eastwards to Newton Stewart and Dumfries. The next decade saw particularly important develop-ments as Orangeism reached Glasgow and Lanarkshire. A lodge LOL No. 106 was established in Glasgow in June 1813 at the Buckshead Tavern, Trongate, and in 1824 the first lodge was established at Airdrie.[23]

Building on these institutional developments, 1821 marks the first attempt at a full ceremonial twelfth of July parade. Only three lodges took part on this first occasion, parading through the prin-cipal streets of Glasgow. Watched by 'an immense concourse of spectators' they were roughly handled and some had their sashes torn off. 'Yet upon the whole', the *Courier* comments, 'the thing went more quietly than expected'.[24]

In 1822 the pattern was repeated. Now seven lodges including those from Paisley and Pollokshaws, assembled to march, contrary to the magistrate's proscription, to Fraser's Hall in King Street. The company met with little opposition during the march since it was unexpected. Once inside the hall, however, they were besieged by a number of 'zealous Irish catholics, most ready to give battle'. Police and even military intervention was required and 127 Orangemen were taken into safekeeping, returning home ignominiously 'with their sashes in their pockets'.[25] A parade was again threatened for the following year but was cancelled and no public Orange processions seem to have taken place in Glasgow till the 1840s.

Hardly portents of the late nineteenth century mass demon-strations, these early outings have a threefold significance. First, they reinforce the sense in which Orangeism in Scotland was an adjunct to already existing bitterness towards Roman Catholics, now particularly focusing on Irish immigrants. This is in some contrast to Liverpool, for example, where this tendency had to some extent been in abeyance since the mid eighteenth century and was actively revived by the activities of the Liverpool Orangemen.[26]

The Glasgow parades were held at the beginning of the Fair Week, the 1822 version taking place on Fair Friday 'the throngest day of the Fair week'. This was fortuitous since the *pièce de resistance* of this holiday ever since the first upswing in Irish migration in the late eighteenth century had been, as Handley notes, the sport of 'hunting the Barneys'. No Irishman was allowed to approach the Fair with impunity and strays were often rounded up, bludgeoned and kicked by Fair bullies. Finally, this element would root about the Saltmarket, the main Irish quarter, breaking windows and clubbing Irishmen out of their homes and ducking them in the Molendinar burn.[27]

Secondly, from coverage of these parades one is given an early indication of bourgeois opinion on the lodges. The *Glasgow Courier* depreciated all assemblies which 'tend to agitate the public mind and to use party feelings', and expressed the vain hope that 'we shall not again be troubled by processions of this kind'.[28] Similarly, a letter in the *Chronicle* in response to the 1821 walk states that:

> With the opinions of the Orangemen the public have nothing to do so long as they keep those opinions to themselves: but what right do the peaceable inhabitants of Glasgow have to be frightened out of their propriety by the wanders through the streets of a set of enthusiasts who...are never against having recourse to the shillelah.[29]

Such feelings of outraged and contemptuous neutrality in the face of what was perceived as an 'alien import' of party feeling were to remain constant in the 'respectable' bourgeois view on the Orangemen's activities throughout the nineteenth century.

Lastly, and on a more general level, the activities of the Orange lodges are testament indeed to the diversity and contradictory tendencies in working class consciousness and practice in the 1800-30 period, one which is sometimes liable to overly optimistic and unitary interpretations.[30]

On the one hand these years certainly did witness a growth of Trade Union activity, political radicalism and even political insurgency, most marked among weavers, cotton spinners and miners in the West of Scotland, possibly influenced by working class Jacobin leadership. Particularly in the years following the French Revolution, radicalism was powerful enough to provoke a crisis for the traditional, paternalistic control structures, accelerating a policy of outright state repression which, as Dickson, notes, represented the only systematic response to unrest till the 1830s.[31]

Paradoxically, however, co-existing with capabilities for joint action and communal solidarity was a heightening tendency in various respects towards sectional conflict. A tangible demonstration was in the quasi-masonic employment of grips, passwords and initiation rituals employed in the early nineteenth century trade unions, as Campbell notes, to guard against the incursions of 'neutral men'.[32] Even more pervasive, though, was the hostile reaction of various sections of the early Scottish labour movement to Roman Catholic migrants from Ireland. This was based on opposition to their religion as much as economic grievances, though the situation was greatly exacerbated by the serious fall in real wages after 1815 and by the employment of Irish blackleg labour after 1817, particularly in the coalfields.[33]

Anti-Roman Catholic sentiments could find expression even at the height of popular radical agitation. In the autumn of 1816, for example, at a public meeting of 40,000 people held at Thrushgrove, near Glasgow, protest ranged from the iniquity of parliamentary representation and government extravagance to the restoration of the Pope and Jesuits in Italy and the Spanish Inquisition.[34]

To return directly to the progress of Orangeism from the 1820s, the emphasis in the early lodges was now broadening beyond their original function as benefit and social societies, as for many their major occupation became increasingly violent provocation and general belligerence towards the Roman Catholic community. In short, the Scottish lodges were beginning to display that same spirit of 'combative sectarianism' which had characterised their Irish counterparts.

Even the indoor celebrations of 'the Twelfth Day' conducted in Glasgow in the period were conducive to faction fighting and serious rioting. In 1829 in the wake of the Catholic Emancipation Bill, the Orangemen had no procession but a body of them met in a Gallowgate tavern, displaying sashes from the window. This irritated a large body of Roman Catholics who had congregated outside to stop the lodge members leaving. Hundreds who had been attending the Fair joined what was now a near riot. There was 'every symptom of a severe popular tumult' had not the police broken up the Orange meeting.[35]

Nor were these incidents confined to Glasgow. In April 1823 there had been a serious outbreak of fighting at Newton Stewart Fair, ending in a victory for the Orangemen who paraded in triumph through the streets the following day.[36] A similar fracas broke out in Dumfries in 1826 and serious party disturbances were also noted at Dalkeith.[37]

These incidents, however, should again be kept in proper perspective, for in terms of their frequency and severity they do not approach similar events in Ireland; nor is there any evidence that the indigenous working class's opposition to Irish Catholics was being widely translated into membership of the Lodges.[38] In fact, the Institution's progress in its first two to three decades was often uncertain and liable to reversal, with lodges 'going down' particularly after the 1820s.

The less favourable cultural context in Scotland, with a strongly generalised 'No Popery' but a weak Orange tradition, has already been cited, but there were other factors in the Order's relative weakness here compared with Ireland.

First, being a working class movement it seems to have been extremely sensitive to the rigours of the economic situation. For in this period the scarcity of labour and high real wages which had existed from the previous century began to be reversed. The re-emergence of a surplus on the labour market facilitated capitalist accumulation – precisely by depressing wages.[39] In this situation members were less willing or able to pay dues; Freemasons' lodges in the period suffered similar problems.[40] Some lodges did survive. Some, indeed, like Glasgow LOL No. 106 and Airdrie LOL No. 19, are still in existence today. A simple explanation here may be the Orangemen's 'sense of history' noted at the outset. Thus in times of constricted finances they would tend to gravitate towards the more prestigious 'original foundations' and pay their dues there rather than to the more recent, and hence less well established, lodges.

Secondly, it is very important to stress the independent attitude maintained towards sectarian disturbances by Scottish magistrates and judiciary, a feature most uncommon in Ireland where protection from legal proceedings was recognised as a major advantage of being an Orangeman. Behind this lay a vital fact for the prosperity of Scottish Orangeism; for if, as suggested above, the proletarian rank and file of the Irish Order had been reproduced in Scotland, indeed often physically transplanted here, its patrician leadership had not. Protestant immigrants were not drawn from the Irish aristocracy, gentry or bourgeoisie, nor had the Scottish lodges succeeded in obtaining support from the indigenous representatives of these classes. Quite simply there is no evidence of any upper class involvement in the Order here in the 1820s.

In these circumstances it was hardly surprising that the deep distrust felt by the state authorities towards popular disturbances generally was also extended to Orange activities.[41] The general attitude is well represented in Sir Archibald Alison, Sheriff of Lanarkshire in the 1830s.[42] An entrenched Tory, Alison was nevertheless unmoved by the Orangemen's' protestations of loyalty, and viewing their processions in a similar light to those of striking cotton spinners and miners which he had also experienced, he dealt with them accordingly. To prevent a Protestant march at Airdrie on 12th July 1834, for example, he personally commanded a squadron of dragoons. He led 28 prisoners back to Glasgow, the ringleaders being later transported.[43]

Until the Burgh Police Act (Scotland) 1892 standardising the law relating to public processions, however, magistrates like Alison faced a confusing system of local controls. They depended either on prohibition by means of statutory powers or common law, as employed in Glasgow against Orange processions in the 1820s and 30s, or an imposition of criminal proceedings 'post factum'.[44]

In this situation, with few magistrates showing Alison's initiative, a great deal in the last instance rested on the efficiency and impartiality of the local police. Again Orange influence was lacking here. Following the 1822 parade in Glasgow, for example, the *Courier* commended the 'promptitude and zeal' of the superintendent and special commissioners of police who readily gave assistance in checking 'a proceeding which was likely to lead to much riot and bloodshed'. A further serious disturbance in 1831 was also apparently curtailed only by the prompt action of Captain Graham in removing offensive Orange emblems.[45]

DEVELOPMENTS IN THE 1830S: THE PARLIAMENTARY REPORT

At such a level of development Scottish Orangeism needed external stimuli to maintain its momentum. In the early 1830s it was to receive these from the aftermath of the Catholic Emancipation Act of 1829, the 1831-2 Reform agitation and the Church of England Disestablishment crisis of 1831-4. Here one can first identify the laying down of a characteristic pattern of cyclical activity, largely in response to events in Ireland, or domestic controversies, in the religious sphere.

Fortunately, this period in Orange history covers the hostile Parliamentary Report on the Institution. Its findings provide further information on Orange activity, as well as providing useful documentary evidence which, although sometimes contradictory, often helps clarify the Order's class composition and numerical strength. **Activity:** A very serious riot in Girvan in 1831, according to the evidence of Cosmo Innes, the Lord Advocate's Deputy in Scotland, marks 'the beginning of the mischief', thus putting an end to the movement's latest period of quiescence.[46]

For several years apparently, Orange processions had been kept up 'from the convocation of Irish in the various manufacturing towns in Carrick'. There had been little physical opposition from either the Girvan townspeople or the Roman Catholic party until the Orangemen had taken the liberty of breaking up Reform processions, which were 'largely under the management of the Scots'.[47] The local inhabitants – or as one indignant letter writer to the *Glasgow Herald* expressed it, 'radicals of the reform persuasion under the new deceitful guise of being patriots and friends of the people'- resolved to prevent the next Orange procession.[48] On learning of this the Sheriff issued a proclamation, but without effect since at the time appointed a party of some 300 Orangemen and their followers appeared, preceded by a cart of whisky, and were met by a hostile crowd. 100 Scots inhabitants sworn in as special constables also proved ineffective in checking the Orange advance. The Orangemen eventually levelled their muskets and as firing commenced 'the constables and people scattered and ran like sheep before a collie dog'.[49] The Orangemen entered the town in triumph (with the whisky cart) and were only persuaded to withdraw by the townspeople's procural of a four-pound cannon.[50]

The tours in 1833 and 1834 by Colonel Fairman, the representative sent by the British Grand Lodge to build up the grassroots movement, further excited activity of this sort with severe rioting occurring in Airdrie and Port Glasgow in July 1834.[51]

Strength. As for the numerical strength and organisation behind such activity, it is wise to treat with some circumspection Fairman's characteristic assurance to the Duke of Gordon that, 'such a flame has been already kindled in North Britain as must speedily burst into a conflagration, not easily extinguished'.[52]

On Fairman's arrival the Institution was limited geographically to the West of Scotland, with Edinburgh an eastern outpost, and was in a chronically insecure financial state. Although he may have given a fillip to some of the ailing lodges, including Neilston which according to its master, Brother Thompson, was 'an almost expiring institution',[53] he was unable to alter these basic structural factors. Thus, the returns of Colwill, assistant to the British Grand Secretary, compiled from the entries of district lodges, show the existence of 44 local lodges in Scotland in 1835. Since the average number in a lodge meeting under a warrant was then 5 and the maximum seldom exceeded 30, this implies less than 500 members for Scotland.[54]

Further geographical diffusion was similarly unimpressive. The lodges were organised in seven districts. Glasgow had the most numerous warrants, twelve in number, including two for Paisley and one for Pollokshaws. Ayr had ten, four of which were in Maybole alone; Innes particularly notes the great number of lodges in the manufacturing towns of Ayrshire.[55] The southwest was still represented, Dumfries having two lodges and Stranraer four, but the nucleus of the movement was undoubtedly moving north towards the rapidly industrialising centres of Lanarkshire. By this date two lodges had already been established in Airdrie and one in Larkhall.

Largely independent of any exertions on Fairman's part, this shift again links up with the influence of migration patterns, specifically Protestant migration from Ulster, on the Institution's progress. For it was precisely into such districts that the bulk of new immigration in the 30's was directed.[56] According to Innes, although 'a considerable number of Orangemen in Ayrshire were Scots', the great majority in Glasgow, Airdrie and Port Glasgow were Irish.[57] The 'Scots' may indeed have been first generation Ulster settlers.

Class: As regards the class composition of the lodges in the early

30s, from the Report there seems a clear continuity from the beginning of the century. Frequent references are made in the enquiry to a membership largely composed of 'the lower orders', 'men in humble life', 'the poor and ignorant'. Fairman's statement that 'they comprise in class and appearance, men perhaps of the best description of the lower orders', does not, for example, square with his preceding statement that they were generally uninformed and unable to write minutes or keep basic accounts – a point confirmed by Innes.[58]

The exception to this basic description was the Royal Gordon Lodge, set up by Fairman in 1833 as 'a gentlemen's lodge', based on the British Grand Lodge. This is the only body at this point for which there is any really detailed information. The minute book gives a list of 40 names and in addition provides an interesting occupational breakdown. Featured among the membership are lawyers (or in the dignified Scottish terminology 'writers'), merchants, naval and military officers, a clergyman and two gentlemen living on their own estates. Of the lodge's office bearers Lawrence Craigie, the secretary, is also a lawyer, while the District Master of Glasgow and Paisley is William Motherwell, a Scottish lyric poet, author of 'The Harp of Renfrewshire', and editor of the formerly anti-Orange *Glasgow Courier* since 1830.[59] Persuaded by Fairman to act as patron over this whole diverse Institution was His Grace, George 5th Duke of Gordon.

Politics: It is not until the early 1830s that the Orangemen come to any political prominence in Scotland, and at first sight this is one instance where a 'social control' approach to the Order seems appropriate. For besides the structure, noted above, of a proletarian rank and file and a leading gentlemen's lodge, the narrative of events in the period, with the involvement of Orangeism in anti-Reform activities at Girvan in 1831, also seems close to the paradigm of 1798, and the Irish gentry's pragmatic use of the Institution against the United Irishmen's rebellion.

Even more explicit, though, were the Orange leadership's stated purposes. There existed high political ambitions among Orange officials such as Craigie and Motherwell to make the lodges the nucleus of a new Ultra-Tory grouping to:

'counter the insidious attempts of those societies who have been so actively at work inculcating seditious principles into the minds of our well disposed and illustrious countrymen...' for if every honest man but does his duty such a storm will be blown about their ears as will advance the enthusiasm of loyalty from one end of Scotland to the other; and the adversary caught in his own snare, we will see everywhere the Orange ribbon banishing the tricolour ensign of revolution.[60]

In writing to Fairman Craigie confided, 'it will be easy by such shows of condescension and liberality to make a complete conquest of the lower classes...'[61]

What actually ensued was frustration and recrimination as attempts at manipulating the lodges for political ends encountered decisive obstacles. These stemmed firstly from the unwillingness of the Tory magnates to identify with Orangeism in Scotland.

Craigie, who had attempted to persuade Lord Douglas, the Marquis of Graham, Lord Cathcart and Sir Archibald Campbell of Succoth to no avail, in his correspondence railed eventually against 'purse proud aristocrats' and 'sluggish Tories'. Giving an insight into the real condition of the Royal Gordon he commented:

> ... is it not a crying disgrace to see petty poor clerks and broken down merchants devoting time, character, and the whole of their fortunes to propagating constitutional principles, while the sons of luxury and wealth are content to have their battle fought for them by those disinterested agents without doing ought to reward them?[62]

Several factors were at work here, including notably many Conservatives' mistrust of friendly societies and convivial fraternities in general. Although ethical rather than political bodies, a particular source of misgivings were the lodges affiliated to federations like the Oddfellows and Foresters, which aroused their prejudices against centralisation.[63] It was, of course, these which, in structure at least, the Orange Institution most resembled.

Specifically in the Scottish context, the apprehension of local aristocrats probably focused more on the Institution's status as an alien importation. Motherwell's biographer McConechy is eloquent here. To his own mind, Orangeism was really 'a particular form of one of those murderous factions into which an Irish society was divided'. It would not have appeared to occur to Motherwell that:

> Whatever the merits real or imaginary of the Orange Confederation might be, its introduction to Scotland could be attended with no benefit whatever and that if it was intended to achieve benefits of a permanent kind, it was only on the soil which had generated it and nourished it that this could have happened. As an antagonist to Popery and Jacobinism it was certainly not wanted in Presbyterian Scotland, and a little reflexion might have satisfied him that the civil and religious rights of the people of this country were not to be upheld through the instrumentality of a Hibernian political fraternity which had outlived the necessity which gave it birth... it had too many of the characteristics of a

sectarian club to be agreeable to sober minded Scotsmen.[64]

Difficulties for the Royal Gordon leadership here were compounded by conflicts with rank and file Orangemen, who proved less than tractable material for manipulative strategies. References to internal difficulties are again frequent in the 1835 evidence of Motherwell and Fairman. At the time of the latter's tour in 1833 fines had been increased to purge the lodges of 'bad characters'. The payment for admission rose from 3/- to 5/- with annual contributions of 2/- in half yearly payments and a Master's Warrant costing 5/- now rose to £1.11/6d.[65] Certain lodges refused to accede to this and were suspended by Motherwell. At the time of the report in fact only two Paisley lodges and the Royal Gordon remained officially operative. The rest persisted regardless.

The 'intemperate' behaviour of some of these proletarian lodges also did not fit the aspirations of the leadership towards political credibility, but although Motherwell expelled 'a great number of immoral and dissolute characters', again the lodges continued to meet without authority. On this whole subject Craigie is again contemptuously outspoken:

> The scoundrels in Donaldson's lodge [a Paisley lodge Warrant No. 178] are a set of thievish gamblers who spend all their money on drink and pay very little respect to their deputy Grand Secretary [ie himself] … we must hold a court martial on these mutineers and suspend them from their privileges.[66]

To fully understand this basic divergence between the Royal Gordon and the proletarian lodges, as in the case of the Irish Institution, one must stress that such Orange watchwords of the period such as 'Protestant Constitution' and 'preservation of the Protestant Religion' did not hold a unitary meaning for the groups concerned. The Laws and Ordinances of 1826 state expressly, 'In the present era our religion is menaced by the arts of Popery and the attacks of infidelity; while our constitution is assailed by fanaticism and faction. Against this double danger the Orange Institution was formed'.[67] The relative weight to be given to each of these dangers was open to interpretation.

Although not lacking in genuine anti-Roman Catholic sentiment, for the leadership of the Scottish lodges, as for the ultra Tories the Duke of Cumberland and Lord Chandos, 'Protestant Principles' were underpinned by a basic *political* understanding and motivation.[68] 'The Protestant Constitution' then, was considered a safeguard against new democratic movements and populist influences and the 'Protestant Ascendancy' was understood as the ascendancy of Protestant Anglo-Irish landlords over Irish peasants, and the right of the Protestant aristocracy to govern Britain. The frequently invoked 'foreign Catholics' phrase similarly implied not only resentment against the separate religion of the Irish, but the difficulties this presented for their political control. Lastly, 'preservation of the Protestant religion' was thought by most aristocratic defenders to refer to the preservation of tithes.

These considerations help to explain, for example, the nature of the Duke of Gordon's involvement with the Institution. Fairman describes him as 'an Orangeman from top to toe', but qualifies this by saying he does not think, 'he gives himself much trouble', though he wishes the movement to be promoted.[69] In 1833 Craigie has to beg Fairman to impress on His Grace the advantages that would accrue from him paying a single visit.[70] His restraint in his dealings with the Scottish lodges is, however, to be contrasted with frequent involvement in the proceedings of the British Grand Lodge, as indicated in the minutes from 1831-5. Here the aristocratic social and political milieu must have a seemed a great deal more familiar. For Gordon it seems the proletarian Scottish body represented merely a third line of defence for the maintenance of the status quo, behind the House of Lords and the Royal Court, and he maintained a well-bred indifference to this form of extra-parliamentary resistance.

Even the adherence of District Secretary Motherwell seems to have had political undertones and astonished his biographer. 'There is no event in his history', McConechy stated, 'which it more perplexes me to account for than this...few men in my opinion were less qualified by habits of study to appreciate the value of the mixed qualities of civil and ecclesiastical polity which that body professed to discuss'. Like many literary figures in the 1830s, such as Coleridge, Southey, and Wordsworth, Motherwell was rather 'a Tory of the old school and all the tendencies of his mind gravitated towards the creed of that old and respectable party'.[71] His poetic works indeed betray certain lingering and romantic Jacobite sentiment, which would have been ill received by rank and file Orangemen.

From the largely working class membership of the ordinary Scottish lodges a much more vigorous and literal interpretation of the 'Protestant' in 'Protestant principles' was prominent. While fuelled by a virulent hatred of Roman Catholicism this was paradoxically not without some 'democratic' input. As suggested in Chapter 1, the key to the anti-Catholic hostility was found in a representation of that religion as an absolutism that had been overthrown by some form of Protestant democratic alliance – so preserving 'the freedom of individual consciousness' and 'civil and religious liberty'. Living examples of Catholic 'mental slavery' were found in the power of priestcraft over the Irish peasantry and their veneration of O'Connell. For the rank and file Orangemen then 'Protestant Ascendancy' could frequently mean not aristocratic domination but the ascendancy of the people over 'Popish' influence, of a religion of freedom over a religion of spiritual timidity and ritualistic observance.[72]

The two camps of Ultra Tory constitutional defence and the pugnacious Protestantism of the rank and file Orangemen united more or less solidly over the issue of Catholic Emancipation. The Tories saw this as a threat to the purity and safety of the Constitution and ultimately 'to aristocratic power', while for the latter group it presented above all a potential encroachment on their Protestant religion.

The alliance, however, seems to prove less sure over the Reform controversy and its aftermath. The Girvan Orangemen, as previously described, were involved in anti-Reform activity in 1831, but against this must be balanced some, unfortunately rather oblique, references by Orange officebearers in the 1835 report. Fairman, for example, comments that he broke up one or two lodges because he did not like the way they were being conducted thinking they were, 'a little irregular not only as Orangemen but as *good and loyal subjects*'. It is also the case that the main object of his missions in 1833 and 1834, besides countering trends towards stagnation and assessing the resources of the brethren, was precisely, 'to inculcate obedience to the laws of the Institution' and secure a strict discipline among those who 'under the taint of *revolutionary and republican notions* had become refractory and mutinous'.[73] One must also conjecture whether it was not this motivation which lay behind Craigie and Motherwell's strictures against what they termed the lodges' rowdy and inebriate members. Certainly in England after the 1829 Emancipation Act Orangeism was temporarily removed from the political stage by 'a certain penetration of democratic ideals among its followers'.[74]

That such 'democratic ideas' could actually check the fulfilment of the highest ambitions of Tory Orange notables such as the Duke of Gordon, to directly control the Orange body and shape it as an adjunct to Ultra-Toryism underlines the independence of plebeian Orangeism and more generally demonstrates the dangers of too intrusive patronage in predominately working class movements.

RE-ORGANISATION AND AN UPSURGE OF ACTIVITY

Further testament to Scottish Orangeism's popular momentum and independence at grassroots is its survival, and indeed expansion, following the loss of its leading figures in the mid 1830's. Craigie, secretary of the Royal Gordon had died in 1834, after which the lodge ceased to be operative and Motherwell, the deputy Grand Master, completely broke down under examination by the House of Commons committee. Sent home to Glasgow he died of apoplexy there on 1st November 1835.[75] The lodges' aristocratic patron, Gordon, followed them on 28th May 1836.[76]

Yet in contrast to the rest of Britain, the Institution in Scotland positively regrouped. The plebeian lodges largely continued to function and a separate Scottish Grand Lodge was formed in 1835, a point overlooked by Sibbet who dates this development only from the 1870s.[77] This seems a more genuine outgrowth than the Royal Gordon. The Scottish Orangemen did again appoint a patrician leader as Grand Master, the Earl of Enniskillen, 'a loyal Ulsterman with a strong Orange and patriotic spirit',[78] but this was really a titular post and the greatest part of his duties were assumed by Brother Clements, a doctor of medicine resident in the Gallowgate, Glasgow. Enniskillen resigned in 1862 and his post was taken over by another doctor, John Leech.

Also unlike the Royal Gordon the Grand Lodge was now able to issue its own warrants for new lodges. Of the first 10 no less than 5 were for Airdrie District, No. 1 for Moodiesburn, No. 2 for Chryston, No. 6 for Drumgellock, No. 8 for Gartsherrie, No. 9 for Shotts, reflecting the further development of Lanarkshire as a powerful centre of Orange activity.[79]

In these circumstances it is rather surprising that, according to official Orange sources, 'there is little information on the activities of the brethren until 1848, when a report of the proceedings of the Grand Lodge was issued, still giving little more than the names of chief officebearers and showing a membership of 660 for Scotland, rising slightly from 1834-5'.[80]

When compared to contemporary external sources, this description appears extremely selective. In fact, important qualitative developments *were* appearing in the plebeian lodges; for while in the immediate aftermath of the 1835 parliamentary report some lodges reverted to their original functions as convivial clubs, many more began to display even more energetically the attributes of fighting societies.[81]

As well as Airdrie and surrounding districts, the industrial areas of Ayrshire were also marked by faction fights in the 1840s. The twelfth celebrations of 1847, for example, were attended by 'riotous proceedings'. At Dalry Orangemen fired on Catholics who had tried to get their regalia. The sheriff and a party of yeomanry arrested some of them and followed others to Kilbirnie and their weapons were confiscated.[82] Similar events threatened at Kilmarnock but the

Orange party's appearance in readying themselves for the fight was so contemptible that one Irish onlooker commented they were 'not worth the bating'.[83] Glasgow too witnessed recurring sectarian disturbance around the twelfth of July. In 1849 two publicans in the Gallowgate were brought before Bailie Orr on a charge of allowing their houses to be used as the public rendezvous of Orange Lodges. Various flags had been extended from their windows 'leading to ill-feeling likely to lead to a breach of the peace'.[84]

Yet incidents such as these are mild by comparison with Orange activity in the 1850s and early 60s. Indeed one of the few points at which the official interpretation does accord with empirical evidence is when it suggests 'a great impetus' or take-off from this period onwards.[85]

The mid century impetus assumed partly the form of institutional expansion reflected in a considerable increase in membership and consequently a number of new district lodges such as No. 20 Rutherglen. Compared with a total membership of 660 listed above for 1848, single Orange demonstrations in Airdrie, Paisley or Glasgow in the 50s and 60s could turn out numbers approaching this figure. However, as indicated in Campbell's table of 'Orange and Green' incidents in the Lanarkshire coalfield, the impetus was also expressed in an acceleration of violent activity.[86]

In the years 1851-60 he records 16 disturbances ranging from an Airdrie waggoner fined a guinea in May 1853 for shouting 'to Hell with the Pope!', to severe rioting and even murder. In July 1853, for example, an Irishman was killed by a mob of ironworkers, and in October of the same year 2 men were stabbed in a party dispute. In July 1857 300 Orangemen returning from a march were attacked and routed by a large number of Roman Catholics. As a result 12th July parades were banned in Lanarkshire for the next 10 years.

Again the Lanarkshire area was reflecting general tendencies in the west of Scotland, particularly in the neighbouring counties of Renfrew and Ayrshire. *The Sentinel*, for example, comments sardonically on 'a grand display of Orange folly and a reckless disregard for the consequences' and gives a useful indication of the nature of parades of the period.[87]

In July 1853 the Glasgow Orangemen had left by steamer for Greenock and joining up with the lodges there, attempted to approach the town:

> In front of the procession marched a stunted Orangeman dressed in Hessian boots and a coat à la Napoleon the whole grotesque garb surmounted by a fierce cocked hat. On the left of this distinguished person marched another fool clad in a

scarlet robe, designed to represent King William...Behind these worthies marched a drummer bold, thumping his instrument with solemn vigour. This musical performance was supported by another character who tried desperately and vainly to bring musical and defiant strains out of an obstinate and rebellious flute. Behind this 'fine band' marched the rag tag and bob tail and all the haughty honours of rampant Orangeism.

When checked by the police, declaring themselves 'True Protestants' they discreetly slunk out of sight into the Gardeners' Arms 'apparently the howf of these queer supporters of our Protestant institutions'. A drunken, violent squabble ensued about the management of the lodge.

Although presenting rather a ridiculous spectacle, the Greenock authorities did perceive in the demonstration the potential for a serious riot, hence their prompt action. A much more violent affray was indeed the outcome of similar demonstration in Paisley some years later.

The authorities in Renfrewshire, unlike Lanarkshire and Ayrshire, did not proscribe Orange demonstrations there in 1859. The Paisley Orangemen, then, were 'bold and confident'. Four- to five-hundred of them mustered and marched to Johnstone but were attacked en route by hundreds of Irish miners. On their return the Orangemen were again obstructed at the Bridge over the Black Cart. The police, however, intervened on the Orange side, and with knives and firearms freely used, several people were injured and killed.[88]

As in the early part of the century, such activities should be located in the broader socio-economic context and related to general developments in the Scottish labour movement. Thus, it was the 1830s to 60s period that saw the construction of Scotland's industrial base, with the development of the extractive industries and the production of capital goods centring on the Clyde Valley. Industrialisation, although very rapid, occurred relatively late and with an uneven development pattern, in Burgess' view representing an extreme form of 'the product cycle'.[89]

These points were vital for capital/labour relations and for the nature of class consciousness. The Scottish economy, for example, became liable to violent cyclical fluctuations as overseas market conditions altered rapidly. These were exacerbated by extreme crises of overproduction, at least till the 1850s.

The outcome here was an enormous increase in the reserve army of labour in areas of industrial expansion, like Lanarkshire from the 1830s and also parts of Ayrshire. In these circumstances class consciousness could be mobilised but the forms of its articulation were frequently incomplete and contradictory. In particular the substantial increase in Roman Catholic Irish migration in the decades following the Famine offered an explanation of recurrent economic crises to many lowland Scots, a great deal more potent and visible than their general experience of subordination to capital.

Yet this is not to suggest that the upsurge of specifically Orange violence around the 1840s and 50s can be reduced to a simple product of a retarded working class consciousness. There is still no indication that significant numbers of the indigenous working class mustered behind the Orange standard in their antipathy towards the Irish. Rather it was Ulster Protestants who continued to form the backbone of the lodges. Settling in increasing numbers in Scotland mid century – as in the 1820s and 30s – they brought with them their traditional assertion of Protestant ascendancy through regular physical confrontation with Roman Catholics. Indeed contemporaries were extremely sensitive to this. The Sheriff of Ayrshire, for example, commenting on disturbances in the late 1850s stated that:

> Of late years numbers of Irishmen amounting to a very considerable part of the population, have become resident in the parishes of Dalry and Kilbirnie where they are employed in the coal pits and ironstone mines…there are amongst them a certain number of Orangemen. And an Orange lodge is established in each of the towns of Dalry and Kilbirnie.[90]

The Courier echoed this, explaining the rioting in Paisley thus: '…it would appear a necessity imposed by the introduction of a *new element in the population* since the opening up of extensive mineral fields in the neighbourhood'[91] (Author's emphasis).

Although aiding the absolute expansion of the Institution and a bolstering of its 'fighting spirit', the large Ulster component in the Order did not further the reception of Orangeism in Scotland. Again the *Courier*'s acerbic comment is representative, and echoes McConechy's strictures quoted above. Censuring the magistrates of Glasgow for not taking draconian action on the disturbances in 1849 it proclaimed, 'These party displays, however well intended, are not for this latitude. They are imports as unwelcome as many of the Irish themselves'.[92]

Besides this growing reputation as a violent and alien organisation, even more immediate problems confronted Orangeism from the late 1850s in the shape of a major schism. Discontent and disaffection began to show itself in 1857, culminating two years later when several of the lodges in Glasgow, Partick, Greenock and Ayrshire seceded from the Grand Lodge of Scotland. They applied for and were granted warrants under the Orange Institution of Great Britain, based in England. Subsequently these two Orange bodies, the original Orange Association of Scotland and the British Institution, pursued separate courses in Scotland.

Such divisions, though, were not as fundamental as those between patrician and plebeian lodges at various points in Orange history. The exact sources of discontent are indeed unclear. Cloughley, Grand Secretary in the 1930s, had no information, but disputes over jurisdiction and administration combined with 'clashes of personality' could be important – certainly for Johnstone of Ballykillbeg speaking in Greenock in 1870 and blaming 'the petty ambitions of individuals who keep us asunder'.[93] This would also fit in with the geographical nature of the split, many of the southern lodges being included, and with the fact that it occurred in a period of expansion in numbers and activity.

In conclusion, by the early 1860s Orangeism in Scotland had gained a high public profile, but largely in terms of a 'party' or fighting society and certainly not as a credible organisational mechanism for propagating militant Protestantism. For, despite apparently favourable developments in the socio-economic structures and ideological climate of Scotland, the Institution did not attract significant bourgeois or gentry support or even mobilise effectively the anti-Irish sentiments of the Scottish working class. Behind this lay a further failure to anchor itself in the specifically *Scottish* tradition of anti-Catholicism and appear anything other than a misgrowth and 'unwelcome import'.

In these circumstances the rapid acceleration in Orange fortunes from around 1865, discussed in the following chapters, is particularly striking.

NOTES

1. R Lilburn, 'Orangeism: its Origin, Constitution and Objects' 1866, Pamphlet in Linen Hall Library, Belfast. Interview with H.S. 2/2/ 1983.
2. *Orange Gazette*, Tuesday, February 19-22; February 21st-March 6th. Scottish National Library.
3. The only 'Williamite Campaign' in Scotland was at Glencoe. Sibbet strives valiantly to clear William III's reputation over this incident. R M Sibbet, '*Orangeism in Ireland and throughout the Empire*' (1939), Vol. 1, XIC, pp.155-171.
4. For the Reformation see G Donaldson, *The Scottish Reformation* (1960), and for a short review R Miles, *Racism and Migrant Labour* (1982), Chapter 6.
5. Eugene Black, 'The Tumultuous Petitioners, The Protestant Association in Scotland', *Review of Politics*, Pt. 25, 1963, pp.183-211.
6. *Ibid*, p.211.
7. *Ibid*, p.186.
8. *A History of the Hereditary Sheriffs of Galloway*, n.d. c1747. Reference

in Lilburn, *op.cit.* (1846).

9. *Loc. cit.*

10. A McClelland, 'The Origin of the Imperial Grand Black Chapter of the British Commonwealth', *Journal of the Royal Society of Antiquaries of Ireland, Vol. 98 (1968).* 'Hedge Masons' appear to have been a source of concern to the official body of Freemasonry.

11. See Chapter 1 for distinction between LOI and RBP.

12. R M Sibbet, *op.cit.*(1939), Vol. 1, pp.400-4.

13. In recognition of its position as the birthplace of Orangeism in Scotland, on 26th October 1929, the Grand Lodge inaugurated a new lodge, LOL. No. O Mother Maybole, *Ayrshire Post* 1/11/1929.

14. *A History of the Counties of Ayr and Wigtown* n.d.; on the formation of the Scottish militia, J R Weston, *Scottish Historical Review,* XXXIV (1955).

15. J Cloughley supports the idea of the role of the Ayrshire militia (*Belfast Weekly News* (BWN) 23/11/1929). It is also suggested in the 1835 parliamentary report on the lodges that Orangemen continued to be involved in the regiment, e.g. letter from Grand Secretary Nixon to an officer in the regiment, J McWilliams, May 16, 1809, concerning regimental lodges.

16. A McClelland, 'Occupational Composition of two Orange Lodges 1853'. *Ulster Folklife* Vol. 14 (1968). See bibliography for sad fate of Kilbirnie lodge records.

17. *First Report for Enquiring into the condition of the poorer classes in Ireland.* Appendix G, Report on the state of the Irish poor in Great Britain (1836) (40) XXXIV 427, p.148. (Hereafter Irish Poor Report).

18. See Chapter 3.

19. *Irish Poor Report* (1836), p.148, W Newen's evidence.

20. T B Interview, 4/4/1983. Scott's evidence in Irish Poor Report, *op.cit.*, p.105.

21. As regards a low profile, there is no mention of the lodges in the *Ayrshire Post*, for example, 1803-5. This could confirm the basically private nature of their early activities. Early friendly society example, rules and regulations FSI 16/108, 1835 at Scottish Records Office (SRO).

22. TB Interview, 4/4/1983.

23. Cloughley, *BWN,* 23/11/1929.

24. *Glasgow Courier* (GC), 14/7/21.

25. *An account of Proceedings at the Orange Procession...(1822)*, Wylie Collection, street literature, Glasgow University Library, Special Collections.

26. PJ Waller, *op.cit.* (1981), p.26. In 1819, for example, the Liverpool Orangemen paraded with lamb, ark and Bibles on poles while a clergyman officiated over the burning of Roman Catholic vestments.

27. J E Handley, *The Irish in Scotland* (1943), p.306.

28. GC, 14/7/21.

29. *Ibid.*

30. e.g. J D Young, *op.cit.* (1979), views the class as simultaneously revolutionary and nationalistic.

31. *Capital and Class in Scotland* (1982), T Dickson (ed), pp.168-177.

32. A, Campbell, *The Lanarkshire Miners: A Social History of their Trade Unions* (1979), Chapter 1.

33. *Ibid* and T Dickson, (ed.) *Scottish Capitalism Class, State and Nation from Before the Union to the Present* (1980), p.174.

34. A Wilson, *The Chartist Movement in Scotland* (1970) p.25.

35. GH, 17/7/29.
36. GC, 13/7/23.
37. *Dumfries Weekly Journal,* 14/7/26. Sibbet, *op.cit.,* Vol. 1, p.705.
38. See Scott's evidence in *Irish Poor Report,* p.105, though the mining districts of Lanarkshire could have been an exception, Campbell, *op.cit.,* (1979).
39. Dickson, *op.cit.* (1980), see Chapter 4 for full discussion.
40. E Jamieson, *Beith Royal Arch Chapter No. 32 1814-1909,* pamphlet n.d. St. Salem lodge collapsed in period 1820-2 through non-payment of dues and migration of members seeking employment.
41. See J L Murdoch, 'Policing public processions in Scotland', *Journal of the Law Society,* March 1983.
42. See Appendix E, biographical index and obituary in *Blackwood's Magazine,* July 1867.
43. A Alison, edited by Lady Alison, *Some Account of My Life and Works* (1888). Alison was a high-ranking Freemason.
44. Murdoch, *op.cit.* (1983).
45. GH 13/7/22. GH 15/7/31.
46. Report from the *Select Committee appointed to Enquire into the Origin, Nature, Extent and Tendency of Orange Lodges in Great Britain and the Colonies,* House of Commons, 1835 [605] xvii, Lane's Evidence, p.141. (Hereafter 1835 Report).
47. *Ayrshire Post,* 16/7/31.
48. GH, 2/8/31.
49. GC 14/7/31. *1835 Report* Lanes Evidence p.29. More violence broke out in 1834 in the town. Fairman's Evidence, p.169.
50. *Ibid.*
51. *Glasgow Free Press,* 16/7/34. *1835 Report,* p27.
52. Proceedings of the Royal Gordon Lodge, June 4th 1833 (*1835 Report,* Appendix No. 2).
53. *Loc. cit.*
54. Senior, *op.cit.* (1966), p.206.
55. *1835 Report,* Introduction, p.9.
56. *Irish Poor Report* (1835).
57. *1835 Report,* Innes' Evidence, p.29.
58. *Loc. cit.*
59. J E Handley, *op.cit.* (1943), dismisses Motherwell as 'a minor poet' but he was very much in vogue in America, and gained particularly favourable mention from Edgar Allen Poe in *Home Journal* 31/8// 1850, and *Sartain's Union Magazine,* October 1850.
60. GC, 26/12/33.
61. *1835 Report,* Appendix No. 22.
62. P Mackenzie, *Letters of the Tory conspirators in Glasgow,* Pamphlet (1935), Mitchell Library, Glasgow.
   Craigie, seems a pathetic figure. He was extremely deferential and ingratiating towards Fairman in his correspondence. His main concern with the Orange body is apparently in projected uniforms and regalia. To Fairman: 'Remember and bring a uniform with you, as we are resolved to want that no longer...' on 22nd of June; a week later; '...will you bring a pattern of a uniform with you? I am getting some King William head buttons over from Belfast. Do you think your waistcoat is sufficiently military for the Institution?'; July 15th 'Are you getting a uniform prepared?'; finally with a note of desperation on July 24th, '*I hope his Royal Highness has sanctioned the project of the uniform.*' (Craigie's emphasis). See Mackenzie's letters 22/6/33, 1/7/

33, 3/7/33, 15/7/33 and 24/7/33.

63. C Hill, 'Robinson Crusoe' in *History Workshop Journal* No. 10, 1981.
64. J McConechy, *Draft of a Memoir of William Motherwell (n.d)*, Robertson MSS. Collection, University of Glasgow Special Collections.
65. *1835 Report*, Appendix 12.
66. Mackenzie, *op.cit.* (1835), letter dated 3/7/33.
67. Lord Eldon was most outspoken on his fears not only for Protestantism and the Protestant ascendancy but for 'freedom as he conceived it'. Cassirer, Ph.D., *op.cit.* (1938).
68. *Ibid.*
69. *1835 Report*, Fairman's evidence.
70. Mackenzie, *op.cit.* (1835), letter dated 24/7/33.
71. *J McConechy, Mss.* (n.d), Loc.cit.
72. See Cassirer, *op.cit.*, (1938).
73. *1835 Report*, Fairman's Evidence.
74. Cassirer, *op.cit.* (1938); Senior, *op.cit.*, (1966), the *1835 Report* also contains the example of Oldham Orangemen expelled for voting for Reform candidates.
75. See *Dictionary of National Biography*, Vol. 2, (1901-1970).
76. *Loc.cit.*
77. Sibbet, *op.cit.* (1939), vol. 2, p.371.
78. Cloughley, *BWN*, 23/11/1929. There is no indication that the noble lord took any active part in affairs of the Scottish movement.
79. *Ibid.*
80. *Ibid.*
81. John Foster suggests a similar shift towards a convivial function took place among the Oldham Orange lodges. *Class Struggle and the Industrial Revolution* (1974), p.219.
82. GH, 17/7/47.
83. *Ibid.*
84. GC, 17/7/49.
85. Cloughley, *BWN*, 23/11/1929.
86. Campbell, *op.cit.* (1979), Appendix III.
87. *Glasgow Sentinel* 16/7/53.
88. GC, 19/7/59. (A list of the injured here also gives a brief indication of early Paisley Orangemen's occupations, noting shoemakers, miners and textile print cutters.)
89. K Burgess, Chapter 5, p.181f. in Dickson (ed.), *op.cit.* (1980)
90. Report to the Lord Advocate of Scotland by the Sheriff Substitute of Ayrshire. *Lord Advocate's Papers AD 58-70*, SRO.
91. GC, 19/7/59.
92. GC. 17/7/49.
93. *Greenock Telegraph* 2/11/70. The tendency towards internal conflict seems endemic to Orangeism at certain periods of its history, notably amid rapid numerical expansion or political stagnation. The RBP was similarly affected in the 1840s. In 1844, for instance, a breakaway Grand Priory of Ireland was formed by members who felt neglected by their brethren in Scotland where its headquarters were then situated. (See Chapter 3 for Ireland and H Senior, *Orangeism, The Canadian Phase*, (n.d.) for parallel colonial developments.)

5

Orangeism in Scotland 1865–1900:
Quantification and Class Composition

The years 1865-1900 mark the real expansion and consolidation of the LOI's mass membership in Scotland. Given the movement's marginalisation in most accounts of class relations of the period some initial grasp of numbers here is important.[1]

There are difficulties in exact computation, but some impression can be gained from newspaper coverage of successive mass demonstrations taking place on or around the 12th of July each year.[2]

The limits on organisational development also become clear, though, in examining the Order's geographical bases of support.

QUANTIFICATION

The Twelfth: 12th of July parades from the 1870s increasingly replaced indoor lodge celebrations, not to mention spontaneous brawling, as the major form of LOI activity. The form of these parades, remaining largely unchanged to the present, was fairly complex and demanding of considerable logistical skill on the part of their organisers.[3] A 'grand demonstration' would be held at a location specified by the Grand Lodge, and all over the West of Scotland 'feeder' demonstrations took place, with the Orangemen mustering and marching through the main streets of their respective towns to the railway station or even, in the case of the Clyde coast towns, the steamer embarkation points. Arriving at their destination they joined in the combined demonstration usually to some field on the outskirts of town, where they were addressed from the platform by Grand Lodge speakers and guests. On the end result James Connolly, in 1906, commented rather perceptively, 'Viewing the procession as a mere league... I must confess some parts of it are beautiful, some of it ludicrous and some of it exceedingly disturbing'.[4]

The first demonstration along these lines was in Glasgow in 1872. On this occasion 1500 were reported to have been present from Glasgow itself and adjacent districts. Twenty lodges represented the Orange Association of Scotland (OA of S) and twelve the Loyal Orange Institution of Great Britain (OI of GB).[5] While not as yet immediately impressive this figure should be compared to the *total* membership of over twenty years before, estimated at 660. It should also be stressed that large independent demonstrations were taking place that day at Airdrie, Slammanan and Ayrshire.

The following year, moreover, such a large triennial gathering was described as 'the greatest demonstration ever witnessed in connection with Orangeism in Scotland'.[6] The *Glasgow Herald* estimated 40-50,000 in the procession. Estimates given by officials for railway transportation purposes the previous week, however, were only 30,000 and apparently not all the seats were filled on the day. Given that the procession was more than two miles long and took 55 minutes to pass a given point perhaps 15-20,000 is more realistic and still a considerable figure.

This is supported by turnout in subsequent years in the 1870s and 80s at grand demonstrations held at Dumbarton, Kilmarnock and Port Glasgow. These attracted an average 8,000, with families and supporters on top of this, the Glasgow contingent alone usually mustering 3,000-4,000. The figure seems to have been less the further the demonstration was held from Glasgow and also appears to fluctuate in response to local manifestations of economic uncertainty. Thus in 1884 'dull trade' was said to have been responsible for the smaller numbers in the Govan turnout, 'having told severely here, the population having been on the decrease for some times past'.[7] Again other demonstrations held simultaneously around Scotland, in Lanarkshire and North Ayrshire could attract in addition a combined total of around 6,000.[8]

Clearly then it is best to treat as hyperbole the then Grand Master George McLeod's claim in 1875 that he stood, 'at the head of 60,000 members in Scotland of such a good and peaceful fraternity... 60,000 loyal men, good and true whose Protestantism could at all times be relied upon';[9] and likewise the *Glasgow News* estimate of no less than 90,000 Orangemen in Scotland in 1878, 14-15,000 of them in Glasgow.[10] Yet nevertheless the figure which the LOI could turn out at its great ceremonial occasions in the 1870s and early 1880s *is* impressive. This growth is paralleled, as Patterson notes, by the LOI in Belfast which expanded from the 1850s but particularly in the 1870s, both cases contradicting the movement's official historians, Dewar, Brown and Long, who indicate the LOI had reacted a quietus from which it only recovered through the enormous impetus received from Home Rule agitation in the mid 1880s.[11]

This is not to say, of course, that the Scottish Institution did not additionally benefit from these political developments. In 1886, for example, the year of the first Home Rule bill a markedly increased complement of 7-8,000 marched from Glasgow to Cowlairs.[12] In addition, 57 lodges turned out at Motherwell, though the Greenock and Port Glasgow brethren numbering over 300 preferred to sail to Rothesay on the new *Meg Merilees*.[13] Over 1,000 also rallied at Ayr.

Progress though was not unimpeded and for the next few years attendances were 'scarcely as large as usual' as the immediate danger of Home Rule passed, though in contrast in 1888 the Glasgow contingent to Thornliebank numbered upwards of 2,000 in 30 lodges.[14]

The 1890s followed a very similar pattern and again the Home Rule issue came to prominence. In 1891 the Glasgow turnout for the march to Jordanhill was 'quite equal to that of former years',[15] and in 1892 with Gladstone's second Home Rule bill the demonstration at Glasgow was 'one of the most imposing ever to have taken place' with a one mile procession of 7,000 Glasgow Orangemen marching to Govan.[16] The Grand Demonstration of 1896 saw 200 lodges at Renfrew,[17] and the following year an estimated 10-12,000 were present at Kilbowie with contingents from Glasgow, Port Glasgow, Greenock, Paisley and Johnstone, while another 10,000 from 8 districts and representing 35 lodges were present at Airdrie.[18]

Fluctuations aside from the evidence of its public outings, the LOI in Scotland would appear at least to have entered the new century with a membership of around 25,000 with around 8,000 of these in Glasgow.[19] Though it is not intended at this stage to provide a systematic assessment of their economic or political weight in Scotland it may help in putting this number in some perspective that the Amalgamated Society of Engineers and the Society of Boilermakers and Iron Shipbuilders, two of the most powerful trade unions in Scotland in the early 1890s, had each around 8,000 members. The National Federation of Mineworkers, revived in 1886, had a nominal membership of 25-40,000 while the Operative Masons, revived in 1892, had 4,000 men affiliated.[20]

The 12th of July marches cannot, however, stand as the only index of LOI development in personnel and activity from the late 1860s. This was after all the point at which the conduct of the Orange year, quite literally, reached its crescendo. For a more adequate account of how the Order sustained its functions, on a day to day basis, it is necessary to consider the LOI's numerical advance in terms of the geographical distribution of its lodges and district lodges, and to note the development of certain power bases.

Local Developments: As suggested, the broad pattern in the earlier part of the century had been a diffusion of Orangeism from its earliest centres of South Ayrshire, Wigtownshire and Dumfries, northwards into Glasgow, Lanarkshire, North Ayrshire and the commercial towns of Greenock and Port Glasgow on the Clyde Coast. In the years following 1865 it is within these areas that the most marked consolidation and intensification of Orange activity occurs.[21]

Besides Lanarkshire and Ayrshire, where the progress of the LOI was acknowledged by the installation of a County Grand Lodge in February 1875,[22] one of the first centres to emerge was Paisley. This had been represented by a lodge, probably LOL No. 3 'Royal Oak' or LOL No. 6 'Duc de Schomberg' at one of the earliest 12th displays in 1822, and had received a great impetus at the period of the poet Motherwell's involvement in the 1830s. It seems to have experienced another spurt of growth even by the late 1850s, witnessing probably the first public 'Orange and Protestant' *soirée* of its kind in Scotland in 1856, with upwards of 700 present.[23] By 1866 it had 10 lodges meeting in their own premises and constituting their own district lodge (No. 6).[24]

While the Orange presence in Paisley tended to remain fairly constant in the latter part of the century, Greenock, another growth point from the 1860s was to continue with a steady development. Indeed, the Rev. Henry Henderson's speech of 1869 boasting '1000 loyal Orangemen in Greenock' is probably not greatly exaggerated, though it may include the figure from neighbouring Port Glasgow.[25] The following year 1,300 were reported as present at the grandest demonstration and *soirée* ever held in the Town Hall under the auspices of the Orangemen of Greenock, where the Rev. Gunn congratulated them on their prosperity: 'He remembered when a very small hall holding about a hundred, could hold them'.[26]

By 1874 these were organised in two districts No. 3 and No. 4 of the OI of GB with a total of 14 lodges between them.[27] The number increased to 15 the following year, with the 5 lodges in Port Glasgow now constituting their own district No. 19,[28] and rose to 17 in the 1890s. Also worthy of note is the existence in the area of a Royal Black Preceptory, St. George's RBP No. 164, and Hunt Chambre District RPB No. 211.[29]

Like the 12th turnout figures, however, such figures cannot go unqualified. For taking an overall view of Scotland, at no point in the late nineteenth century did the LOI's geographical stronghold extend beyond the West of Scotland. Certainly 25,000 were estimated to have attended the 12th parade in Edinburgh in 1902, with William Johnstone of Ballykillbeg commenting that the proceedings would have been the most imposing seen in Scotland if the weather had been more favourable.[30]

But this reflects the Order's efficient transport arrangements rather than an improvement in the Capital's status as an eastern redoubt. The *Glasgow Observer*, for example, had noted only a few years earlier that the Orangemen there 'bulk so meagrely... that they thought it advisable to hold their social in the Conservative rooms... rather than make any public display'.[31]

Even within the West of Scotland variations in support were evident. This is demonstrated in the case of Glasgow, where amid rapid and widespread development, large areas of the West and South remained largely uncultivated. The earliest 'Orange area' at the beginning of the nineteenth century, was Candleriggs and Blackfriars in the old city centre. This was the site of the major Orange Halls and Grand Lodge Headquarters till 1914,[32] forming No. 2 district and No. 24 Candleriggs sub-district with a complement of over 600 in 1878.[33]

By the 1840s and 50s though, new growth areas were already apparent. (See Fig. 2). These included Partick which formed district No. 1 of the LOI of GB as well as No. 15 of the Scottish Association. Most noticeable though in this period was the beginning of the spread eastwards: first into Townhead with LOL No. 167 'Auchenairn Volunteers'; then to Camlachie and Calton, with districts Nos. 17 and 37 respectively; to Parkhead, district No. 21 with 7 lodges; and to Bridgeton, which had previously only 2 lodges, now becoming district 31.

This shift was steadily reinforced with many more lodges in these areas in the late 1860s and 70s. Expansion now also took place westwards with the establishment of Anderston district No. 41 and Whiteinch and Partick No. 46. Again from the late 1870s and 80s the Institution expanded more definitely south of the river. Kinning Park, for example, which in 1878 had been 'only a small but comparatively recent foundation' with 2 lodges, in the 1880s had a total of 8 lodges with a probable membership of 250-400. Districts were formed in Govan No. 42, and Gorbals/Hutchesontown No. 50. Bridgeton also underwent further development during this period with the creation of a further district No. 44 on its eastern boundary. From this area came the 'new men' in the LOI, W. Young and J. McManus, rising to prominence in the Grand Lodge in the late 1880s.[34]

To sum up then, by the closing decades of the nineteenth century the LOI had displayed a very uneven pattern of development. It was still firmly rooted in the West of Scotland, with notable centres of growth in Glasgow and surrounding counties but it had failed to have any significant impact either in the Highlands or in Edinburgh and the East.

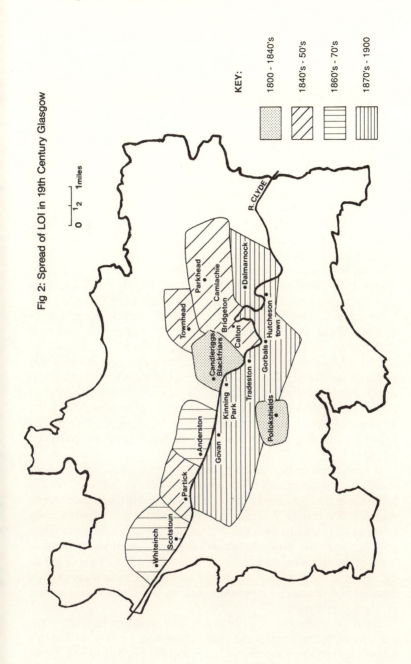

Fig 2: Spread of LOI in 19th Century Glasgow

KEY:

1800 - 1840's

1840's - 50's

1860's - 70's

1870's - 1900

CLASS COMPOSITION: THEORY

Having dealt with initial quantification, we can now move on to the more qualitative aspects of Orangeism's nineteenth century advance, and consider the Order's class composition. From anecdote and folklore the strongest impression is that the LOI found its constituency among skilled workers, in the West of Scotland acting as a major lever to recruitment and advancement in the shipyards and engineering works. Superimpose on this an acquaintance with much of the sociological theory on working class sectionalism and the LOI becomes hypostatised as a labour aristocracy movement, albeit of some vaguely 'deviant' nature.

Some corroboration for this is found among the general academic literature with a bearing on the Institution. Smith appears to see it in this light.[35] Melling also discusses it in the context of skilled male workers and the development of an artisan culture.[36]

In such accounts, of course, the major focus of interest is elsewhere. Here, however, where the focus *is* directly on Orangeism, such 'commonsense' assumptions cannot go unchallenged. The historical evidence, in fact, strongly militates assimilating the LOI into the labour aristocracy type of analysis. Doubts also arise over the theory itself.

The substantive developments which have promoted the adoption of the theory for Scotland are fairly straightforward. The 1850s onwards witnessed a massive shift to the manufacture and export of capital goods, thus integrating Scottish capital more closely with the fortunes of British capital in the world economy, and giving an enhanced standing both to the industrial bourgeoisie and to skilled labour.[37]

A prominent feature of this period was also a greater comprehensiveness in the hegemony of liberalism, though this shift was possibly less dramatic in Scotland. Thus, for example, although there was a mid century revival in Trade Unionism and a greater propensity towards joint action, with the first regular Trades council in Glasgow in 1858, the products which emerged shared the distinctive traits of the British model unions.[38] These included a view of political action in terms of pressure in the existing parliamentary parties, advocacy of franchise extension and an acceptance of classical political economy.

Such developments in expansion and stability prompted the backwards projection to the mid nineteenth century of Lenin's labour aristocracy concept, which originally applied to the 1890s and 1900s. There are different definitions of the basic concept but Foster provides a useful example. He suggests that the process of 'liberalisation' or stabilisation around the 1850s was rooted in a historical reorientation of the British ruling class in the face of a 'revolutionary working class', an integral part of this reorientation being precisely the fragmentation of the labour force with strategies to encourage 'sub-groupings' in the working class and more efficient forms of social control.[39]

Increasingly though the labour aristocracy concept has met with less than equivocal acceptance. In the face of criticism Moorhouse neatly codifies three responses. First there is the almost dogmatic retention of the concept without qualification. Most recently, as already noted, Smith states, 'It is impossible to think of the nineteenth century without the term. It has been an organising concept of most of the research into the nineteenth century labour movement'.[40] Secondly and 'the new insipid orthodoxy' according to Moorhouse, is a critical acceptance of a revised concept like Gray's with its less ambitious and more indefinite claims for explanatory power and sometimes allied with a culturalist problematic. The third position, however, is that the concept has little analytic value and should now be disregarded.[41]

The 'middle course' here is not necessarily preferable. The immediate problems, as Gray himself admits are twofold.[42] It is difficult, despite Hobsbawm's precise criteria, for example, to identify empirically a division between labour aristocrats and others. This might work for some specific occupations and localities but the very diversity of the Scottish, not to mention British, experience confounds almost any procedure of generalisation. Moreover, even if one can isolate this prized group, as Smith believes possible for Glasgow and Liverpool,[43] the extent of its analytic power is still left unclear; whether it is merely to denote the empirical delineation of social structure divisions within the boundaries of the working class, or more ambitiously, though with less precision, whether it can aid conceptualisation of the relationship between economic classes, class consciousness and state agencies.

Gray believes the value of the concept is that it is concrete and conjunctural but, as Clarke points out, the type of division indicated by the 'labour aristocracy' may not be just a unique historical phenomenon but the particular form of a more general tendency towards complexity and differentiation. For expansions and movements in capital do not necessarily unify and homogenise labour even in the direct relations of production.[44]

In this way structural divisions within localities, industries and indeed other internal divisions such as those based on gender, ethnic or religious categorisation, which cannot be simply explained in terms of occupational tendencies, should perhaps be the starting point of an analysis of working class relations and consciousness, rather than an implicit principle of unity. To employ the labour aristocracy device as some sort of historically contingent factor, to explain the 'gap' between the working class's theoretical destiny and its actual history in the nineteenth century displaces these central features. This is particularly significant in the Scottish case where a major sectional divide was between the indigenous Scots population and the migrant Roman Catholic Irish. Indeed for an understanding of the nature of class relations in Scotland and the LOI's position in them, a rigid retention of the labour aristocracy analysis does not mark a great advance on the traditional economistic approach and may close off more radical overtures.

Similarly in analysing the internal dynamics of Orangeism, reliance on the labour aristocracy concept can obscure the central distinction between 'rough' and 'respectable' in the working class, which, as Moorhouse suggests, is by no means coterminous with hierarchies of skill and pay.[45] As subsequent discussion will show, this distinction is not only vital in understanding Orangemen's self-perceptions, but also provided the terrain on which many rank and file/leadership conflicts were waged.

CLASS COMPOSITION: HISTORICAL EVIDENCE

No attempt was made in the preceding sections to offer an explanatory analysis of the LOI's general expansion in the later nineteenth century or its increasing presence in certain areas. A simple hypothesis can be made, drawing particularly on the experience of Glasgow, that, as in the earlier period, these closely follow the shift of population and the development of industry in the West of Scotland. In turn this involves the obvious assumption that the class basis of Orangeism must follow closely on the occupational and industrial structure of its specific locations. In other words at grass roots level in Scotland, it was still overwhelmingly an organisation of the industrial working class, both skilled and unskilled, albeit with a significant petty bourgeois component.

The following breakdown of membership for the latter part of the nineteenth century does reinforce these points.

For this breakdown four main areas were selected for detailed examination. This was determined to some extent by the availability of sources, but is also designed to illustrate the differing material contexts for LOI development. Two burghs with distinct industrial and occupational structures are examined, Greenock and Paisley, based respectively on commerce and on textiles and crafts. Also considered is the Glasgow conurbation, a heavy industrial area and one of the largest centres of the Scottish LOI. Finally as examples of the Order in varied county settings, attention focuses on Lanarkshire and Ayrshire.

The names of Orangemen in these areas were gathered from sources such as newspapers and pamphlets, and checked against electoral registers, Post Office directories and Fowler's directories to determine occupation. The majority of this sample are officebearers, but certainly at private and district level these are strongly representative, as in Ireland, of the general character of the Institution's rank and file. They were, for example, democratically elected and the turnover of personnel throughout the period studied does not suggest a self-perpetuating group. [46] Nor were the officebearers likely to be the most literate among the rank and file, since the nature of lodge meetings and degree work did not set a particular priority on this.

The largest and most representative sample of names came from Greenock and Paisley, where *soirées* and meetings were frequent and well reported. It was possible to set out findings here in the tables in Appendices B, C and D. Glasgow also provided a large sample but, as discussed below, it probably represents only a small proportion of Orangemen in the city, therefore more general secondary sources were employed as a supplement. This was also the case in Ayrshire and Lanarkshire, and with the former interviews with contemporary Orangemen and ex-Orangemen were also used. The names and occupations available for Glasgow and the counties are included in the biographical index, Appendix E.

Greenock: Turning first to Greenock, the dominant characteristic of labour here was its unskilled and casual nature. This is expected from a primarily commercial and distributive centre, though during the nineteenth century Greenock's status as a port had to some extent declined as the deepening of the Clyde enabled ocean-going ships to reach Glasgow, and sugar refining, textiles and new enterprises in engineering had expanded. [47]

LOI membership here shows a close correspondence to these general circumstances throughout the period under study.

Of the 53 names, from 1870–86, for which occupations have been located, 16, the largest group, are listed as 'labourers', only one of whom is apparently in a supervisory position. A further 10 are in unskilled work or depressed trades, seaman, gatekeeper, tenter, for example, 5 fall into the rather ambiguous and amorphous categories of 'joiner' or 'engineer' while 6 are more definitely in skilled trades, but significantly include those tied to the volatile nature of the local economy, sailmaker and fitter. The 12 remaining might be designated petty bourgeois and are mostly shopkeepers, an ironmonger, a grocer (and interestingly 2 wine and spirit merchants) with a sprinkling of clerical workers, an insurance agent, a 'broker', and a single representative of the professions - a veterinary surgeon.[48]

The majority (62%) of the LOI's Greenock membership in the 1870s and 80s was drawn then from that section of the working class, principally defined by its less regular and well paid employment. Indeed the dominance of this strata is probably understated above. For a further 40 names it was not possible to determine occupation, and the nature of the sources employed, post office directories, electoral registers, suggest it would be precisely the unskilled and casual labourers who were omitted.

This impression of class composition is confirmed for the later period. The 1892-3 post office directory gives a very full listing of LOI officebearers. Of 38 names for which occupations can be found 16 are listed as 'labourers' or in unskilled trades, 3 are janitors or watchmen, 11 are in the 'fitter', 'joiner' category or in other skilled trades, 6 are small shopkeepers (one a spirit dealer) or insurance salesmen, 1 is a fireman and 1 a policeman.[49]

A further significant dimension in the Greenock case is also the extent of LOI members' residential concentration.[50] Like Candleriggs in Glasgow, the original 'Orange area' of Greenock in the 1850s and 60s and site of the Institution's Hall, had been Cathcart Street and the Wellpark area towards the older centre of the town, and here the Orangemen retained a strong presence. From the 1870s onwards, however, the real muscle of the membership was to be found in the area of new tenement flats on the higher ground to the south of the town and close to the sugar refineries and foundries - Drumfrochar Road, Prospecthill Road, Ingleston Street, with Mill Street as its axis (see Fig 3).[51] Even among the petty bourgeois element, several had business premises or residences in this southern corner. In 1892-3 indeed the southern concentration is particularly prominent. Seven officebearers are resident in Drumfrochar Road alone, 3 in Dempster Street, 5 in the Ingleston Street/Baker Street area.[52]

By comparison, for example, in the 1870-86 period 4 officebearers' names were located in Cathcart Street, 6 in Drumfrochar Road, 3 in Prospecthill Road, 3 in Ingleston Street, 3 in Crescent Street, 3 in West Blackhall Street and 2 in Market Street,[53] still a significant concentration of 48%.

Although anticipating the discussion below on the LOI and labour migration it should be stressed that this was precisely the area of heavy Protestant Irish settlement, 34.2% of residents here being of

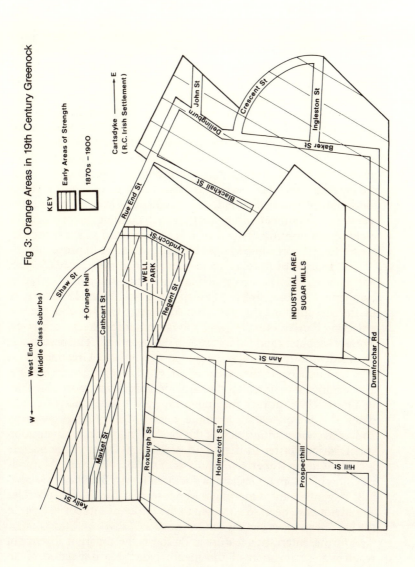

Fig 3: Orange Areas in 19th Century Greenock

KEY

Early Areas of Strength

1870s –1900

Cartsdyke ⟶ E
(R.C. Irish Settlement)

W ⟶ West End
(Middle Class Suburbs)

+ Orange Hall

WELL PARK

INDUSTRIAL AREA
SUGAR MILLS

Kelly St

Market St

Cathcart St

Shaw St

Rue End St

Lyndoch St

Regent St

Blackhall St

Bellingburn

John St

Crescent St

Baker St

Ingleston St

Roxburgh St

Holmscroft St

Ann St

Prospecthill

Hill St

Drumfrochar Rd

Irish birth.[54] The Roman Catholic Irish seem to have been similarly concentrated in the old decaying part of the town and the neighbouring burgh of Cartsdyke to the east.

In this way a possible parallel emerges between Greenock and Liverpool in terms of the LOI's physical ghettoisation and significant casual and unskilled component. The two centres of course also shared an economic structure rooted in commerce rather than heavy industry.[55] It is dangerous, however, to extend the Liverpool comparison in any sustained manner to Scotland as a whole. If one looks at Paisley, for example, a comparable burgh to Greenock in size and location, its pattern of class affiliation has a quite distinct emphasis.

Paisley: Unlike Greenock, Paisley from the late eighteenth century enjoyed a tradition of skilled labour based on high quality textile production with a strong radical culture. In the period under study the local economy had become dominated by thread mills and was more vulnerable to fluctuations of demand, but also represented were a large number of urban crafts, coach building, tailoring, shoemaking and printing. The town in addition acted as a commercial centre for the surrounding agricultural districts of Renfrewshire.[56]

The sources provide a smaller sample than the preceding case, but the impression is of a much larger artisan and petty bourgeois component in LOI membership than Greenock. From 35 names, 26 fit this description, the patternmaker, shuttlemaker and drapers reflecting Paisley's textile basis, though other shopkeepers, clerical workers, cobblers and tailors are also represented.[57] The percentage is considerably higher, 74% compared with 30% for Greenock. This may well understate the extent of unskilled involvement,[58] but it is also significant to note that the Order in Paisley was more able than in Greenock to attract the much desired 'better class of candidates'.[59] A R Pollock, for example, owner of a drysalters company and 'convenor of antiquities' of the Paisley Philosophical Institution was District Master in the 1870s and 80s.[60] Other office bearers include William Robertson, Minister of the local Primitive Methodist Church; Thomas Graham, a doctor; and Mr. Smellie of Gallowhill, a 'gentleman'. One might suppose that these local notables would not have been so attracted to the Order had its social basis in the area been more similar to Greenock's.[61]

A further interesting feature in Paisley is the apparent absence of residential segregation of the membership. No indication of an Orange area comparable to the Mill Street/Drumfrochar Road example above emerged. Generally, as McCarthy indicates, Paisley was free from Greenock or Liverpool's degree of residential segregation on religious lines, although the Roman Catholic Irish had originally tended to settle in the decayed areas such as the Sneddon and parts of the new town.[62]

Glasgow: Moving on to the case of Glasgow, the impression is of a hybrid of the two patterns of class affiliation outlined above, with a thorough mixture of unskilled, casual, artisan and petty bourgeois. Unfortunately a detailed tabulated breakdown is not feasible as it is for Greenock,[63] nor are occupational lodges found as they were on occasion in Belfast thought they may have existed in a 'de facto' sense.[64] Conclusions, then, must remain rather tentative. However, working from the premise of the links between the local industrial structure and the occupational and class basis of the LOI, clearly a strong representation is to be expected from the industrial working class - with Glasgow from the 1870s becoming a major centre for heavy engineering and shipbuilding and metal manufacture. Significantly, the outposts of Orangeism in areas of the city where it was otherwise not represented were also working class outposts in otherwise bourgeois residential areas. In the College parliamentary division which covered large areas of the West End, for example, the only district with any sizable LOI presence was Cowcaddens which, as McCaffrey notes, was characterised by an unskilled working class population, high density housing and a local economy based on foundries and chemical works.[65]

Beyond this it becomes difficult to determine the relative weight of unskilled or artisan components of membership. Nor is the general economic context conclusive. Glasgow's base in heavy industry, ensured an occupational structure where the skilled workers, in the broadest definition, dominated. But Treble still estimates 27.16% employed males were unskilled, and as Smith suggests this may actually underestimate those in the 'unskilled' category with the difficulty in precisely identifying the status of the growing designation of 'handyman'.[66]

Only in a few localities for which a limited breakdown is possible can one suggest a predominance of one component or the other. In Partick (like East Belfast), its local economy relying on shipbuilding and engineering, the strength of the skilled working class element is indicated by a number of those from the boilermaking and engineering trades among office bearers in No. 16 and 46 districts. While Anderston is probably similar in this respect, both Cowcaddens and Maryhill present important contrasts. The industries of the former were noted above and in the latter case 'a pocket version of Hades' on the 12th,[67] large areas were occupied for railway purposes or by large public works in the 1870s and 80s. Heavy industry characteristic of elsewhere in the city had not yet penetrated. In both cases the

LOI tended to reflect the unskilled nature of the general working class composition, with occupations of officebearers ranging from labourers, and moulders to a railway signal maker. In all other areas, however, even this limited breakdown is difficult from the sources. These are also areas of a more diverse class base. Camlachie, for instance, with its chemical works and Beardmore's furnace at Parkhead had some of the worst slum housing in the city, Little and Great Dovehill and the Rookery but also the new artisan tenements of Annfield and Bellgrove.[68] It is similarly difficult to specify with any accuracy the size of the petty bourgeois component for the various localities but the biographical index suggests a fair presence, again often in the shape of insurance collectors and shopkeepers.

Clearer is the lack of ghettoisation of the LOI's membership when compared with Greenock or Liverpool, despite the Order's increasing presence, sketched above, in areas like Calton and Bridgeton. There had been in the 1830s a range of buildings in Bridgeton known as 'wee Belfast' occupied by weavers from Northern Ireland,[69] but such examples are few from the 1870s onwards due in part to the tenement system.[70] Whiteinch and Partick were reckoned by contemporaries to be 'Orange' strongholds, for example, but the term is used loosely with no distinction usually made here in anecdotal evidence between LOI members, Protestant Irish and even indigenous Protestants, the actual degree of residential segregation is doubtful.[71] This was translated into electoral terms. As Hutchin-son points out there were no 'Protestant' wards in the city though some were 'skilled' or 'unskilled', and the Roman Catholic Irish were similarly distributed throughout wards and parliamentary constituencies.[72]

The LOI's diversity even within the West of Scotland is confirmed in looking briefly at its county strongholds in Lanarkshire and Ayrshire.

Lanarkshire and Ayrshire: Campbell, in his study of the Lanarkshire coalfields, indicates the strength of Orange membership there among coal face workers who had achieved a precarious quasi-craft position drawing on the independent collier tradition.[73] Later in the century Orangemen were also increasingly drawn from the iron and steel works in Lanarkshire. McDonagh notes that many Protestant Irish were employed in largely skilled capacities, particularly in the original Tube and Iron Smelting Works such as Kipps, Bairds, and Lloyds 'Sun' and 'Britain' branches, which employed Roman Catholic Irish only in the capacity of Puddlers' labourers, and later blastfurnacemen. Though new works in the 1890s were less able to select their workforce.[74] This area is also interesting, she suggests, in its marked residential segregation particularly in the case of the mining villages of Harthill and Larkhall which were the local centres of the Order.[75]

In the case of Ayrshire membership was similarly drawn from the mining community in the small southern villages such as Patna which boasted 2 lodges in the 1870s.[76] Though also represented in membership in the south were agricultural workers suggesting a similarity with some of the Ulster counties, Tyrone and Fermanagh.

This group was also present in the lodges in North Ayrshire, in the Dalry and Kilwinning area lodges, Districts No. 9 and 14, for example, but overall here as in Lanarkshire the heavy industry workforce predominated.[77] The heart of Ayrshire's industrial area around Ardrossan, Saltcoats, Stevenston, Irvine and Kilwinning was indeed described by contemporaries as 'a little Lanarkshire' with ironworks, mining and a variety of manufacturing. In 1873 the Garnock area alone had 31 out of 61 of the ironstone mines in the country.[78]

Thus, for example, the village of 'the Den' near Beith, which was based around a single small pit and had a population of just over a hundred, had its own lodge from the 1890s, until the pit was exhausted in the 1920s and the community dispersed.

From the 1880s a new potential component was added when steelworking was introduced in the area by Merry and Cunningham at Glengarnock. The steelworkers seem to have provided the backbone of the LOI in the Garnock Valley, though the lack of sources makes it impossible to specify whether a skilled element predominated. Merry and Cunningham apparently employed members of the Institution in all capacities including that of labourer and blastfurnacemen.[79] These workers were housed in company housing based on the design of miners rows, but unlike some of the Lanarkshire villages at no point did they become 'Orange' enclaves, instead containing a significant Irish, and later even Lithuanian, Roman Catholic population.[80]

ORANGEISM AND SECTIONALISM

Two related issues emerge from this straightforward descriptive account of the LOI's class composition: first, the relation of Orangeism to sectional practices in the workplace; and secondly, the question of what motivated the various sections of its membership *as* Orangemen.

For Gibbon the LOI was influential among the Protestant working class in Ulster because it enforced the Protestant monopoly in skilled trades.[81] In the Scottish case this view is again reinforced in popular mythology. In truth the relationship between religious sectarianism and sectionalism seems to have been a great deal more

historically contingent. The basic analytic point would be to delin-
eate this empirically. Unfortunately, for the nineteenth century this
appears an almost impossible work of historical recovery, with the
nuances of possible occupational discrimination most unlikely to
reach official Trade Union and industrial records. Only partial
insights can be offered.

The skilled component in LOI membership in Scotland has been
noted above. Again, for the involvement of the Institution's members in the organisations of this section of labour, the evidence is
more likely to be circumstantial than documentary. The local
branch of the Boilermakers' Society in Airdrie, for example, traditionally met in the Orange Hall in Baillie Street, as did the Bakers
Union (and still were meeting there in the 1950s).[82] The Amalgamated Society of Engineers (ASE) similarly used the Coatbridge
Orange Hall from 1877-1931, and did not have a single Roman
Catholic member till the 1930s.[83]

Here it seems most likely to have been the case, as Patterson has
suggested for Belfast, that while skilled men could employ discrimi-
nating practices *qua* Orangemen, their sectionalism was in fact dependent on their prior status as craft workers in trades with restrictive rules of entry and apprenticeship. Orange ideology, in other
words, determined that those already in a position to exercise craft
control would do so in a specific way.

To take the ASE example again, this union catered for a highly
skilled membership being exclusively restricted to those who had
served a lengthy full apprenticeship. The largest component in
Lanarkshire were indeed Scots whose main interest was in maintaining the high standards of entry to the trade rather than the more
political aspects of Unionism. This is illustrated in 1897 by the
refusal of the Coatbridge branch to accept an invitation to join the
workers' parliamentary committee.[84] Some Protestant Irish, principally those from the Belfast shipyards and probably including many
Orangemen, were eligible to join and a number did. However, it
seems more likely that the exclusive nature of the trade precluded
the less well educated and connected Irish Roman Catholics from
membership, rather than an active LOI inspired discrimination
policy. Indeed the National Iron and Steel Workers' Union which
accepted all grades of iron workers, including semi and unskilled,
did have a majority of Roman Catholic members.[85]

Some contrasting examples may, of course, be found. Sectarianism
may have been more weighted as an explanatory factor in cases where
employers actively pursued a hierarchical structure of employment
along religious lines, as noted above in some of the earlier Lanarkshire

Ironworks. But overall, the impression of Orangeism as a vocabulary for maintaining prior mechanisms of exclusion is persuasive.

Following on from these points, one might expect in sectors of unskilled labour unprotected by strong craft unions that Orangeism would have more decisive material effects. Patterson, for example, notes that 4 out of 6 of the occupational lodges in Belfast in 1889 were focused on work of this nature.[86] This general area, of course, is also a fertile ground for anecdotes: Thayer, for instance, suggests that in dockwork in Liverpool if a gang boss was Irish he would hire only Irish gangers and similarly if he were Protestant he would hire only those of his own faith. A sign language grew up that would indicate to the gang boss to which religion the job seeker belonged. If he fluttered his fingers by the side of his cheek in the imitation of a flute player he was a Protestant; and if he gave the sign of the cross he was a Catholic. According to Thayer, the story goes that every morning the workers would line up at the docks for jobs and in the confusion one unwitting Catholic or Protestant would find himself in the wrong line 'Got a job for me, mate?', would ask the Irishman (crossing himself),. 'Not bloody likely' would come the reply from the foreman (fluttering his fingers). In many cases, Thayer was informed, such a miscalculation would find the offender being quick-stepped onto the edge of the pier and thrown in the Mersey.[87]

Again in reality the situation is a complex and historically variable one for which formal sources are of little assistance. It seems that as an agency for selective recruitment, the LOI would, in fact, have competed strongly with the connections of family and friends already in the work place. There may, of course, have been some overlap between the two, but it also is probable that practices of exclusion and prejudice would be conducted by a much larger section of the working class in Scotland than were members of the Order.[88]

In these circumstances, the traditional role of 'marginal privilege', the term employed to denote the relative political and economic advantage of the Protestant working class in the Ulster case, seems in need of reassessment.

Although it has been suggested above that sectionalism and craft awareness are primary material circumstances allowing the promotion of a sectarian ideology germane to Orange membership, crucially this ideology was more likely to have been the product of *external* factors. The dynamics of sectarianism then were not simply reducible to the work place, and may indeed have drawn more on ideological and political factors than the economic level. The question perhaps was more one of territoriality or intercommunal relations than production, with the entry of Roman Catholics into the workplace being seen as an unfavourable shift in the overall balance of forces.

In this way, it has been argued for Ulster that even more significant than marginal economic privilege was the wider regional context within which differentiations existed, Unionist ideology having a much less substantial social base if located simply in the privilege of a section of the Protestant working class. Instead its hegemony lay, Patterson believes, in the contrast it drew between an expansionary regional capital in the North and Southern underdevelopment.[89]

Such an analysis may seem irrelevant to the LOI in Scotland, but following the argument that the most substantial and significant component of the Institution's membership were Ulstermen, the transfer of such conceptions of ascendancy may, in fact, be a crucial factor in its practice here. While their very inappropriateness in the quite distinct Scottish social formation could simultaneously have acted as a block on the LOI's future progress.

MOTIVATION

The most basic and yet the most potentially perplexing problem remains, namely the motivations of the LOI's varied rank and file membership. Why were they Orangemen? What did it mean to them to be an Orangeman?

Some initial material factors can be cited. The network of lodges seems to have retained its original informal benevolent function paralleling the provisions of the plethora of benefit and friendly societies in the nineteenth century such as Foresters, Gardeners, and Ancient Shepherds. The Imperial Orange Council meeting in Glasgow in 1912 hoped to standardise these by becoming an approved friendly society under the Insurance Act; the Orange and Protestant Friendly Society which resulted registering 26 branches in and around Glasgow the following year.[90] By the twentieth century the Institution was also increasingly engaged in more general charitable work such as that undertaken by the Loyal Orange Widows Fund set up in Belfast in 1906-7.[91] There may also have been the hope, however ill founded, as indicated above, that for those with little job bargaining power positive discrimination might work in favour of one of 'the brethren'.

Beyond this, however, in attempting to grasp what, for instance, Orangeism contributed to its members' wider self-conceptions and how it interacted with images forged in the work place, a sociological analysis such as this, remaining largely at the level of social structure and class relations, begins to look rather inadequate.

The first impression here is of a certain 'identity' conferred by affiliation. For the skilled worker or shopkeeper this may have been a further enrichment of the existing perception of his role, with a demarcation even from his fellow craftsmen or business rivals. For the unskilled an alternative identity outwith the workplace was offered. Here, too, the elaborate proliferation of degrees, particularly within the RBP, had the important function of internal differentiation, providing a recognised hierarchy of status to which the novice could aspire.

A 'respectable' or 'decent' standing among the working class, akin to that conferred by the Temperance Societies, etc, of the Liberal beehive may have been a motivation for some Orangemen. One is frequently struck by the pathetic dignity of Orange 'speechifying' and their prolix resolutions, which do seem indicative of working men striving for 'respectable' or perhaps more accurately 'educated' status.

It is more likely though that many of this group may have gravitated towards the quasi-masonic RBP. With more of an esoteric and allegorical emphasis on ritual, this was, as suggested, viewed informally as the 'sedate' order as opposed to the 'rag tag' LOI.[92] For the majority of the LOI rank and file the sources for this identity are more diffuse and insubstantial.

One point here which can be drawn from the section on Orange ideology is the sense of belonging to some form of elite or vanguard (or at other times bulwark), conferred by adherence to the Order. If Protestantism was 'the purest form of evangelical Christianity', 'the religion of the Bible', Orangeism was in turn, as Grand Lodge personalities never tired of stressing, 'True Blue' Protestantism *in action*. It is probably in *this* sense that the Orangeman felt himself to be 'marginally privileged'. Whether a genuine or bastard religiosity animated the ordinary member is rather missing the point. For to subscribe to 'The Protestant Religion' had much wider resonances than church attendance, being intertwined precisely with claims for political and territorial ascendancy.

The identity promoted here was potently expressed in almost ritualistic confrontation with Roman Catholics, most significantly in the triumphalist celebrations surrounding the 12th of July. This specific form of plebeian Orangeism, typified as traditional 'combative sectarianism', was a vital dynamic but, as stressed throughout this study, could bring the LOI into conflict with the ruling class bloc and state agencies and produce internal conflicts. The official historians of the Irish Order capture the attitude of mind with great clarity:

What mattered to the ordinary man was to be able to feel that his own position and living and those of his family were secure. He wanted to go to fairs and markets without being cudgelled there, or waylaid on his return, and to use whatever roads he wished. When reports of disorder, intimidation and 'agrarian' crime came from the South, the Northern Protestants refused to allow the slightest self-assertion to 'the other side' lest the same occur in his own neighbourhood. On the 12th of July... he marched with his lodge, behind its flag and drums and fifes, wearing his regalia (cockade, ribbons, scarf or sash) and, armed with his yeoman gun, to show his strength in arms where he thought it would do most good. *Where you could walk, you were dominant, and the other things followed.*[93] (Author's emphasis)

Two final points should be briefly outlined here, the *total* world view offered by Orange ideology and the total nature of the Orange community. A cornerstone of the former was Orangeism's all embracing world conspiracy theory, which focused on Papal and Jesuitical machinations and which could in turn be employed to 'explain' a vast range of topical features, ranging from the politics of the Liberal party to the Franco-Prussian war. As for the second, it is vital to grasp that besides its economic and charitable role, the Order had a considerable social and cultural function in predominantly working class areas like Partick, Kinning Park and Bridgeton. The limited requirements for Orange pageantry, flutes, banners and regalia, more simple than that of Freemasonry, could be fairly easily mustered there, affiliation fees moreover were modest and paid at monthly lodge meetings rather than the masonic system of heavy annual subscription or test fees.[94] Weekly band practices and the regular pattern of initiations and degree work offered valued recreational opportunities, in Greenock indeed there was a 'Sons of William' Quadrille party.[95] At the last membership even conferred the right to an Orange funeral.[96]

The thread which ran through these actions was, moreover, a convivial, not to say bibulous one, and eventually in the 1960s this was to be given formal recognition by the setting up of social clubs attached to lodges and providing a vital source of income.[97] Temperance lodges were also found though. There were a few in Glasgow and surrounding areas by the end of the century, such as LOL No. 217 'Harthill Temperance' and LOL No. 440 'No Surrender Total Abstainers' of the Gallowgate.

A possible index to the total nature of such provisions is the small number of ordinary Orangemen who are to be found in outside organisations such as Temperance and Friendly Societies. Paisley and Greenock, already examined, present very similar patterns. In Paisley, with the exception of District Master A R Pollock in the Philosophical Society, no names were identified in other Paisley societies, benevolent, trade and religious. Nor contrary to current popular assumptions, were Orangemen found among any of the officebearers of the town's masonic lodges, Renfrew County, 'Kilwinning' Lodge or Paisley 'St. Mirren'.[98] In Greenock only the most peripheral involvement was found in benevolent, temperance and sporting clubs, with one William Swan, an Orangeman, being described as 'key keeper' in the Weavers' Society. Again there is no representation apparent in the lodges of Freemasonry, Kilwinning No. 12, St. John No. 175 and the Royal Arch Chapter No. 17, nor in the town's main religious societies, the Greenock United Bible Society and Association, or the YMCA and the Working Boys' and Girls' Religious Society. The one exception here with some Orange participation, although by no means a domination in its committee, is the Greenock Young Men's Protestant Association instituted in 1862. This has a constitution which reads like an extension of the order's own, its object: the study of the Bible and Romish works, enlightenment of Protestants as to the real character of Popery in its religious, social and political aspects, and the conversion of Romanists.[99]

NOTES

1. See Dickson, *op. cit.* (1980).
2. Cloughly BWN, 23/11/1929.
3. In 1873 for example when a major demonstration was held at Glasgow contingents from Paisley, Govan, Greenock, Port Glasgow, Lanarkshire, West Lothian, Edinburgh and the East had to be organised and conveyed GH 16/7/73, or GH 13/7/76 for Kilmarnock demonstration.
4. *Forward*, 12/7/1913, 'July the Twelfth'.
5. GH, 13/7/72. There are, of course, difficulties of precise quantification with all these figures. In this respect official Orange accounts of turnout tend often to be wildly exaggerated, including wives and friends of the brethren, though those prepared by the LOI for the railway companies involved (in the interests of expense) are probably more reliable though still over the mark. If these are taken in conjunction with eyewitness reports culled from a collection of contemporary newspapers of various political and religious hues, from the *Glasgow News* (Tory) to the *Glasgow Observer* (Roman Catholic) then some estimate, albeit imperfect, is possible.
6. GH, 16/7/73.
7. GH, 13/7/84.
8. GH and *Glasgow News* (GN), e.g. 13/7/74 Broomhouse; 13/7/75 Dumbarton; 14/7/78 Rutherglen; 13/7/80 Hawkhill; 13/7/81 Johnstone; 13/7/82 Maryhill; 13/7/82 Coatbridge; 13/8/87 Paisley.
9. GN, 13/7/75.
10. GN, 13/7/78.

11. Dewer *et al. op. cit.* (1967). Also argued by J M Barkley *A Short History of the Presbyterian Church in Ireland* (1959).
12. *Govan Press*, 17/7/86.
13. GH, 13/7/86; GN, 13/7/86. Perhaps a sentimental attachment, she had spent the 1884 season on Belfast Lough: G Duckworth, G Langmuir, *Clyde River and Other Steamers* (1972), p. 54.
14. GH, 13/7/88; GN, 13/7/88.
15. GH, 13/7/91.
16. GH, 13/7/92.
17. GH, 13/7/96.
18. GH, 13/7/97.
19 Current estimates of LOI membership in Scotland range from 50-80,000. The lower figure is probably more realistic. In 1966 for example the General Secretary, John Adam, said 50,000 were present at the 12th in Glasgow, 35,000 at Airdrie, 15,000 at New Cumnock and 4,000 at Paisley. The police, however, had been told by lodge officers to expect 20,000 in the former case with perhaps 50% of this actually present on a rough head count. In these circumstances *The Scotsman*'s estimated 40,000 members in 1966 and increase of c.10,000 by the 1980s may not be improbable given the events in Ulster in the intervening years. *The Scotsman*, 8 and 9/7/1966.
20. Marwick, *A Short History of Labour in Scotland* (1967).
21. Appendix A, listing District Lodges.
22. For CGL Ayr see GN 2/16/75.
23. *Report on the Protestant and Orange Soirée held in Paisley on 5th November*, published by J & R Parlane (1856). 'Paisley Pamphlets' collection Paisley District Library.
24. Paisley Directory 1866-7 lists:
    No. 3 Royal Oak, No. 4 King William
    No. 7 Victoria's, No. 15 Queen Elizabeth
    No. 17 The Diamond, No. 18 Cromwell
    No. 22 True Blue, No. 27 Royal Inniskilleners
    No. 74 Prince of Orange, No. 102 John Knox
    Place of meeting: Orange Hall, 12 High Street
25. *Greenock Telegraph* (GT), 5/11/69.
26. GT, 2/11/70.
27. GT, 31/1/74
    No. 3 district numbers: 82, 90, 108, 111, 112, 179, 189, 157.
    No. 4 district numbers: 80, 107, 115, 136, 173, 190.
28. GT, 12/7/75.
29. GT,16/10/74, 3/11/74.
30. GH, 13/7/1902
31. *Glasgow Observer*, 18/7/94.
32. GH, 711/5/1814 for opening and dedication of new Headquarters in Cathedral Street.
33. GN, 13/7/78.
34. For Kinning Park see GN,13/7/78.
35. Smith, *op. cit.* (1983).
36. 'Scottish Industrialists and the Changing Class Relations in the Clyde Region c.1880-1918' in T Dickson (ed), *op. cit.* (1982).
37. See Dickson, *op. cit.* (1980).
38. Marwick (1967), *op. cit.*, p. 91.
39. Foster, *op. cit.* (1974), see pp. 203-4, 237-8, 248-9, 254.
40. Smith, *op. cit.* (1983).
41. H F Moorhouse, 'The Marxist Theory of the Labour Aristocracy',

Social History, Vol. 3 (1978).

42. R Gray, *The Aristocracy of Labour in 19th century Britain c.1850-1914* (1973).

43. Smith, *op. cit.* (1983).

44. J Clarke, Crichter & Johnstone, *Working Class Culture* (1979). This, of course, is a large part of what Penn argues (see Chapter 2).

45. Moorhouse, *op. cit.* (1978)

46. For revised Orange constitution see GN, 18/12/1875.

47. R D Lobban, 'The Irish Community in Greenock in 19th Century' in *Irish Geography*, Vol. 6, No. 3.

48. See Appendix B on 'Greenock Orangemen 1870-86'. The very rough distinction between skilled/unskilled has been maintained varying occupations to denote this. The Greenock Orangemen were certainly not well enough off to afford band uniforms. GT, 13/11/84.

49. *Post Office Directory, Greenock 1892-3.*

50. See Appendices B and C Greenock Orangemen for addresses.

51. *Ibid.*

52. *Ibid.*

53. Appendix C, 'Greenock Orangemen 1891-3'.

54. Lobban, *op. cit.*, suggests this Protestant/Roman Catholic distinction in housing lasted well into the 20th century.

55. P J Waller, *op. cit.* (1981), T Gallagher also stresses parallels here, *Glasgow: the Uneasy Peace*, (1987), p. 15. Kirk, *op. cit.* (1980) suggests similar residential polarisation in Lancashire and Cheshire, pp. 87-8.

56. M McCarthey, *A Social Geography of Paisley* (1969).

57. See Appendix D, 'Paisley Orangemen'

58. The category of 'labourer' is much less common in Paisley directories. Some occupations such as 'cowfeeder' presented a problem of classification. (It means dairyman.)

59. See Cloughley, *loc.cit.*, for an example of these aspirations.

60. See Biographical Index, Appendix E.

61. *Ibid.*

62. McCarthy, *op. cit.* (1969).

63. See Biographical Index for Glasgow Orangemen.

64. Patterson notes there were 6 of these with 259 members in 1899, *op. cit.* (1981).

65. J McCaffrey, *Political Reactions in Glasgow Constituencies at the General Elections of 1885 and 86.* PhD University of Glasgow (1970).

66. Smith, *op. cit.* (1983), J H Treble, 'The Navvies' in *Journal of Scottish Labour History* (1972).

67. *Glasgow Observer* (GO), 14/7/1900.

68. McCaffrey, *op. cit.* (1970), J B Russell, 'The Municipal Burgh of Glasgow in (1911)' Similar were Bridgeton and Calton.

69. W Guthrie, in *Transactions of the Old Glasgow Club*, vol. 1, p. 83.

70. F Wordsall, *The Tenement - a way of Life* (1979), and particularly Smith, *op. cit.* (1983) on 'The natural societies'.

71. *Parker Smith Correspondence*, Strathclyde Regional Archives, Babington Smith to PS 22/1/90 'Is it true there is a large body of Orangemen in Partick. We were told there was a large body among the Irish working men'. A rare example of the distinction made.

72. I G C Hutchinson, *Politics and Society in Mid-Victorian-Glasgow 1846-86*, University of Edinburgh, 1975, pp. 140-50, an important point when considering LOI political practice.

73. Campbell, *op. cit.* (1979), Chapter 1.

74. A M McDonagh, *Irish Immigrants and Labour Movements in Coatbridge*

and Airdrie 1891-1931, B.A. Dissertation, Strathclyde (197?) (Department of History), p. 34. In Dumbartonshire colliery owners set up two adjacent villages, Croy for Catholics and Twechar for Ulster Protestants, S and O Checkland, *Industry and Ethos: Scotland, 1832-1914* (1984).
75. *Ibid.*
76. GH, 13/7/74, LOL No. 47 'Faith Defender' (Patna) and LOL No. 83 (Patna).
77. Interviews with H S, J McF.
78. J Strawthorn, *Ayrshire - Story of a County* (1975).
79. J E Shaw (ed), *Ayrshire 1745-1950: a Social and Industrial History* (1953), and interviews above.
80. Interviews above; for Lithuanians see K Lunn, 'Reactions to Lithuanian and Polish immigrants in the Lanarkshire Coalfield 1880-1914', *Journal of Scottish Labour History Society*, No. 13, May 78.
81. Gibbon, *op. cit.* (1975), p. 137.
82. *The Book of Airdrie being a complete picture of the life of a Scottish Burgh*, by 'Its Inhabitants'. (Of course, this is not conclusive proof of Orange affiliation - the Airdrie and Coatbridge Operatic Society also held rehearsals there!)
83. McDonagh, *op. cit.* (197?), p. 43.
84. *Ibid.*
85. *Ibid.*
86. Patterson, *op. cit.* (1981).
87. G Thayer, H G Hanham, 'The Protestant Party' in *The British Political Fringe* (1965). H G Hanham and G Thayer (ed.).
88. Interviews, HS, JMcF, TB. A further volatile factor intervening in the 1890s here was the revival of unskilled and general unionism, though following on the Orange involvement in unions suggested above, this development should not be automatically counterposed to the LOI. The most interesting point would be what, if any, influence had Orange affiliation on the political motivation of such unions - a very difficult question to pin down empirically.
89. Patterson, *op. cit.* (1980).
90. GH, 18/3/1912 and J Smith, *op. cit.* (1983), p. 174. For an example of the type of provisions made, see *Patna Loyal Orange Permanent Society Rules and Regulations*, c1872, FS4 101. It paid £2.10/- funeral money for a member, £1.10/- for his wife.
91. *Imperial Grand Black Chapter of Belfast Centenary Souvenir Brochure* (1983).
92. Suggested in HS interview in these exact terms, 9/11/1982.
93. Dewar and Long, *op. cit.* (1967), p. 83.
94. J McF interview for this information.
95. GT, 26/12/75.
96. For an example, GN 27/5/74.
97. Joyce, *op. cit.* (1980), p. 257, notes the importance of the lodges' social functions in the industrial towns of the English North East. Bruce, *op. cit.* (1985), p. 201, on the social clubs developments.
98. *Paisley Fowler's Directory* 1868-1880s.
99. *Greenock Fowler's Directory*, Greenock Post Office Directory 1870. Some of the leading Grand Lodge figures such as McLeod and Wetherall did have greater links with outside bodies (see Biographical Index).

6
Absolute Strength and Relative Weakness

The historical account of Scottish Orangeism raises a further substantive problem. For although the late nineteenth century movement increased significantly in absolute strength, in relative terms when compared to Ulster and other concentrations in Liverpool and the Commonwealth, its influence on society and politics remained fairly limited. This unfavourable feature had also characterised the 1799-1865 period. We begin though, by considering the Order's numerical and geographical expansion.

INSTITUTIONAL DEVELOPMENTS

In Cloughley's official account a central role in the process of expansion is accorded to the resolution of the 1859 schism of the Orange body, when, 'happily, leaders on both sides reviewing the progress of the past and with the vision of a great future, began to realise that their mission could best be fulfilled by a union of the forces'.[1] Unlike much of the official history there is at least some explanatory power in this, for a large body of lodges had actually seceded in Partick, Glasgow, Greenock and Ayrshire, and pursued a separate course from the Orange Association of Scotland with potentially destructive results. They fielded rival candidates, for instance in the Glasgow School Board elections in 1873 and 79, dividing the Orange vote.[2]

The actual process of negotiation and settlement was a great deal more acrimonious than Cloughley admits, and it was not until June of 1877 that the 'happy union' could finally be reported in Grand Lodge minutes, the united Order adopting the name of 'The Loyal Orange Institution of Scotland'.[3]

As had been the case with the healing of a similar schism in Canada over 20 years earlier,[4] the union did prove a happy one, promoting at least a sounder financial basis. Within a year two new districts were founded, one in Dumfries the other in Motherwell.[5]

It is implausible that such institutional developments were themselves sufficient condition for expansion, although they probably acted as useful adjuncts, facilitating, for example, the organisation of elaborate 12th celebrations. An alternative explanatory framework is clearly required. For this we must examine more sustained developments occurring on the levels of politics, ideology and the Scottish economy.

POLITICAL ISSUES

Vital here was the prevalence, from the late 1860s onwards, of galvanizing issues for the LOI. These seem relevant to the continuing cyclical nature of much of the Institution's activity, as indicated in the varying figures for 12th turnout.

The first such issue was the crisis throughout 1868 over the Liberal government's intention to disestablish the Church of Ireland, a Bill for the purpose being finally introduced in March 1869. This was followed by successive Disestablishment crises which shook the church in Scotland in the early 1880s and during the 1890s.[6] By 1879 the Orangemen were also faced with the prospect of the re-establishment of the papal hierarchy in Scotland.[7]

An even more decisive factor in stimulating the Institution's progress, was the Liberal attempt at Irish Home Rule, in the Bills of 1886 and 1892. As we shall see these were particularly important in forging links with West of Scotland Conservatives.

In comparison, ritualism in the churches, a 'portmanteau term of abuse' equating those clergymen who practised liturgical ceremony with crypto-Catholics,[8] did not have the same currency in Scotland as in Liverpool, although resolutions against it were passed at successive 12th gatherings.[9]

THE IDEOLOGICAL LEVEL

Since the Scottish Churches and their links with Orangeism will be dealt with in the next chapter, remarks here concentrate on the various *lay* channels for the communication of a powerful anti-Catholic ideology, and the extent to which these provided a favourable climate for the Order's own positions.

Dating from the beginning of the early nineteenth century, for example, a 'No Popery' press had sprung up, with William McGavin's paper *The Protestant*. This was followed, in 1851-2 by *The Scottish Protestant* edited by James Gibson, Minister of the Free Kingston Church, Glasgow; *The Glasgow Protestant Watchman* 1854; *The Protestant* II 1873-4 and *The Shield and Protestant Journal* in Greenock in the early 1870s.

As Billington noted for the American case, these publications were intertwined with a variety of anti-Catholic societies, established under clerical and bourgeois lay guidance.[10] In America and

England two types could be identified: those like the 'Irish Evangelical Society' aiming to convert Roman Catholics to Protestantism, and those like 'the British Society for Promoting the Principles of the Protestant Reformation' designed to protect the country from Catholicism by disseminating the dangers of the system. In Scotland it is the latter which predominated. Typical here were the Protestant Laymen's Association, the West of Scotland Protestant Association and the Protestant Missionary Society, the latter two merging in January 1884 to form the Scottish Protestant Alliance.[11]

The West of Scotland Protestant Association had been founded in Glasgow in 1835 by a number of ministers and laymen:

> Impressed by the dangers of Popery, ascent to power of Roman Catholics in the legislature, the zealous efforts made by the Church of Rome to regain her ascendancy, the loose notions of religious principle unhappily prevalent among large numbers of Protestants and the magnitude of the Roman Catholic population in Glasgow[12]

The purpose of the association was by means of public meetings and the press, to expose 'the pernicious tendencies of the Popish system, extensively diffusing information respecting the character and history of the Church of Rome and arousing Protestants to the duties to which they have been specially called'.[13]

Similarly the Protestant Laymen's Association in the inaugural issue of their paper trumpeted:

> ... perhaps the most dreaded species of infidelity, at present, is that which pretends to be *the* true church known as Popery. There we have a notable example of the effects of laying aside the teachings of the Bible and substituting the devices of men. Here erring man assumes the prerogative of the Saviour, mummery supplants the place of meetings and rights are made to serve the purposes of righteousness. Our aim is to watch the operations of the enemy and warn the people of their danger; our more special sphere being that of the working classes. As they are the most numerous, most willing to part with money, and the most easily accessible portion of the community, they are therefore most exposed to the attacks of the enemy and deserve a large measure of the attention of the Christian philanthropist[14]

'The working classes' which such bourgeois societies sought to reach do indeed provide a further interesting case for study. It is Pelling's view, for example, that 'the ordinary working class in the Victorian era were too preoccupied with the necessities of day to day living to spend time on the niceties of religious doctrine'.[15] This can probably be extended to Scotland if the 'niceties' are taken as referring to church membership or attendance. As Bullock and Drummond indicated the problem of the 'unkirked' weighed heavily on Scottish churchmen, with the three main presbyterian denominations competing fiercely for members in an age of strong secular pressures.[16]

Active church connections though, as suggested earlier, are by no means the only basis of motivation for popular militant Protestantism largely defined in negative terms as anti-Catholicism. The involvement of large sections of this class in active 'No Popery' agitation, one prominent example being the rioting which surrounded the peregrination of the demagogue 'Angel Gabriel' throughout Scotland in the 1850s.[17]

Workers had, moreover, their own anti-Papal society, the 'Working Men's Evangelistic Association' (WMEA), formed in 1870 by 'Pious operatives to stem the flood of Popery in Glasgow and to offer effective opposition to infidel propaganda coming to Glagow at select intervals from London'.[18] Under its auspices *The Protestant* was published, a newspaper engaging more in gossipy calumny, ridicule and stirring calls to arms, than coherent theological exegesis.

Thus its first editorial:

'Our battlestar shall be that which shone on the plains of Bethlehem when his epiphany was who came from the Father to console Israel and cleanse the Temple ... Advance! Unfurl again our unconquerable banner of blue that for ages struck terror into the Papalini – D.G. it is destined to float in triumph when the cross overcomes the crucifix and crescent and the cry shall arise 'Soldiers of Christ, our Captain appears!...The Lord is on our side, here we say as the Lutheran braves said when contending with the eldest son of the Church at Sedan – Forward!'[19]

Here one can speculate on the extent to which such sentiments are influenced by direct bourgeois proselytisation, or by the 'lived experience' of the working class. Again it is necessary to emphasise that the familiar control/consent couplet admits more reciprocity in practice than is often acknowledged. One strength of Thompson's analysis of early nineteenth century Methodism is precisely that it can place beside each other as explanatory factors, direct indoctrination and the psychic consequences of the experience of counter revolution.[20] It seems likely for nineteenth century Scotland too, that popular 'No Popery' may have contained historically variable elements of active bourgeois missionising, such as that of the Protestant Laymen's Association. But the virulence of its language and activity indicate it was also firmly rooted in the material conditions of

working class existence, to some extent, for example, in the experience of Roman Catholic Irish migration.

A fairly receptive environment did then exist in Scotland for the
LOI, and this must have had a role in its expansion. The defusing of
a previously sympathetic environment in the USA following the Civil
War was, for example, an important factor in thwarting a similar
expansion of the 'Know-Nothings' and similar anti-Catholic group-
ings there.[21]

Clearly this is also important in underlining the need for a similar
demarcation to that employed for the early history of Orangeism,
between the Institution proper, and a much wider body of militant Protestantism, often erroneously dubbed 'Orange' by contemporaries.

However, to go further and state that the role of the ideological
environment was a decisive *causal* one, leads to several difficulties.

'No Popery' or 'anti-sacerdotalism', as Best describes it, was after
all a major force throughout England in the nineteenth century, and
yet the Order there was restricted largely to Liverpool and parts of
Lancashire, with only a weak representation in the South East.[22]
There are also chronological objections. The suggestion is probably
correct that 'No Popery' was not uniformly persistent in the nineteenth century.[23] In Scotland it seems to have exhibited a very
uneven pattern, related to specific events like Catholic emancipation
in 1829, the restoration of the Papal hierarchy in England in 1851
and the promulgation of the Doctrine of Papal Infallibility in 1876.
This finds correlation in the dates of the establishment for the
newspapers and societies above.

The most febrile period for anti-Catholic agitation was from the
early 1830s to the late 1870s, when the atmosphere was one of
frenetic 'revival' and self confident optimism, Protestantism viewed
as on the march towards conquest of the world.[24] This was not to say
such agitation was dormant in the years from 1880 to 1900, for the
politics of Home Rule from 1886 were frequently animated by
religious fervour, but again it is difficult not to concur with Best that
'by the end of the 1870s the self appointed leaders of Protestant
opinion were increasingly feeling an uncongenial isolation'.[25] While
it is true that the LOI enjoyed a similarly uneven path of progress,
experiencing rapid growth in the late 1860s and early 1870s, the
crucial point against a causal link is that such expansion continued
apace, *particularly in the 1880s* at the very point when more general
forms of 'No Popery' were already on the wane.

A further difficulty arises. If the ideological environment was a
truly active factor in the LOI's growth, one might expect closer links
between it and the bourgeois anti-Catholic societies. As it was, the

Protestant Laymen's Association, for example, does not seem to have had a large LOI involvement, 2 out of 12 directors in 1879.[26] The West of Scotland Protestant Association had also wished to distance itself from the LOI at its outset disclaiming 'all identification with party names and interests and presenting a centre for rallying for those who prefer the welfare of Protestantism to the objects of political faction'.[27] At the 12th rally of 1875 MWGM McLeod, for his part, was equally contemptuous of the Association, 'the most prominent association in Scotland beyond our own', for sending a deputation to London to invite Gladstone to a great Protestant demonstration. 'What are they doing?' he queried, 'What are they worth? Who can rely on their Protestantism?'[28] Not surprisingly then there were no LOI representatives at the mass meetings in the Glasgow City Hall on Vaticanism in 1875 and on Papalism in 1876, held under Association auspices.[29]

Rivalry seems to have abated to some extent by the time of the Association's amalgamation to become the Scottish Protestant Alliance. A few of its directors after 1884 *were* Orangemen. F Y Henderson, its Hon. Secretary, was also treasurer of the Grand Lodge from 1881 and Peter Hutcheson had been in the Grand Lodge in the 1870s. Yet again this is only 2 out of 10 directors. In fact, at no time from its annual reports do Orangemen number more than 2 out of 19-20 directors 'in toto'.[30] The Protestant Alliance then was not simply 'Orange dominated'. Much more prominent, certainly among its vice presidents, are scions of the Glasgow Conservative Association, J A Campbell, Sir William Anstruther, Archibald Orr Ewing, although some of these, like W C Maugham, were themselves frequent visitors on Orange platforms.[31] In fact, the only Protestant society for which Orange links are appropriately close was not one of the bourgeois associations but the popular Working Men's Evangelistic Association of which Deputy Grand Master Wetherall was President and Orangeman and evangelist H A Long was guiding spirit.[32]

Finally, the greatest danger in over-stressing the autonomy and efficacy of the ideological level is that one finds oneself positing as a causal factor some 'cultural detritus' of anti-Roman Catholicism, a deeply engrained attitude unchallenged by actual experience. The point here is rather to distinguish between the genesis of the Scottish 'No Popery' ideology, rooted in the sixteenth century and the specific course of the Reformation in Scotland; and how elements of this ideology came to be reproduced in definite circumstances in nineteenth century Scotland. Vital here are developments at the economic level, with the migration of both Roman Catholics and

Protestants from Ireland into the Scottish labour market. The effects of the former were largely indirect, while the latter can be assigned a much more active role in LOI expansion.[33]

CATHOLIC IRISH MIGRATION

The heavy post-Famine waves of migration leading to permanent settlement in the 1840s and 50s, were predicated on an already well-established pattern of seasonal migration mid-summer to assist in harvesting. The census of 1841 revealed 126,321 of Irish birth in West Central Scotland, around 5% of the population, 15.93% in Glasgow though taking in those of Irish extraction Handley believes 10% for Scotland as a whole is more realistic. In 1851 207,367 Irish born were reckoned including 18% of the Glasgow population.[34]

The main dynamics behind this persistent exodus, for the most part Roman Catholic Irish, are found in the collapse of the nascent domestic industries in Ireland, and the increased rate of farm consolidation, with an increase of cattle and dairying production and consequently a lower demand for agricultural labour and withdrawal of leases. Most affected were North and Central Ireland for in the South and West widespread migration was prevented by severe impoverishment. Settling in areas of high labour demand, the vast majority of migrants were employed in semi- and unskilled manual work in sectors which were essential to the development of industrial capital in Scotland, roadmaking, bricklaying, canal cutting and harbour and railway construction.[35]

With this type of material it is possible, as Campbell indicates, to hold up a highly impressionistic case for a close correlation between the frequency of general sectarian activity and the volume of Catholic Irish immigration.[36] Charges, for example, were often made against this group that they deprived the native Scot of employment and lowered the rate of wages. Gallagher argues the latter was undoubtedly the case with the Irish working longer for lower rates of pay, while Handley who at points seems determined to refute every charge ever made against the Roman Catholic Irish in Scotland, characteristically rejects these suggestions too.[37] He points out, probably correctly, that most of the labour performed by them was actually created by the Industrial Revolution and was not sought as employment by Scots. Similarly he argues that as demand exceeded supply in sectors such as coal mining and iron making, where the Scots and Irish did appear to compete, there was in reality room for both. Kirk, in his study of the Irish in North East England, also notes there is not much to support the contention that the Irish brought a general lowering of wages at least from 1850-75, though the sectors in which the Irish were concentrated did not experience similar wage rises as elsewhere.[38]

More research is required here for the Scottish case, but in a sense its results need not be totally conclusive for the theme of immigration and reaction. Popular attitudes and the reproduction of popular ideologies like 'No Popery' are not the single product of cultural atavism, yet neither will they permit a simple reduction to the level of economic 'facts'. Contemporaries' commonsense beliefs regarding the Irish and wage levels, and competition in the workplace, may stand in need of qualification or factual correction. Some partial and local basis for fears of economic downgrading, for example, could be reinforced by and reproduced by the visible signs of increased migration and by reports from other areas, but whether 'correct' or not such beliefs were steadfastly held and provided incentives for action.

Beyond this one must be highly sensitive of adopting the 'post hoc ergo propter hoc' type of argument, either for general anti-Irish sentiment or for LOI activity in particular. This argument was itself, as Handley indicates, current in the nineteenth century among those concerned for the threatened moral and spiritual turpitude for the native Scot, simply attributing anti-Roman Catholic developments mid century to a build up in the Irish population. For if numbers were the prime mover, one would have expected the general offensive to have coincided with the waves of post-famine migration in the 1840s and 50s. Further, in assembling the data for the whole nineteenth century in the form of a line graph, one would expect indeed an uninterrupted and continuous climb falling off around the 1860s and 70s.

In fact in the 1840s, as Foster notes for Anglo-Irish relations in Oldham[39], political co-operation between Scots and Irish, to take one indicator, although limited was by no means completely precluded. Wilson, for example, notes a good deal of fellow feeling towards Irish Roman Catholics from the Scottish Chartists.[40] Though few Roman Catholics took an active interest in the early stages of the movement, by the 1840s a generation of Irish born in Scotland had already grown up to identify with the political aspirations of their fellow workers. Many Irish people consequently took part in the Chartist demonstrations of 1849. John Daly, for example, addressed a meeting in Glasgow stating that 'prayers and petitions are the weapons of cowards, arms were the weapons used by the free and the brave. They could best help Ireland by keeping the army in Scotland'. Chartists and Irish fraternised at Edinburgh, and in 1848 in bread riots at Glasgow the Irish were particularly active. In a list of those arrested 14 out of 31 were Irish by birth.[41]

As regards the overall pattern of immigration and reaction during the nineteenth century, anti-Irish feeling, indeed, appears not simply continuous and coterminous with immigration trends. In fact one sees in Scotland, as Miles suggests, a much more uneven tendency towards an increase and decline of reaction in a cyclical form that can be related to specific events.[42]

Again looking back specifically at LOI activity, these remarks hold good. First the Order's numerical advance took place from the 1860s, precisely the point at which the numbers of Roman Catholics of Irish birth and descent were beginning to stabilise and even decline. To take Glasgow as an example, the number of Irish born in 1851 was 18% of the total population, by 1871 this had fallen to 14.4%, by 1891 to 13% and by 1901 to 8.7%.[43]

In the 1840s and 50s, however, when one might have expected a take off in LOI activity in accordance with the increased numbers of Roman Catholic Irish, the evidence suggests instead sporadic violent outbursts, but a weak institutional basis with far short of 1,000 members.

Nor does the Institution's geographical basis suggest a particularly close fit with the volume of migration. The three Scottish towns with the highest Irish settlement 1876-1901 were Greenock 19.1%, Dundee 15.6% and Glasgow 13.1%.[44] Greenock may indeed provide some correlation with its significant LOI presence, but in Dundee no important Orange outpost developed. Walker notes only two rather 'down at heel Orange lodges'.[45]

Another interesting example was Paisley whose Irish community had become fairly stable in numbers as early as the 1840s, but which was an Orange growth point from the 1850s.[46] The major influx had, in fact, been in the 1813-21 period and the town probably took less than its share of post-famine immigrants. The number of Irish born increased by only 2% after 1841, so that by the second half of the nineteenth century they constituted only 5.6% of the population.

ULSTER PROTESTANT MIGRATION

Clearly a correlation cannot be forced between the volume of Roman Catholic Irish settlement and LOI expansion. However, as already suggested for the 1799-1865 period, there was an active and direct link between developments in the lodges and the labour migration of Irish *Protestants*, mainly from the counties of Ulster.

Contemporaries outside the Order certainly seem to have made this link.[47] The official account too places central importance on the impetus it gained from Ulster migration. Cloughley states:

Many young Ulstermen crossed the channel to find employ-

ment in Scotland. True to their principles they joined up with
the Order in Scotland and the membership increased considerably, ever since the loyal Ulster immigrants and their
descendents have rendered yeoman service to the Institution[48]
The actual evidence here is very persuasive, though methodo-
logical problems arise in giving an exact enumeration of Protestant
migration, since the census does not yield religious data. At a rough
estimate perhaps about one-third of all Irish immigrants were
Northern Protestants, this high percentage already being indicated
in the 1830s. Here the census indicated 35,534 Irish born inhabitants in Glasgow, while Clelland estimates 26,965 Catholics in the
city.[49] For the later period exact evidence is fragmentary, as indeed
is indicated by the frequency with which the table below is reproduced in various accounts. Ravenstein suggests the greatest number
of Irish migrants to Scotland, at least for the period 1876-81, were
from Ulster, and within the province from the 4 most Protestant
counties, Antrim, Down, Tyrone and Armagh.

MIGRATION FROM ULSTER TO SCOTLAND 1876-81

Total Irish Immigration	42,297	
From 9 Ulster counties	35,194	83.2%
From 4 Protestant counties	24,811	58.7%[50]

The Ulstermen's presence was moreover translated into more tangible organisational form. A number of societies seem to have
sprung up particularly in the 1886s, such as the 'Glasgow Antrim
and Down Benevolent Association', its object, 'to cultivate and
maintain a friendly intercourse between the natives of Antrim and
Down residing in Glasgow and the neighbourhood and raise a fund
for temporary relief...'[51] Similar was the Irish Protestant Association, its aim, 'to manifest...unswerving loyalty to the British crown
and show that not all Irishmen are Home Rulers'.[52]

Whatever the exact dimensions of migration though, it is clear
that Ulster Protestants entered the labour market in quite different
conditions to those described above for the Roman Catholic Irish.
Frequently Protestants arrived as permanent settlers to secure
skilled or semi-skilled employment to which they had already been
recruited in their county of origin. Many, for example, were recruited by advertisements in the Belfast newspapers for specific jobs
in the mines and later in the iron and steel works in Lanarkshire and
Ayrshire. Here the skilled labour supply could be a problem. They
often travelled to Scotland using warrants sent by their firms, and
went directly to houses allocated by their new employers and near
the company school where their children would be educated. Higher

grade railwaymen, such as goods guards, tended to be recruited in a similar way, as were many tram drivers and transport workers in Glasgow later in the century.[53] Finally in 1902 Harland and Wolffs shipbuilders themselves established a yard in Glasgow and introduced directly a large complement of their Belfast workforce.[54]

Not all Ulstermen were Orangemen, of course, and some must have resented contemporaries' frequent implications that they were. Some of the first migrants had indeed been radical refugees from the '98 rebellion. John Ferguson, instrumental in publishing 'the Green Flag of Erin' and a leading figure in the Irish National League in the 1880s, was a Protestant from Belfast and suffered accordingly from the sectarian and clerical elements in the league.[55]

Yet logically there does seem to have been a strong and positive link between this thriving community of the late 1850s and 60s, and the progress of Orangeism. To return to the example of Dundee, this city had a high Irish born proportion of the total population (15.6%) but little LOI development. The important point here is that the Irish whom the Jute Mills attracted were overwhelmingly Roman Catholic, with relatively few Ulster Protestants.[56]

Indeed, the Ulster connection adds another facet to the motivation for LOI membership, in that the lodges could become a familiar point of reference in a new country, in a time of some inevitable economic and social dislocation. The lodges in Greenock in the 1860s and 70s regularly organised an annual pilgrimage back to Belfast for the 12th celebrations there, a tradition which persists in Scotland.[57]

The exact extent of Ulster involvement in the late nineteenth century is difficult to specify, though indicators suggest it was considerable. One is struck, for example, by the large number of prominent officebearers at Grand Lodge level of Ulster descent: T Macklin, Councillor H B Wilson, J McManus, Dr J E Fairlie, W McHaffie, Rev. J U Mitchell, J Cloughly, J Wyllie, Rev. T Patrick, Rev. Gault and T Wetherall.[58]

Also interesting here are the colourful epithets attached to many of the lodges, LOL No. 27 'Paisley Royal Inniskilleners', LOL No. 79 'Shamrock and Thistle', LOL No. 148 'Killyman True Blue', LOL No. 289 'Derry Maiden Light', LOL No. 179 Glasgow 'Ballykillbeg'.[59]

Official documentary evidence is not widely available. Orangemen leaving their own lodge in Ulster would be presented with a transfer certificate which was presented on arrival to the master or secretary at the appropriate local lodge in Scotland, but these have frequently been destroyed. In the case of Glengarnock LOL No. 100 though, 13 of these certificates do survive for the years 1906-14, which apparently does not represent all the transfers from Ulster lodges during this period.[60]

To sum up, it is difficult to provide a discreet equation for the LOI's late nineteenth century advance. As in the early part of the century, however, the incidence of Ulster Protestant immigration to Scotland does seem a vital process in providing a future constituency for the LOI. In addition, some prominent ideological forms in Scotland provided a sympathetic environment, albeit in a rather passive sense. Important, too, in delineating the finer contours of activity was the availability of appropriate political issues.

RELATIVE WEAKNESS

Notwithstanding its general progress, we must now turn to an analysis of the Scottish LOI's *weakness* in comparative terms. For, against the numerical advance in Scotland which resulted in around 25,000 members at the turn of the century, should be set the LOI in Ulster. With one-third of Scotland's population, Ulster had some 1,500-2,000 local lodges with around 100,000 members.[61] Even when set against other significant importations of the Institution, Scotland does not compare particularly favourably. In Canada, for example, by 1843 a total of 83 lodges were in existence, while by 1870 there were over 1,000 lodges and the membership totalled 100,000 out of a population of around 4 million. With the opening up of the country westwards, the Order spread and by World War 1 numbered 150,000 adherents.[62] Liverpool provides another instance, for although Orangeism arrived here around the same time as it did in Glasgow, in the former case the order was 17,000 strong by the 1880s, while in the latter only around 8,000 could be regularly mustered.[63]

Naturally the Order's position in Scotland.as in the early part of the century, again defines reduction to a single causal factor. Subsequent chapters will discuss Orange relations with ecclesiastical and political bodies, focusing on the broad features of Scottish society which combined to marginalise the movement. For the moment, though, we can concentrate on certain intrinsic features associated with Orangeism in Scotland.

The first of these can be conveniently summarised as the *'Ulster factor'*, though here a distinction must be drawn between the indigenous Scots' reaction to Ulster migration and their perceptions of the LOI as an Ulster Institution.

Sibbet, for example, notes approvingly 'the wonderful intimacy' which had existed since the early Plantation days between Scotland and Ireland.[64] Scottish migrants themselves had originally played a significant part in this settlement, transplanting their own presbyterian Protestantism. In turn the Church of Scotland report of 1923 was moved to comment, 'Nor is there any complaint of the presence of an Orange population in Scotland, they are of the same race as ourselves and are readily assimilated to the Scottish population'.[65]

Relations were probably not always in this idealised state of harmony. McDonagh suggested that in Lanarkshire they tended to be a community within a community, distrusted by some Scots ironically as 'Ribbonmen', a Catholic secret society. There may also have been some resistance from the original settlers to the second generation of immigrants marrying out.[66] Yet the Ulster Protestants do seem to have been more easily acceptable than the Roman Catholic Irish, and to have achieved a greater degree of integration.[67]

And still, despite becoming fused in the public mind with the favourably received Ulster population, the Orange Institution provoked a decisively more suspicious and hostile reaction from all classes of indigenous Scots, who condemned its preoccupations with 'Irish issues and quarrels'. Frequently, this was compounded by their recognition of two further unwelcome Orange characteristics, ironically similar to host perceptions of the Catholic Irish. The first was the Order's violent nature, with a transplantation of that tradition of 'combative sectarianism' which had been vital to the Order's functioning in Ulster. Second was its reputed propensity for drunkenness. In practice these elements were intertwined, often being jointly invoked whenever one was called into account.

Significantly here, we witness an important continuation of that 'contemptuous neutrality', noted for the 1820s and 30s, towards what was viewed as an import of 'alien' party feeling to Scotland. Thus even the *Glasgow News*, which had proudly proclaimed in its first edition that 'Glasgow is the head and heart of Protestantism in Scotland'[68] stated in its editorial on the 12th celebrations of 1874:

> We seem never able to escape from the possibility of the turmoil which occurred at the Boyne being resuscitated and sounding in our ears. There is seldom any healing element in the wings of the sun which dawns over the North of Ireland on the 12th. On the contrary it is a dispute and confusion of the most disgraceful kind. To the Saxon or the Scot who is a lover of social concord and has a taste for upholding the law, these rows are perfectly unintelligible. We can understand people differing from each other in their religious sentiments: but their disputes...ought to be conducted by words and not by blows. It is simply absurd to think that in Great Britain where freedom of opinion is an established rule, either one course of

the other could be furthered by the bludgeon.

The absurdity of these wretched quarrels between Protestant and Catholic is evident to all out of the immediate range of their influence...The quarrel is one of the most foolish and groundless the world has ever seen[69]

The Tory satirical magazine *The Bailie* had a 'poem' in similarly disapproving tones:

The Twelfth

Hurroo! for Billy,
The Streets perambulate,
Sport your Orange Lily,
And duly celebrate
The Twelfth.

There's a brick – lift it,
We'll maybe need it now,
When 'tis hurled swift it
Makes or ends a row,
On Twelfth.

Gather all your Bands now,
Let's kick up a dust,
Come a show of hands now,
In Gladstone we've no trust
This Twelfth...[70]

Equally telling is that the Orangemen themselves felt these problems keenly. In 1856 at the pioneering Paisley *soirée*, significantly the experiment was hailed as a bold one not so much because of Roman Catholic antipathies, as because of 'almost universal Protestant prejudice'. The display it was felt had indeed to go a long way to prove 'we are not mere party zealots but among the best, most loyal and trustworthy of our Protestants'.[71]

To assist in this respect the Rev. Jas. Stewart was anxious since most of his audience were 'natives of the sister Kingdom and therefore...in a great measure strangers to Scotland', to stress that, 'in the battleground of religious controversy...the two [Ulster and Scotland] are brethren and shoulder to shoulder they will stand or fall. Study, therefore, [he enjoined], the peace of the people among whom you dwell, for in their peace you shall have peace'.[72]

His colleague the Rev. Fraser was more aware of the uphill nature of the task. He explained:

In this country Orangemen are usually shunned as returned convicts, many intelligent and conscientious men avoid them

as they would a mad dog. If I found my notion of an Orangeman from prevalent opinions, I would describe him thus: An
Orangeman is a senseless bigot who sports Orange lilies in
summer and is especially fond of fighting and marches on the
12th July, and who delights to sing 'Boyne Water' and
'Croppies Lie Down'; and to drink strange toasts about the
glorious pious and immortal memory about brass money and
wooden shoes; who uses wicked prayers about the Pope,
breaks the law and shoots Papists whenever he can. Unfortunately, ...when an idea fastens itself in ; the mind of a
Scotchman it is as difficult to get out as a burr of a Scots thistle,
when it has wrapped itself up in the fringe of his plaid.[73]

There may have been an element of truth in this observation, for
in 1869 William Johnstone of Ballykillbeg,guest chairman of the
Greenock Orangemen's *soirée* was still lamenting along similar lines:

Orangeism was a system in which John, Pat and Sandy might
take an interest ... It had grown more rankly on Irish soil than
English or Scotch, and the reason for this was that in Ireland
they had more to contend with, and above all the battle for
reform in the three countries was fought and won on Irish soil[74]

The following year he expanded on this theme:

In Scotland you are misunderstood and misrepresented, you
are spoken of as though you were a mere Irish faction, a foreign
import brought to disturb the peace of the country. You are no
such thing (hear, hear). If you were rightly understood and
your principles looked into you would soon be found to be the
true apostolic descendants of John Knox. If other people have
forgot the contest waged in Scotland for an Open Bible, the
Orangemen have not forgotten it.[75]

The extent to which each of the unfavourable elements of
'Irishness' and 'violence' were stressed was, of course, historically
variable. From the 1870s onwards, for example, the dynamics of
confrontation and territoriality in most of Scotland became increasingly confined within 12th processions, rather than in spontaneous
faction fights. Violence now tended to be less prominent in perceptions of the main body of the Order, though by no means did it
disappear, as witnessed in the newspaper coverage of various fracas
surrounding Orange bands in the early 1880s.[76] More·generally,
coverage of the LOI activities became highly routinised with the
regular heading 'The July Celebrations', a formally structured report, buried well amongst other domestic news.[77]

Such treatment was often rather quizzical and patronising, but
still retained a strong perception of the LOI as a curious *Irish*

importation. This, for example is seen in a sentimental piece in the *Glasgow Herald* 'Orangemen's Day and an Incident'. Written as late as 1908 it would surely have brought little comfort to the Scottish Grand Lodge. Focusing on one of the marchers the *Herald* comments:

> The face is curiously Irish...but not all the sombre vicissitudes of navvydom have quenched the Celtic fervour in this old Orangeman's soul. ...the Orangemen's walk is essentially the pageant of the proletariat; the rank and file of the demonstration are not men of many clothes. But the best such as it is is donned for the ceremonial – hats of a historical, almost archaeological value, and suits of a like giddy antiquity....
> Those men who step out jauntily at the sound of the fife and drum are for the time being true sons of dead heroes...put in a general way they feel the Twelfth is the appeal of their fathers' faith to their personal protection, and what they lack in broad knowledge they have in heart fervour.
> They 'walk' and 'demonstrate', 'listen' and 'applaud', 'move' and 'resolve' all with a quaint seriousness and earnestness that savours of a reverential past, and arrests attention because it is so manifestly aloof from bread and butter interests of the instant present. In short the phenomenon belongs to 'the sectarian mania' of sturdier years[78]

Here too one can trace a continuation of an attitude of dismissiveness and even contempt towards the Order by reason of its predominantly working class basis, identified in literate bourgeois opinion as early as the 1820s and 1830s.

A further constant element throughout the nineteenth century period was the impression given to those outside the Order that 'the Orangeman anywhere is seldom a teetotaller and a tipsy Orangeman is nothing if not provocative'.[79]

Along these lines, an ex-Orangeman pontificated in 1877:

> If the principles of Orangeism were faithfully adhered to, the Order would be a great Christian and political factor in the affairs of the country, for the fundamental necessity of its existence is the defence of the Bible and the Crown....But in reality the spectacle presented by many of the brethren on their return from the 12th in Glasgow was disgraceful. If they had the decency and forethought to remove their colours before they get tipsy it would not have been so bad...[80]

Nor were the regular lodge meetings in Scotland any improvement on ceremonial occasions. 'In nine out of ten cases the lodges meet, transact some formal business and then order in refreshments.

Orangemen themselves know as well as I what the "refreshment" part of the business means'. In short, he earnestly protested:

> The masses of the Orange body both in Scotland and Ireland are composed of ignorant and illiterate people, whose highest notion of the principles of their Order is a big drink and an ignorant detestation of the Pope. This will not help to forward the case of Orangeism, nor will it induce intelligent and respectable people to join the Order[81]

These negative impressions help further reconsideration of Smith's view of an unproblematic dichotomy between the Labour Movement and Orangeism, as introduced in Chapter 2. For they suggest that the antipathy, or at least apathy, of the 'Scottish Working Man' towards the Institution had sources other than his own 'liberal commonsense', important though this may often have been. If, for example, the LOI was perceived as an 'Ulster' Institution, and a violent and drunken one at that, what attraction would membership hold for the indigenous Scottish worker, frequently employed in a skilled trade where Roman Catholic Irish exclusion was already a *fait accompli*? What indeed would be the point of an annual ritualistic assertion of 'Protestant Ascendancy' in such circumstances?

If indeed secrecy and elaborate ceremonial were the native worker's requirements, the Masonic Order must have appeared the preferable alternative. Freemasonry was much more widespread in Scotland than the LOI. In 1879 it was calculated to have 69,255 members in lodges holding to the Grand Lodge and over 1,000 in dormant lodges.[82] It had distinguished partrons among the Royal Family, aristocracy, municipal leaders and major employers of labour,[83] and claimed ancient historical roots in Scotland, springing from the continental masons who built the twelfth century Abbey at Kilwinning.[84] The Masonic Lodge at Maybole, for example, No. 11 St. John founded in 1734, easily predated the first Orange lodge there in 1799.[85] High entry fees and annual subscriptions, moreover, promoted a strong artisan and bourgeois membership, while above all by the standards of Scottish society the organisation was eminently respectable.

In short, Scottish Freemasonry was all that the Orange Grand Lodge desired for its own movement.

NOTES

1. *Belfast Weekly News*, 23/11/1929.
2. eg. GN, 29/1/74.
3. BWN, 723/11/29. In Minutes of Grand Lodge meeting 2/6/1877 is the following paragraph. 'The most important item of home news is the happy Union of all Scots into one body under the supervision of one Grand Lodge. All agree in ascribing the honour and advantages of this happy union to the untiring exertions of the Most Worthy Grand Master'.
4. H. Senior, *op.cit.* (nd.), Union took place in 1856 at Brockhall, p.52.
5. BWN, 23/11/29. Other institutional moves during the period may also have been of some importance, particularly in covering other potential areas of membership. As early as 1875 juvenile lodges for boys (girls were not admitted till 1917) had been sanctioned by the Grand Lodge, and the first opened in Paisley where it still functions. At first progress was slow with only 10 lodges in operation in 1904 though from this date the Grand Lodge undertook to positively encourage them and by 1905 membership had doubled. In 1908 they began to hold their own annual demonstrations.

Grand Lodge, however, seems to have been a great deal more circumspect in admitting women to the Order – though women were often present unofficially, even at the first recorded public march in Glasgow in 1821. In 1901 a proposal from W McIntyre and W McRoberts of Greenock to institute separate Orange Lodges for women was turned down. In 1907 the proposal was again made by Glasgow District No. 24 resulting in a commission whose report was unfavourable. As Cloughly comments though 'the ladies were not to be easily put off' and in 1909 the Grand Lodge finally decided to issue separate warrants. On 17th November 1909 the first lodge was instituted in Govan with Sister Harriet Wilson as Worthy Grand Mistress. By the late 1920s 176 women's Lodges were in operation, with No. 42 in Govan having over 400 members.
6. See J Bullock and A L Drummond, *The Church in late Victorian Scotland*, Vol. 3J (1978).
7. J Fleming, *A History of the Church in Scotland* (1927).
8. Waller, *op.cit.* (1981).
9. *Glasgow Observer* 16/7/98. See Chapters 7 and 10 below.
10. R A Billington, *The Protestant Crusade* (1938), p.l9.
11. GN, 29/1/84.
12. *2nd Statistical Account of Scotland: Lanark*, p.701.
13. *ibid.*
14. *The Glasgow Protestant Watchman*, No. 1, 4/3/54. Original in Glasgow People's Palace.
15. H Pelling, *Popular Politics and Society in Late Victorian Britain* (1968).
16. Bullock and Drummond, *op.cit.* (1978). See also R. Howie, *Churches and Churchmen in Scotland* (1893).
17. Handley, *The Irish in Modern Scotland* (1947), p.95.
18. *WMEA 10th Annual Report* (1879), p.5. In Glasgow Collection, Mitchell Library.
19. *The Protestant*, No. 1, 1873.
20. Thompson *op.cit.* (1968), Chapter 11.
21. Billington, *op.cit.* (1938).
22. See Sibbet *op.cit.* (1939), Vol. 2, on the South East.
23. G F A Best, 'Popular Protestantism', p.138, in R. Robson, *Ideas and*

Institutions of Late Victorian Britain (1961), pp.113-42.

24. For a splendid portrait of an evangelical Christian of the period, see Edmund Gosse, *Father and Son* (1907).
25. Best, *op.cit.* (1967), pp.137-8.
26. PLA Annual Report 1879, Glasgow Collection, Mitchell Library.
27. *2nd Statistical Account of Scotland :Lanark*, p.701.
28. GN, 13/7/75; GH, 13/7/75.
29. GN, 6/10/75; 16/11/76.
30. See Annual Reports 1885-93, Glasgow Collection, Mitchell Library.
31. See Chapter 8.
32. See Biographical Index, Appendix E.
33. Again here an important analytical distinction has to be made between the progress of the LOI and the more general development of reaction towards the Irish in Scotland. Failure to specify which of these is at issue at any given point, can lead to obviously tautological conclusions. One of the most frequently cited factors in the hostile attitude of the Scottish people is precisely that of Orange agitation.
34. See Handley, *op.cit.* (1947), Table, p.44.
35. *ibid.*, and R. Miles,*Racism and Migrant Labour* (1982), for useful short discussion. See also J Treble, 'The Navvies' in *Journal of Scottish Labour History* (1972), pp.227-247.
36. Campbell, *op.cit.* (1979), Appendix III, pp.316-319, 'Table of Incidents Involving Irishmen...'
37. Handley, *op.cit.* (1947), p.43, T Gallagher, Glasgow, the Uneasy Peace (1987).
38. *Op.cit.* (1980), p.86.
39. Foster, *op.cit.* (1974), p.333.
40. A Wilson, The Chartist Movement in Scotland (1970), p.223. Also L.C. Wright, *Scottish Chartism* (1953), p.172, p.197.
41. Wilson, *loc.cit.* (1970).
42. Miles, *op.cit.* (1982), Chapter 6, pp.135-145.
43. 1911 Census Table in McCaffrey.Ph.D *op.cit.* (1970).
44. In E Ravenstein, 'The Laws of Migration', *Journal of the Statistical Society*, No. 48 (1885).
45. W M Walker, *Juteopolis* (1979), p.121.
46. McCarthy, *op.cit.* (1969).
47. For example, *Govan Press*, 6/7/89; GH, 12/7/1902.
48. BWN, 23/11/29.
49. See Cassirer, Ph.D *op.cit.* (1938); 1831 Census Parl. Report 1833 xxxviii, Estimate of Clelland, p.1600.
50. Ravenstein, *op.cit.*, p.167-224. An important factor was obviously close geographical proximity and the frequency of steamer crossings. See Handley, *op.cit.* 1947.
51. *Glasgow*, GPO Directory 1885-6.
52. Inaugural meeting in Edinburgh, GN,18/12/86.
53. McDonagh, *op.cit.* (197?) p.48, and *Govan Press*, 6/7/89. Letter 'A son of the soil'.
54. B Murray, *The Old Firm* (1984), for a discussion of this in relation to Glasgow Rangers F.C. I G C Hutchison, Ph.D, *op.cit.* (1975), pp384-404, also suggests that Scots returning from work in the Belfast shipyards were instrumental in Orange expansion. This is plausible but difficult to substantiate empirically.
55. I S Wood, 'Irish Nationalism and Radical Politics in Scotland 1886-1900', *Journal of Scottish Labour History*, June 1975, No. 9.
56. Walker, *op.cit.* (1979), p.121 and n. Also pp.114-5.

57. *Greenock Telegraph,* (GT), 12/7/69.
58. Appendix E.
59. Methodically listed in newspaper reports of successive Twelfth demonstrations.
60. Interview T.B. In the author's possession is Thomas McFarland's certificate issued in 1915 by LOL No. 457, Seskenore, Co. Tyrone.
61. Sibbet, *op.cit.* (1939), Vol. 2, Dewer et al., *op.cit.* (1967).
62. Senior, *op.cit.* (nd) p.91 ff.
63. Waller, *op.cit.* (1981), p.167.
64. Sibbet, *op.cit.* (1939), vol. 2, p.141.
65. Handley, *op.cit.* (1947), pp.287-8
66. Interview H.S., 1/9/1983 said his father had forbidden him to marry a 'Scotch girl', and told him to look for 'one of his own kind' (he disobeyed).
67. See *Irish Poor Report* (1835) for situation in 1830s.
68. GN, 15/9/73.
69. GN, 10/7/74.
70. *The Bailie,* 16/7/84.
71. *A Report of the Protestant and Orange Soirée held in Paisley on 5 November 1856,* Paisley District Library.
72. *ibid.*
73. *ibid.*
74. GT, 5/11/69.
75. GT, 6/11/70.
76. For a sample of troubles see *GN* 29/7/78, 25/3/79, 15/7/79, 9/5/81, 9/8/81, 13/9/81, 4/10/81.
77. See *Glasgow Herald* reports late 19th century/early 20th century, e.g. 9/7/1900.
78. *GH,* 11/7/1908.
79. *Glasgow Observer,* 16/7/84.
80. *Scottish People,* 16/7/87.
81. *Loc.cit.*
82. *GN,* 8/8/79. Probably more accurate than LOI figures. The Masonic Grand Lodge was more administratively efficient than its Orange counterpart and had less to 'prove'. C Harvie suggests that by the 1920s a tenth of adult Scots males were members, in *No Gods, and Precious Few Heroes – Scotland, 1914–1980* (1981), p.100.
83. See regularly Freemasonry Column in *Glasgow News,* 1873-85.
84. J Wyllie, *A History of Mother Lodge Kilwinning* (1879).
85. *ibid.*

7

The Scottish Churches

This chapter will illustrate how Orangeism's alien and disorderly reputation reacted with the Scottish social formation's cultural uniqueness, as represented in the Scottish Churches. Ecclesiastical relations represent probably the Order's least successful adaptation to Scottish conditions, and demonstrate the continuing relevance of Mc Conechy's remark in the 1830s that Orangeism, identified as a creature of the Irish episcopal establishment, '... was certainly not wanted in Presbyterian Scotland'.[1]

BACKGROUND TO THE SCOTTISH CHURCHES

It is useful to start from an examination of major developments in the Scottish churches, for in Scotland the schismatic tendency of Protestantism was particularly well developed, resulting in a morass of ecclesiastical divisions and reunions (see Fig. 4).[2]

The discussion also indicates the class basis of the major ecclesiastical bodies, and emphasises the unique configuration of religion and politics in Scotland, both points which are important in considering the determinants of Orange-ecclesiastical relations.

By the late eighteenth century, the Church of Scotland had become characterised by doctrinal rigidity and circumscribing state links. Difficulties also arose due to its parochial structure, originally planned for a rural society. In particular, the Kirk's traditional social responsibilities for poor relief and education were now becoming prey to the secularising and urbanising forces accompanying capitalist development in Scotland.

In these circumstances dissent first arose from the increasingly advancing urban bourgeoisie, particularly prosperous independent tradesmen and commercial proprietors, those to be enfranchised by the 1832 Reform Act. It was this group, for example, which formed the backbone of the Relief Church, one of the earliest secession bodies.

When in 1847 this merged with the United Associate Synod to form a new denomination, the United Presbyterians, it was again grounded in urban bourgeois support. Bullock and Drummond

Fig 4: Divisions in Scottish Presbyterianism 1730-1920

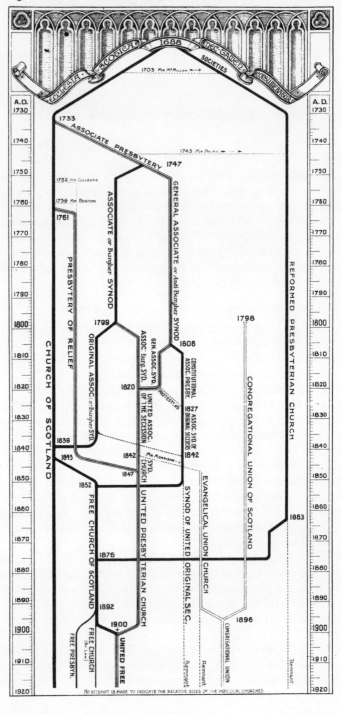

No attempt is made to indicate the relative sizes of the individual churches

describe it indeed as 'the one class church' recounting that one of its congregations was so wealthy that the cards for its annual congregational meeting bore the inscription 'Carriages at 10 p.m.'.[3]

For such United Presbyterian congregations the main line of attack was on the traditionally intimate Church and State relation, rooted in Calvinist doctrines and expressed in the established status of the Church of Scotland. Now they believed it stood in need of fundamental reconsideration. Actively questioning the tenets of scholastic Calvinism, they advanced instead the 'Voluntary Principle', the concept of the church as a spiritual society animated and sustained by stalwart Christians and disassociated from contaminating secular powers. In this they were guided not only by their reading of the New Testament, but by their frustration as a rising class, with the limitations in administration, preaching and pastoral work of a National church, which no longer seemed capable of representing them. In this way Voluntaryism was thoroughly in keeping with the dominant ideology of political economy which held that any government action was an interference with personal liberty and the play of market forces.

The Established Church was able to weather these secessions, but a much greater threat was posed by the 1843 'Disruption', which brought a national 'Free Church' denomination into existence. As in the emergence of the Relief Church the basic question was still the relevance of the historic Calvinist standpoint that the Christian church was the household of faith and should so impress itself on the surrounding secular community, that the standards of the gospel became the rule of life for society at large.

Here, though, the test for the church-state link was posed by the question of lay patronage – the right of the senior heritors, usually major local landowners, to secure the appointment of parish ministers.[4] Here too the secession was led not by laymen as in previous dissenting movements, but from the Kirk's own clergy. These were the 'Evangelical' party led by the Rev. Thomas Chalmers, men who had been coming to prominence from the 1830s, but were prevented from becoming dominant in the Kirk, precisely by the institution of patronage, since the landowners' candidates were usually orthodox 'Moderates'.

Placing a great reliance on Biblical inspiration, these Evangelicals stressed the independence of the Christian community from State control. Initially at least, they did not embrace the Voluntary principle – as Chalmers expressed it 'we go out on the established principle; we quit a vitiated establishment, but would rejoice in returning to a pure one'.[5]

The Church of Scotland suffered a severe setback; as the Rev. Norman McLeod commented, 'the best ministers and the best portion of our people have gone.' Difficulties were faced in filling vacant pulpits and often, 'schoolmasters, worn out probationers and men of dubious morale and training' were recruited.[6]

Meanwhile the new Free Church made rapid progress, crucially drawing on the same class as the old dissenting presbyterians, in particular on small employers in urban areas. Contributions to various Free Kirk schemes amounted to £1000 per day, although less than one-third of the Scottish population were members, and a rapid programme of church building was undertaken, coherent with their claim to be a real 'National' church. In 1843-4, for example, over 50 churches were opened and a total of £320,000 raised.[7] Except for the North and West Highlands, however, the working class failed to enter the Free Kirk, largely alienated by the Toryism of its original founders and its increasingly introspective Calvinism.

During the 1840s and 1850s the United Presbyterians similarly progressed, attracting more wealthy industrialists, such as John Clark the thread magnate of Paisley. Consequently, as Bullock notes, the laymen who made decisions in these matters now frequently resolved to move their churches out of areas uncongenial to them socially, sell the buildings at a shrewd profit, and rebuild them in the districts where their moneyed members were settling. Thus when Cambridge Street, in the centre of Glasgow, showed signs of declining the wealthier members of the United Presbyterian congregation there, with Dr. Eadie as their minister, removed in a body to the new and aesthetically impressive Landsdowne church, built in the wealthiest part of Great Western Road. On Sunday 6th December 1863 the new church was opened, and as the first of the congregation arrived they found a notice pinned to the front door:

> The Church is not for the poor and needy,
> But for the rich and Dr. Eadie.
> The rich step in and take their seat,
> But the poor walk down to Cambridge Street.[8]

The collection (counted on Monday to observe the Sabbath) amounted to £1231.5/9d. When in 1884 the United Presbyterian church similarly moved from Wellington Street to the crest of University Avenue the collection at the opening service was £1,100 – a most tangible demonstration, suggest Bullock and Drummond, of this denomination's social and material advance.[9]

By mid century the three main presbyterian churches in some

areas such as Glasgow were almost equal in following with the Church of Scotland slightly in front.[10]

In the late 1860s and 70s this situation was already beginning to alter, as the established church pulled ahead more decisively. One factor here was the continuing support of the local gentry, farmers and members of the legal establishment but another was the positive attitude of many of the working class, particular in rural areas towards 'the Auld Kirk'.[11] This was further reinforced by its retention of a clear sense of parochial responsibility for poor relief, and by a more liberal approach from the established clergy as the old 'Moderate' leadership died out.

During the same period the Free Church faced serious financial difficulties with the death of some generous donors. Factional wrangles absorbed much energy and its major church building effort proved over-ambitious, with one-third excess capacity resulting.

The United Presbyterians faced similar problems with a loss in prominent backers, though, as suggested above, it remained wealthy and avoided internal divisions at the cost of expansion.

This background of tension and stagnation brought a particular energy to attempts to *disestablish* the Church of Scotland, which marked the period from 1874 to 1895. The original anti-Voluntary position of the Free Kirk had already been overtaken by events in the 1870s. The removal of patronage by the 1874 Act again raised the question whether the root grievances of the original dissent over the Church and State relation had been removed and whether the Establishment was really free from the Erastian* taint of Lutheran state churches or even the Church of England. The suspicion here was that 'the interests of evangelical truth could not be safe in a church where elements of the old 'Moderatism' survived under a modern guise'.[12]

The Free Kirk and United Presbyterian campaign for Disestablishment and Disendowment was chiefly orchestrated through the medium of the Liberation Society and later the Scottish Disestablishment Committee. Most significantly though this crisis decisively aligned the rival churches with the rival political parties.[13]

Thus it was to the Liberal party that the Voluntaryists turned as the most likely vehicle to achieve their objects, its conversion, they hoped, being secured through the persuasion of party leaders and its popular associations.

This was, of course, no departure for the United Presbyterians' urban bourgeois membership who were solidly Liberal, always viewing the party as potentially sympathetic to church and state

*Subordinating church jurisdiction to the state.

separation. As regards the Free Kirk though, a tradition of Toryism had originated with Chalmers and those who retained their belief in a purified national church. A substantial minority remained Conservatives in the 1870s and 80s, well represented by Rev. James Begg of Edinburgh and the layman, William Kidston of Glasgow, although the majority of Free Churchmen were now convinced Liberals, particularly alienated by Tory government action around the Disruption and the 1874 Patronage Act, and by the hostile attitudes of Tory landowners like the Duke of Buccleuch towards their Kirk.

In these circumstances the Church of Scotland became drawn more to the Conservatives, as upholders of the establishment principle. A number of prominent clergymen, like the Rev. Dodds of Glasgow, began to address Conservative associations and even use the pulpit to support the party.[14] In turn the latter gave its active support to the large public meetings organised by the Kirk against disestablishment and to its Church Defence Associations organised in 1885/6 and the Laymen's League established in 1890. Again though this process was not without exception and, as Hutchinson notes, two broad bands remained outside the Kirk and Tory alliance: firstly, the Whig wing of the Liberals, the 'Liberal Churchmen' with a significant representation from the large mercantile bourgeois like Sir Charles Tennant and Sir James Lumsden, and secondly the 'Broad Churchmen' among the Kirk's clergy, Liberals in politics and theology like Professor Caird.[15]

These alignments were naturally shaken by the emergence of the Liberal Unionist party, who drew significantly on the Whiggish sections of the mercantile and professional bourgeoisie. The bitterness of ecclesiastical rivalry persisted throughout the period of study and beyond, as Kellas suggests, helping to sidetrack the Liberals from confronting the increasing desire of the working class for independent political representation, and, moreover, preventing church unity till as late as 1929.[16]

ORANGEISM AND THE CHURCHES:
THE NATURE AND EXTENT OF RELATIONS

The second step here is to specify the precise contours of Orange-Church relations. Here a comparative perspective is again useful, though secondary sources for Ulster, Liverpool and Canada though are rather disappointing. Senior, for example, suggests the early Canadian lodges offered an improvised substitute for a church, at a time when clergymen were sometimes more difficult to find than an Orange warrant. Though some episcopal clergymen did take a prominent role as members.[17]

Details are very sketchy for later developments. The Order seems to have had some Baptist links and had a Minister, D F Hutchinson, as Grand Chaplain of the Provincial Grand Lodge of Nova Scotia.[18] One interesting point though is that the Canadian Orangemen unlike the Scottish did not develop a single entrenched position in favour of the Established Church. Ogle R Gowan, for example, Grand Master in the 1840s, had headed a government committee which recommended that financial reserves for the Anglican clergy, provided by the state, should be divided among all the legally recognised denominations, and later he forcefully expressed his distaste for a 'state priesthood'.[19]

As for Liverpool, there is even less precise detail on ecclesiastical links. Here Anglicans and Nonconformists were fiercely at odds over the established nature of the Church of England, though they tended to be united in practical terms by an evangelical alliance against High Church Anglican practices and Roman Catholicism. In these conditions the Orangemen adopted a more unambiguous State-Church policy than in Canada, generally supporting Church of England candidates in the school board elections. This promoted support from the Anglican clergy – the Rev. Richard Hobson, for example, proclaimed himself 'attached to the Protestantism of Orangeism' although he never joined 'that honourable organisation'[20] – but nowhere is the extent of this support specified.

More fruitful, for comparative purposes is the case of Ulster, though again exact data for the later period is lacking. Although, as suggested, the LOI at its foundation was free from gentry control and formal links with the Established Church of Ireland, and some of its original members were themselves presbyterians, this situation was reversed fairly rapidly. As a result of an anticipated attack on tithes and state endowment episcopal clergymen were drawn into much closer association, and by 1828 15 out of 25 members of the Grand Committee of the Orange Grand Lodge were from this body. This set the typical pattern for lodges, particularly in Antrim, Down and North Londonderry, consisting of landlord, rector and curate, servants, and agricultural labourers.

Given this episcopal, gentry dominance, presbyterians, largely drawn from the Northern bourgeoisie and veering towards Liberalism, remained aloof from the Order in the first half of the nineteenth century. There were exceptions to this such as Rev. R H Shaw of Island Magee and Rev. Henry Cook of Belfast. The latter, as Tory and a bitter opponent of Catholic emancipation, formed an alliance with the landlords and the LOI. In spite of protests from other members of the synod of Ulster he spoke at a rally in Hillsborough, organised by the Orange gentry, at which he pledged presbyterian co-operation and an alliance with the Established Church.[21]

This, in fact, prefigured the demise of 'denominational rigidities' in Ireland, and the decisive shift of the presbyterian bourgeoisie away from a republican and radical past and towards a staunch Toryism in the face of Fenianism and Home Rule crises. Prominent among them from the 1860s were many presbyterian ministers who now eagerly embraced Orangeism, attracted by its official stand on Temperance and Sabbath observance, and irritated by the withdrawal of the old 'Royal Bounty' originally granted by William III to the Presbyterian Church of Ireland.

By no means did these developments go unobserved or uncriticised by some presbyterians. The following outburst from the *Christian Banner* in 1878 displays considerable anxiety over the contamination of the presbyterian spirit with Orange influences:

> The 12th of July has once more come and gone and with it the usual amount of Orange eloquence and Orange valour. With one or two exceptions the clergy of the late established church had all the abusive declamation as well as all the Orange lily and No Surrender rhetoric to themselves. Hundreds of presbyterians, however, we are told, went on the Sabbath before the 12th to hear the men who from parish leaders and schoolmasters were manufactured into curates... These presbyterians could not... have more effectively dishonoured the memory of their mighty dead, had they on the 12th of July last gone to the churchyard of the Old Grey Friars in Edinburgh, exhumed the sacred dust of the dead and flinging it into the Firth of Forth, they could not have shown greater disrespect to those sainted sons of the blue banner who died for the rights of the Redeemer and the liberties of their Country.[22]

Despite these strictures, in the years that followed leading presbyterian figures like Rev. Hugh Hannah and Rev. Thomas Drew were central in the Orange anti-Home Rule campaign. At this point one witnesses a most thorough interpenetration between the Orange Institution and both of the major Ulster churches, with a large body of clergy taking an active role in the business of Grand, Provincial and Local Lodges.[23]

On the other hand, the leading Orangeman, Col. Saunderson, was also one of the foremost laymen in the Church of Ireland. He even had a private chapel in the grounds of his estate and usually conducted the service and preached the sermon there himself, 'not caring for assistance even in the reading of lessons'.[24] These close ecclesiastical links still, indeed, characterise the Irish LOI in the present day, its official historians Dewar, Long and Brown are clergymen, as is present Grand Master the Rev. Martin Smyth, a minister of the Presbyterian Church of Ireland.[25]

A stark contrast is presented by Scottish Orangeism. At its low state of development in the early nineteenth century, as indicated, the Order here had no significant involvement from the clergy of any denomination and even by the time of the 1835 Parliamentary Report only one clergyman, an English episcopalian Rev. John Jervis Bently of the 'Royal Gordon', was a member.[26]

With its general expansion in the 1860s the Scottish Institution found its first real clerical enthusiast in the Ulsterman Robert Gault, minister of the Free Kirk in Glasgow Kingston and superintendent of its anti-Popish mission. Gault was himself an Orangeman, prone to inflammatory speeches at the Order's November *soirées*. He was, moreover, most willing to receive his brethren in his church and on the 12th of July 1868 the Glasgow Orangemen met in Brunswick Street and marched to Kingston 5-6 abreast. The episcopal link also seems to have remained in this period and in 1868 200 members of the Order walked to the Episcopal Church in St. James Place, Coatbridge, resplendent with Orange necklets and Bibles.[27]

Yet compared with the extent of Church of Ireland support and the reorientation of a large body of the presbyterian clergy in Ulster towards the Order in the same period, such developments appear rather insignificant.

Moving on to the 1870s and beyond, further ecclesiastical links did develop. Indeed, looking at the apparent proliferation of ministers on Orange platforms it might even seem possible to assimilate Ulster and Scottish experience.

For the period 1873-1900 43 clergymen were identified on public Orange platforms. These appearances were spread throughout the West of Scotland and unlike the Order's political links no significant local variations are apparent between the cases of Glasgow, Paisley and Greenock. Many of these figures were moreover frequent visitors and the figure of 43 is surely an understatement of the total of clerical supporters in the 30 years' span.[28]

Beyond this, considerable caution must be exercised. First, among this number, the representation from the various denominations was unbalanced. No less than 27 of those whose denominations could be identified were from the Church of Scotland, 6 were Episcopalians, 6 were Methodists and 2 were 'Independent Congregationalists'. Only 2 were from the Free Kirk, Robert Gault and the Rev. Fraser of Paisley, and there were *no* United Presbyterian representatives. Secondly, 27 is only a tiny minority of Church of Scotland ministers considering there were no less than 1113 Kirk congregations in Scotland in 1854, for example.[29]

Thirdly, it is also essential to distinguish between the 'fellow travellers', willing to guest at the fairly sedate November *soirées* and make expansive gestures of support there, and those, like their Ulster counterparts who were actually prepared to become members of the Order. This might involve acting as Grand Chaplains, and even appearing at the considerably more rowdy 12th parades. If this distinction is made, clerical involvement swiftly appears less impressive. It is striking how frequently ministers at Orange meetings feel compelled to emphasise they were not actually Orangemen. The Rev. Paton, for example, stressed he 'did not wear Orange colours', but he 'cherished its principles as warmly at heart as any of them'.[30] Similarly the Rev. Hugh Ramsay of Baillieston told his Royal Black Preceptory audience he was 'not a member of the Order' though he 'thoroughly believed in the principles the brethren professed'.[31] Thus only nine of the Church of Scotland ministers were themselves Orangemen, three of the Episcopalians, one Free Churchman (Gault), both Congregationalists and one of the Methodists (Rev. William Robinson of Paisley).

Fourthly, a point which will be developed below, it is interesting to note how many of this number were *Ulstermen* – a total of six, three of the Kirk Ministers, both the Congregationalists and Gault.

Finally, even the native Scots ministers who did join the Order were not prominent or influential churchmen, some were indeed reckoned as mavericks by their contemporaries, and consequently carried little weight in the life and work of the Kirk. The Rev. J K Campbell, for example, was actually a former United Presbyterian. minister who the *Greenock Telegraph* commented '... changed his political colour of late and overcame his previous prejudices... against Orangeism'.[32] Joining the Institution around 1879, he seems to have swung to the most reactionary extremes of Toryism, sponsoring a resolution attributing increased papal aggression to the non-enforcement of the 1829 Catholic Emancipation Bill's guarantee clauses and calling for the Bill's repeal.[33]

An even more intriguing case, though, is the Rev. Robert Thompson of Ladywell Parish, Glasgow – 'Rubbart' and 'something of a rantipole' according to *The Bailie* magazine, for whom he was a favourite figure of ridicule.[34] Certainly an ardent self-publicist, Thompson was very prominent in the Order in the early 1870s. He had much wider ambitions, though, standing as an independent Protestant candidate in the Kilmarnock parliamentary election in

1868, the Glasgow municipal election in 1883, and later in the parliamentary division of St. Rollox in 1890 and 95, as an 'Independent Protestant Working Man's candidate' embracing a populist 'Protestant democracy'. He also managed to gain election to the Glasgow School Board in 1885, and was principal of his own, very short lived, 'Southside University'.

His conduct was at times embarrassing, even to the Orangemen. In 1883, for instance, he threw the Greenock November *soirée* into uproar when he attempted to use his speech to publicise his municipal candidature. Another minister on the platform objected to him introducing 'extraneous matter at this social gathering'. At this Thompson became very excited shouting, 'You are a trimmer, sir, you are a liar, sir, and you gave me the cold shoulder, sir'. Provost Binnie chairing the meeting vainly tried to pacify him and only after several other interruptions was he persuaded to offer the other clergyman his hand 'to show we are Christian ministers'.[35] He had similarly disrupted a municipal banquet in Glasgow the same year, protesting noisily at the presence of the Roman Catholic Archbishop Eyre at the festivities.[36]

In these circumstances the eccentric divine's position in the Established Presbytery of Glasgow was extremely marginal, and he was refused the position of Moderator which should have been his by rotation for 1884. An amendment proposing the Rev. McLeod of Govan in his stead was accepted 42 to 14 with the most distinguished and respected Glasgow ministers in favour. Rev. Thompson in retaliation proposed a variety of motions including one of 'no support for the pervert Marquis of Bute, a papist, in the Glasgow University rectorial election' but these were overwhelmingly defeated.

These points on personalities, coupled with the general level of involvement of Kirk ministers point clearly to the crucial distance between the two bodies – further confirmed by the lack of representation from the Orangemen in local Church Defence Associations and the Kirk's large anti-Disestablishment rallies.[37]

DETERMINING FACTORS IN CHURCH RELATIONS: ORANGE IDEOLOGY

One factor militating against closer ecclesiastical relations was presented by the positive elements in the Orangemen's own ideology, which stressed its role as 'the only body where Protestants of all denominations could unite against the common enemy, especially resisting papal aggression on the British constitution'.[38] 'We take credit to our Institution for being one in which all general Protestants are equally welcome whether Episcopalian, Presbyterian or whatever else and in which they are associated together in a movement which strengthens them in the feelings of Christian brotherhood and so promotes their spiritual welfare'.[39] For Johnstone of Ballykillbeg the Order was quite simply the foremost religious organisation, 'Protestantism in action'.[40]

Such ambitious claims to be superior to competing denominational interests, 'differing from one another on minor points',[41] as Paton dismissed them, were very likely to alienate the more orthodox religious bodies who were actually pursuing those interests, interests which *they* genuinely believed were essential for the well-being of the Christian church in Scotland. In particular the Orangemen's definition of themselves as the 'leaven' of pure and scriptural Protestantism was liable to offend the Free Church which, as noted above, had been anxious to lay claim to a very similar role as the true 'Church of Scotland'.

More specific elements, though, in the Institution's ideology on the church and state relationship also contributed to the alienation of the dissenting bodies. First, largely drawing on their experience of the Irish Church, the Orangemen most strongly opposed disestablishment and 'Voluntaryism'. The latter was denounced in the strongest terms by McLeod, '... The voluntary principle has been and still is one of the main influences – outside the Church of Rome – by which Popery has been advanced to political power and state position within the three kingdoms and therefore Voluntaryism must be resisted as one of the chief assistants of Popery'.[42]

The United Presbyterians often explicitly incurred the LOI's wrath, but the Free Kirk was also liable to attack, once it moved from its original 'purified establishment' position. Dr. MacKnight of Ayr, for example, saw them as twin foes, calling on his audience to:

> buckle on their armour against the disestablishment movement carried on by the UPs, who were a body professing belief in the Bible, all except the 13th Chapter of Romans, teaching the magistrates power under God, and the Free Church which is a body divided against itself... they left the Church of State believing in the principle of church and state and now a great number of its ministers were Voluntaries.[43]

This attack was further pressed home from the late 1870s, notably by Thomas Macklin and Samuel Geddes both themselves Free Churchmen; as Geddes, Master of Lodge No. 690 commented:

> I and many thousands of Orangemen belong to dissenting bodies... but the time has come to remove to more wholesome quarters. The Free Kirk position leaves no alternative, for

Orangemen are bound by solemn obligation to support the Protestant Religion as established by William III in 1689, hence they are no disestablishers.[44]

At times criticism from Orange platforms even extended to the Free Church's lack of concern for the poor, as contrasted with the Established Church. The Rev. Hutcheson of Newhall Parish reported in 1878 that his district had been said by the Free kirk to be too poor to support a minister, but his Church of Scotland predecessor had stepped in: 'he did not go to proselytise but to preach to the poor, the halt, the maimed and the blind and God forbid the Church of Scotland should ever cease to care for the poor.'[45]

THE INSTITUTION'S NEGATIVE REPUTATION

Such barbs were offensive enough in themselves, but when combined with what many dissenting clergymen viewed as the unsavoury reality of Orangeism they were seen as arrogant and insupportable.

The antipathy of the bourgeois-dominated United Presbyterians and Free Churches was roused in the first place by the proletarian and stridently populist tone of many of the local lodges. Secondly, we have also described the extremely negative reputation the Order had gained during the nineteenth century for drunkenness, disorder, and importing an alien party spirit into Scotland. It was now that this had one of its most baneful effects; for such 'attributes' sat uneasily with the overwhelming concern for individual conduct and personal morals which particularly characterised the dissenting Churches.[46]

One of the best illustrations of the reactions the LOI aroused among the dissenters is provided by the Greenock Free Church controversy of 1876.[47]

The circumstances of this case were very complex, but basically it had transpired that a congregation of Ulster settlers in the town had formed themselves into an independent 'Orange Congregational Church', meeting in the Orange Hall in Cathcart Street under the direction of the Rev. Dignum and later Rev. Charleton, both themselves Ulstermen. In time they had applied to be accepted into the Church of Scotland. The Kirk had permitted this, but some of its ministers, such as Rev. Bryce, had been anxious to score a point against the Free Church, and at a meeting of the Church of Scotland presbytery in December 1875 claimed that the 'Orange Church' was in fact a defection from the 'Frees' – provoked by their increasing 'Voluntaryistic' proclivities. Claims for similar defections and a cry of 'the Free Church on the wane' were quite prominent in the mid 1870s as Disestablishment became a more contentious issue.

The Greenock Free Church presbytery was outraged. The substance of their argument was that the congregation had always been
under false colours, being composed almost entirely of Orangemen.
In these circumstances it appeared to them to have a profound 'political' or 'party' motivation rather than a religious one. Significantly,
however, this was entwined with ridicule of the Irish origins and the
general social standing of the Orangemen. As an Orange correspondent summed up, to the Free Churchmen, 'Orangemen are detestable
and in everything are to be avoided and excommunicated'.[48]

Thus the Rev. Bonnar, taking to task his Kirk opponents, began
fairly inoffensively by challenging the facts of the Rev. Bryce's claims
for 'the new established church'. 'This,' he explained, 'was a congregation of Irish presbyterians and had been advertised week after
week in the paper as 'the Orange Established church', they dropped
the name afterwards in deference to the choice or antipathies of the
body which they were meaning to join' [the Church of Scotland]. He
went on though to recount (to great laughter from the presbytery)
that one of the Orange church had made a slip of the tongue, saying
that '... for the last twelve months he had watched the progress of the
Order – not the congregation – and he thought they would now take
a leading part in the town's elections and other local matters... To
form a congregation upon such a basis', Bonnar continued 'was a
scandal and an outrage on the Christian religion. Why these gentlemen would not sit at the Lord's Table as disciples but as politicians,
and they would go forth from worship down through the thor-
oughfares of the town to agitate... .Their minister, moreover, would
have to be one with themselves in Orange politics and one with
themselves in everything... .And where', he asked, ending on a note
of sarcasm, 'would the Orangemen get a man in Scotland that would
sympathise with them in Orangeism?'[49].

Bonnar's contribution seems to have unleashed similar sentiments from his Free Church colleagues. The Rev. Nelson, for
example, commented, it was singular that whilst other unions with
which they, as ministers, had to do there was always a great display
of Orange blossom – in this case the Orange blossom is carefully
concealed by Mr. Bryce and his Orangemen – they best know the
reason why'. Nevertheless he hoped 'their minister would do much
good, especially among the low *Irish*... ' (author's emphasis); while
the Rev. Stark said 'two or three families had left his church because
he would not attend a certain meeting and make a speech in favour
of Orangeism... but he did not think that their friends in the
established church need be overjoyed by getting three hundred
Orangemen (laughter and applause)'. For his part the Rev.

Thompson took the more common positive viewpoint on Irish Protestant migration. 'It gave one pleasure to see them gradually rise in social position, to see their children marrying and intermingling with Scottish families...'. However, '... he had dealings with Orangemen and complied with a request to attend one of their meetings. He looked on that gathering as a social gathering of those who belonged to Ireland. He was allowed... to make a speech on anything he liked, and he took advantage to speak on toleration (laughter).... .The audience appeared to be very well pleased with his speech (laughter). He was well pleased with his speech (renewed laughter) and he was invited to come back again. But they afterwards began to bring speakers to their meetings who discussed Disestablishment and such things, men whose sentiments were in direct opposition to his own and since then he had given up attending their meetings'.[50]

With the hostility voiced here it is at first sight surprising that the Order found any Free Church champions like the Revs. Gault and Fraser. In fact these were drawn from the 'old guard' of the Free Church who followed Chalmers both in his Toryism and his commitment to the establishment principle. Already by the 1870s they were steadily dwindling in numbers. Fraser, for example, a frequent visitor to Paisley Orange platforms, died in 1879; his obituary described him as a 'thorough constitutionalist' in his opinions, a Free Churchman but opposed to Disestablishment and an ardent pamphleteer against the latter.[51]

Finally, in the case of the Church of Scotland, the Order's class composition may have been less problematic than for the dissenters, given the responsibility the Kirk felt, as the 'national church', to minister to all sections of Scottish society. A large part of its membership, as noted above, was itself drawn from the working classes in the rural areas. In addition, the LOI's positions on 'Voluntaryism' would be more positively received by this body, particularly in the midst of Disestablishment agitation.

However, considerable reticence on the Kirk's part towards Orange links was still apparent. The negative features of the Order also seem relevant here, for although less individualised the ethos of respectability still had a commanding presence in the Church of Scotland. The image of the 'tipsy Orangemen', for example, was likely to arouse great distaste among ministers, given the church's growing commitment to Temperance. As Fleming indicates, the Kirk had been slow to act at first and identify itself with the Temperance movement but in 1848 a Temperance committee was appointed and by 1853 more than 400 ministers in Scotland were abstainers.[52]

In the Greenock case, for example, there seems to have been a significant lack of enthusiasm among the Established Kirk presbytery for their new congregation. In fact, they seemed embarrassed by the whole affair and were unwilling to reply to the Free Kirk's charges. 'Perhaps the presbytery may see', commented Rev. Murray its Moderator, 'that it is more conforming to its dignity that no such reply be given forth'. In fact, Bonnar's charge is probably correct that the Irish church's 'Orange' epithet was dropped to save their feelings.

Also revealing are some of the statements from the small minority of ministers who were willing to give the LOI public support. Again these placed stress on the Orangemen's conduct. 'If Orangemen are true to their colours, they will not forget the church', stated the Rev. Park, '... and they will not fail to have the ministers rally round them'.[53] Apparently his advice was not well heeded and years later a Coatbridge Minister, Rev. Tait, was compelled to rebuke the local Orangemen for their poor church attendance.[54] Even the eccentric Rev. Thompson offered advice to his 12th audience. He had just returned from a trip to Italy and had visited the Pope's summer palace. 'If you saw a Pope', he declared, 'you would see he was not half as good looking as the men here, if you would only wash your faces' [55]

SCOTTISH SOCIETY

The pejorative connotations of Orangeism, however, provide only a partial explanation of the lack of links with the Scottish churches. Similar difficulties after all were faced and largely surmounted by the LOI in Ulster. In fact, as suggested, its negative reputation here was effectively compounded by features rooted historically in Scottish society and beyond the Order's control.

Gallagher, for example, suggests that the Disruption may have had a debilitating effect on militant Protestantism generally in the Scottish churches, and this seems most plausible.[56] Certainly one should not underestimate the strength of anti-Roman Catholicism which did exist, as expressed notably by James Begg and the Free Church's ultra Conservative wing.[57] However, the ecclesiastical controversies promoted by the events of 1843 and the earlier schisms also qualify Miles' view that the Church of Scotland was characterised by anti-Catholicism and opposition to Irish immigrants, because its position as the *National* church in the Scottish 'Proto-state' was perceived to be threatened by them.[58] In fact, the Kirk's established position had been consistently challenged by dissent from as early as the eighteenth century and most notably by the combined UP body in the nineteenth century. From 1843 it had an even more formidable rival in the Free Kirk, which struggled vigorously to become recognised as the true National Church of Scotland in the eyes of the Scottish people. The Greenock Free Church case indicates how in practice the bitterness of such rivalry left little energy for active 'No Popery' in the churches. If indeed the Kirk had played the role that Miles identifies for it as the most institutionalised expression of anti-Catholic and anti-Irish sentiment in Scotland, this might have offered the LOI an opportunity of dialogue with a central pillar of Scottish society. In reality it proved an increasingly uncongenial climate for Orange sentiments, even when Church union was at last appearing on the horizon in the 1920s.

Far from being Orange partisans the views of many leading ministers may have been influenced by the Rev. Dr. Flint, a leading Churchman, Professor of Divinity at Edinburgh from 1879-1903, when he wrote:

> Let us hope, that... the time may not be far off when even the greatest religious differences in opinion among us, will not be felt to be incompatible with unity in Christ and the exercise of all Christian graces and duties towards those who differ from us in doctrinal views.[59]

Besides the Disruption, another factor in Scottish religious life was important in marginalising Protestant militancy in the churches and with it Orange involvement. This was the limited extent of ritualism as a *cause célèbre*. It was the anti-ritualist movement in Liverpool, as well as anti-Catholicism, which promoted a 'low church' Anglican and Nonconformist rapprochement and may have permitted Orange/Anglican links. In Scotland, however, where the use of organ music in churches was considered by some like Begg to be an abomination, ritualistic practices and concern with the 'externalities' of worship were extremely rare in the major Scottish denominations.

Only a few 'ritualist outrages' came to public attention. Rev. John Charleston of Thornliebank, for example, advocated responsive prayer in public worship and the observance of Holy Week festivals. His congregation seems to have included many Ulster Protestants and Orangemen who had come to work in the local thread mills,[60] and a petition with 207 names was sent to the Paisley presbytery in 1896 expressing their 'greatest dismay'. Charleston eventually left the Church of Scotland in 1901 and became a Roman Catholic. Questions of ornament and ritual were again raised in the case of Rev. T N Adamson at Barnhill in 1901-4, including charges of genuflection before a 'popish altar', and even a Free Church minister, Rev. Stuart Mills, was suspended for 'popish and superstitious practices'.[61]

The High Church movement in Scotland instead found its most authentic expression in the Scottish Church Society (scs). This body, much influenced by the idealist categories of nineteenth century thought, rejected much of Puritanism and Moderatism, turning sympathetically to the purer features of the pre-Reformation church and the neo-Catholic tradition pioneered by the Rev. Milligan of Aberdeen. It differed from the contemporary evangelism, as Fleming notes, in the prominence it gave to sacramental doctrine and its stress on the historic continuity of the church from earliest times. Unlike its English counterpart, however, it had little interest in ritual and ceremonial, and actually expelled the erring Rev. Charleston for his 'Romish practices'.[62]

In fact, a useful indicator of the relative absence of High Church controversy in Scotland was the *progress* of the scs. Its membership was never very large, only 91 in 1900, but its influence, Murray concludes, was out of proportion to this; three former moderators joined and three members became moderators from 1892 to 1914.[63] It was, of course, the Rev. John McLeod 'the priest of Govan' and an energetic scs apostle who was appointed moderator of the Glasgow presbytery in preference to the Orange Rev. Thompson. In contrast opposition to the scs was lead by a 'marginal man' in the Church of Scotland, the Rev. Jacob Primmer of Dundee, like Thompson an eccentric who held Protestant 'conventicles' and disrupted successive General Assemblies.[64]

The effects of the Disruption and the lack of effective anti-ritualist movement combined to limit militant Protestantism in the major denominations. It is Bruce's belief, for example, that the majority of ministers were not anti-Catholic, and that the overt racialism of the 1923 General Assembly report 'The Menace of the Irish Race to Our Scottish Nationality' was the work of a small, relatively powerless group.[65]

A set of more specific factors also lay behind the LOI's ecclesiastical marginalisation. These are basically related to the Institution's position as an importation, and to the disjuncture between the social formations of Ulster and Scotland, in particular in this case between denominational characteristics and alignments.

As previously emphasised, a central role in the mid century development of the LOI was played by Ulster migrants. It is probable, as both Barkley, and Bullock and Drummond suggest, that a very large proportion of these were communicants of the Church of Ireland, given this denomination's overwhelming predominance in the history and progress of the Order in Ireland.

This episcopal body had a Hanoverian and Constitutionalist

background in Ulster, and its churchmanship was strongly Protestant and highly coloured with evangelism. Like the Kirk, as a former National church, it drew strongly on the aristocracy and gentry but also assumed a responsibility for the working class. The latter's representation was strong in the counties, though non-churchgoing became a problem in Belfast in the late 1880s.[66]

The Scottish Episcopal Church into which Orangemen, as former communicants of the Church of Ireland, would have been received was a very different body in terms of history, worship and class composition. It had been a mainstay of the Jacobite rebellions in Scotland, for instance, and as Thatcher notes, it was not until 1792 that the penal laws to which it was subject were repealed.[67] At that time there were only 40 Episcopalian priests in Scotland and it took a considerable time before the church could expand. Even by the 1830s there were only 6 or 7 congregations in Glasgow and the West of Scotland. In the 1840s and 50s many churches were built, though the South Western diocese numbered only 40 or 50 clergymen.

Moreover, although congregations were predominantly working class in the North East, in the West and Edinburgh the strength of expansion in the early nineteenth century lay in the anglicising gentry. Unlike its Irish counterpart, though, the church seems to have had little concern for poor relief, or sense of duty towards the less privileged sections of society.

At this level of development then, the Scottish Episcopal Church was markedly unprepared for the influx of thousands of migrant workers from Ulster. The rector of St. Andrew's-by-the-Green in Glasgow, for example, claimed 10,000 Episcopalians in the city in the late 1830s, but bewailed that 4,000 of them were Irish and destitute.[68] More commonly it seems this group was received, not in the mainstream of the church, but by missions largely catering for the poor. Several of these opened in Glasgow, one of the first being formed in Bridgeton in 1805 by the Rev. Aitchison. Seats were free and collections for the half year amounted to £7.10/-, an indication of the congregation's lack of prosperity.[69] A similar mission, St. Luke's, was founded in Springburn in the 1870s, built expressly for 'the English and Irish of the artisan class'.[70]

Besides the logistical problems of finding a hospitable congregation, further serious difficulty confronted the episcopalian Orange migrant, in the strongly High Church nature of the Scottish Episcopalians. In fact, in Scotland most of the principles of the Oxford movement were in operation long before the days of the English Tractarians and 'Puseyites', including the divine origin of the

Church, apostolic succession and even the real presence of Christ at the eucharistic sacrifice. Increasingly, moreover, even in Glasgow and Edinburgh it was the old 'Scottish rite', strongly liturgical in character, which was employed in services. Such 'ritualism' would, of course, be abhorrent to an Orangeman reared in the Irish episcopalian tradition of unadorned services and stern doctrinal preaching.

Yet problems of transition also confronted Ulster Orange settlers who, like Geddes and Macklin, were presbyterians, usually communicants of the Presbyterian Church of Ireland. While the General Assembly of this Church had condemned Disestablishment, and from the 1860s began to display profound Tory sentiments, crucially at the time of the 1843 Disruption it had allied with the Free Church, regularly sending two representatives to its assemblies. This then became its sister church in Scotland, and the receiving body for its communicants arriving here.[71]

In this way, whereas men like Macklin who ... had read from Plato, Plutarch, Aristotle and Cicero etc, all who love to witness the truth of National religion ,[72] might have found a more congenial place of worship in the Church of Scotland, with its growing rapport with the Conservatives and championing of the Church and State link, they were, in fact, directed to membership of the Free Church. This was, as illustrated earlier, the bulwark of Liberalism in Scotland and its position on the autonomy and independence of Christian society seemed to be converging with the United Presbyterians on the voluntary support of the Gospel. (This explains why the reception of the Greenock Ulster congregation into the Church of Scotland was reckoned by some as a gain from the Frees.)

Furthermore, even if Orangemen were willing to enter the Free Kirk, with its unwelcome political and ecclesiastical orientations, they may also have faced difficulties by the frequently strict admission to Communion among the dissenting bodies. New members were usually admitted by resolution of the Kirk Session and testimonials and certificates from their previous church had to be produced. Young persons were examined in the Shorter Catechism and scriptural knowledge and if satisfactory received tokens of entry. Even the sacraments of marriage and baptism were celebrated in accordance with this discipline and a fee was charged for registration.[73] Given anti-Orange prejudices, not all congregations may have been particularly willing to be co-operative here.

The vital contribution made by these dislocations is indicated not only in their explanations of the weaknesses but also the strengths in Orange-Church relations. Notably these include the important presence of episcopalian clergymen as members of the LOI and on its platforms. These were either ex-Church of Ireland vicars, some of whom had come to Scotland after disestablishment in 1868, like the Rev. James McCann of St. Paul's Glasgow; or more commonly evangelical 'low church' Anglicans unhappy with Scottish Episcopalianism. The Revs. Halliday and Hodgekinson, Grand Chaplains in 1899 and 92 respectively, and ministers of the Free Episcopal Church of England 'Emmanuel' Church in Camlachie, were representative of this group, as was Rev. Bradshaw of St. Luke's Mission.

Secondly, the general situation also helps explain public links between Methodist ministers and the LOI; for the Methodists had a significant following in Ulster dating from the time of Wesley's tours in the late eighteenth century, Larne being a notable centre.[74] Blending with initial familiarity with the lodges would also be that High Toryism which had characterised sections of the church since the role of Wesley and Bunting, and which found resonance in the Order's claims to defend Crown, Constitution and the Protestant Religion.[75]

Primitive Methodists of the more radical tendency were also represented though. Rather than a political motivation, it seems here that their common situation as 'strangers in a foreign land', as Bullock expresses it, drew these otherwise rather uncommon bodies together. Even in 1901 the Primitives had less than 1000 members in Scotland.[76] In other words they may have been grateful for the opportunity to speak on the LOI's public platforms, although, like their Wesleyan counterparts, 'common Protestantism' was usually not sufficient to persuade them to join the Order.

Thirdly, frustration with those Scottish churches which should have received the Orangemen as members was important in driving the LOI to set up its own churches, 'Independent Congregational' bodies with the Ulster ministers J U Mitchell and T W Patrick. In 1881, for example, C I Paton laid the foundation stone of the latter's new Congregational church at Rutherglen at the cost of £2000. He was subsequently presented with the silver trowel as a token of 'the brotherly love which should be held by Orangemen and all true Protestants'.[77]

This frustration also seems to have led the Orangemen into a close relationship with the lay evangelist, H A Long. Interestingly Long's background was cast in the 'low church' Anglican tradition as curate at St. Silas's in Glasgow.[78] The relationship, though, did not always run smoothly, due largely to personal rivalries. Long seems to have been a rather egotistical character and strongly

resisted Grand Lodge attempts to alter candidate selection in the
'Knoxite' voting confraternity he had founded for the Glasgow
School Board elections.[79]

Finally, the disjuncture between the ecclesiastical situations of
Ulster and Scotland was also liable to produce a result particularly
feared by the Grand Lodge, namely that the Orangemen would stay
away from the churches altogether. The Rev. Tait's remarks in 1894
have already been noted and one of the main motivations of the
Orange Church's foundation in Greenock was precisely that 'large
numbers of our brethren who come from the sister isle attach
themselves to no congregation at all, and we wish to get hold of
them'.[80] Thus the Order's unsavoury reputation, which itself had
contributed to its marginalisation in Scottish religious life, was again
reinforced.

NOTES

1. J McConechy Mss., *loc. cit.*
2. J Bullock and A L Drummond, vol. 1 *The Scottish Church 1688-1843*
   (1973); vol. 2 *The Church in Victorian Scotland 1843-74* (1975), vol. 3
   The Church in late Victorian Scotland 1874-1906 (1978) are very useful
   and are used extensively below. For a legalistic account of Church and
   State relations, see F Lyall, *Of Presbyters and Kings* (1980), and for a
   spirited early account see Fleming, *A History of the Church in Scotland*,
   vols. 1 and 2 (1927). See also Bruce, *op. cit.* (1985), for an excellent
   analysis of Protestant factionalism, Chapter 4, 'The Protestant Popes
   and Internal Conflict', pp. 108-121. Figure 2 is copied and reduced
   from Coloured Diagram by Rev. R Waterson and N Brown. (n.d.).
3. Bullock and Drummond, *op. cit.* (1975), p. 51.
4. See John Galt's *Annals of the Parish* for the sufferings of the Rev.
   Balquidder as 'The laird's man' in his new parish. He had to climb
   through a window to gain access to his church.
5. A J Campbell, *Two Centuries of the Church of Scotland* (1930), pp. 206-
   23.
6. J H S Burleigh, *A Church History of Scotland* (1960), p. 147.
7. Fleming (1927), *op. cit.*, p. 58.
8. Bullock and Drummond, *op. cit.* (1975), p. 46.
9. *Loc. cit.*
10. Various surveys of church membership and attendance were made in
    the period, e.g. R Howie, *The Churches and Churchless in Scotland*
    (1893); and J Rankine, *Handbook of the Church of Scotland* (1888), but
    these are unreliable given their often partisan inspiration. The census
    of 1851 also included denominational data, but this was claimed by
    some contemporaries to be weak methodologically. See Hutchinson,
    Ph.D, *op. cit.* (1975), pp. 55-58, for discussion.
11. See Bullock and Drummond, *op. cit.* (1975), Chapter 5, 'The Na-
    tional Church'.
12. Fleming, *op. cit.* (1927), p. 64.
13. J G Kellas, 'The Liberal Party and The Scottish Church Disestab-
    lishment Crisis', *English Historical Review* 79 (1964), pp. 318-9.
14. For a typical lecture, see GN, 16/2/74.

15. Hutchinson Ph.D, *op. cit.* (1975), pp. 55-58.
16. The UPS and Free Kirk united in 1900 forming the United Free Church, which in turn united with the Church of Scotland on 1st October 1929.
17. Senior, *op. cit.* (n.d.), pp. 7-8.
18. *Ibid.*, pp. 63-65. He was editor of the anti-Fenian *Burning Bush* in the 1860s in Canada.
19. *Ibid.*, p. 36 on Clergy Reserves Question.
20. Waller, *op. cit.* (1981), p. 93.
21. De Paor, *op. cit.* (1973), p. 46.
22. In J M Barkley, *A Short History of the Presbyterian Church in Ireland* (1975), p. 37.
23. See Dewar *et al.*, *op. cit.* (1967).
24. R. Lucas, *Memoir of Col. Saunderson MP* (1908).
25. The latter is the author of the pamphlet *The Message of the Banners* (n.d.), an official 'reading' of Orange Insignia.
26. *1835 Report*, *loc. cit.*
27. *North British Daily Mail*, 13/7/68, 14/7/68.
28. For the various clergymen see Appendix F. The names were collected from 12th July and *soirée* reports in *Glasgow News, Glasgow Herald, Greenock Telegraph, Paisley Daily Express, Paisley and Renfrewshire Standard.*
29. Bullock and Drummond, *op. cit.* (1975), p. 112.
30. GN, 6/11/84.
31. GN, 28/8/76.
32. GT, 16/11/78.
33. GN, 8/11/79.
34. See *The Bailie* 248, 495, 576 with 2 portraits.
35. GT, 3/11/83.
36. GN, 6/10/83; and GN, 8/11/83 for Presbytery meeting.
37. e.g. GN, 21/10/85, 22/11/85, 13/11/85.
38. GN, 4/11/76.
39. GN, 12/9/81.
40. GN, 6/11/74.
41. GN, 12/9/81
42. GN, 3/7/77.
43. GN, 3/11/77.
44. GN, 29/11/81.
45. GN, 11/11/78.
46. Bullock, *op. cit.* (1975), p. 51.
47. GT, 30/12/75, 27/1/76 for Free Kirk meeting.
48. Letter from R Madill in GT, 28/3/76.
49. GT, 30/12/75.
50. *Ibid.*
51. GN obituary, 7 22/9/79. Funeral 29/9/79. The local Orange Lodges were in attendance.
52. Fleming, *op. cit.* (1927). Also see E King pamphlet, *Scotland Sober and Free* (1979).
53. GN, 12/11/73.
54. McDonagh, *op. cit.* (197?), cites *Coatbridge Express*, 7/11/94.
55. GH, 13/7/81.
56. Gallagher, *op. cit.* (1987), p. 34.
57. Early Begg pamphlets in Murray Collection, Glasgow University Library Special Collections.
58. Miles, *op. cit.* (1982), Chapter 6 (though this point does not bear the

major theoretical weight of his argument in the chapter).

59. *Life of Professor Flint* (n.d.), p. 436. One prominent Kirk minister, Rev. Donald McLeod of Park Church had even attended a service at the English Roman Catholic College in Rome, where Cardinal Newman had preached. S Smith, *Rev. Donald McLeod* (1926), p. 62.

60. D M Murray, *op. cit.*, *The Scottish Church Society 1892-14: A Study of the High Church Movement in the Church of Scotland.* D.Phil, University of Cambridge, 1976.

61. Fleming, *op. cit.* (1927).

62. Murray, *op. cit.* (1976), p. 261.

63. Murray, *loc. cit.*

64. S Bruce, *op. cit.* (1985), pp. 38-42.

65. *Ibid.*, p. 46.

66. R B McDowall, *History of the Church of Ireland*, p. 15.

67. B Thatcher, 'The Episcopal Church in Helensburgh' in *Scottish Themes; Essays in Honour of Prof. S G E Lythe*, (1976), J Butt (ed).

68. Bullock and Drummond, *op. cit.* (1975), p. 62.

69. *Ibid.*

70. Thatcher, *op. cit.* (1976).

71. Presbyterians were excluded from Trinity College Dublin till 1793, but even after this date there was a tradition of Irish presbyterians coming for higher education to Scottish universities, particularly Glasgow. This may have been the background of Macklin, a Classics professor.

72. GH, 14/7/73.

73. Barkley, *op. cit.* (1959), p. 37.

74. *Official History of Larne*, Guidebook (1979).

75. E P Thompson, *op. cit.* (1964), Chapter 11. See also R Currie, *Methodism Divided* (1976).

76. Bullock and Drummond, *op. cit.* (1978).

77. GN, 12/9/81

78. See Bibliographical Index, Appendix E

79. GN 17/3/82. The LOI sought support for W C Maugham.

80. GT 27/1/76.

8
Leadership and Rank and File Relations

The Order's leadership responded in most definite terms to its retarded progress in Scotland. Its tactics concentrated on the conduct of plebeian Orangemen, with attempts to mould this towards the prevailing ethos of respectability. Paradoxically in this the Grand Lodge met with some measure of 'success'. For although its admonitions and interventions produced tension and conflicts with the rank and file, internal relations were characterised less by that 'limited class consciousness', and disruptive factionalism which Patterson identifies for Belfast.[1]

The first explanatory factor here was the class composition of the Scottish Grand Lodge which distanced it less from the ordinary Orangemen than its Ulster counterpart. Second, as explained in depth in Chapters 9 and 10, was its consequently greater ability to balance the demands of Protestant defence, with the simultaneous exigencies of forging political alliances to become 'a power in the land'.

Whatever the exact resonance the Order's unfavourable reputation had in fact, the attitudes of contemporaries towards it do point above all to the salience of a *rough* as well as respectable element in its membership.

A full reconstruction of this division within the Institution is not possible. Even in general application a definition of terms is difficult, beyond the basic injunction previously encountered, that rough-respectable distinctions should be seen as 'tilted across hierarchies of skill and pay, relating as much to personal qualities and effort in the face of circumstances as it did to the world of work'.[2] An excellent practical example of these nuances is provided in Bone's description, in 1901, of two very different types of 'Protestant Working Man'. Of the first:

> His bonnet and blue turned down collar are characteristic. He
> is a time-served workman, a fitter. He lives in a tenement in
> Govan and his house consists of a room and kitchen. He is
> married and has four children and as likely as not his name is
> John Macmillan. He is not, however, a domesticated man. His

wife is too much with him in the room and kitchen house, and
instead he takes to football and drink, by way of a reaction
against the dullness of a machine-made existence. His wife aye
washing; his own work the same week in, week out... .No
wonder he took to the streets for his recreation and joined the
Kinning Park 'Rangers' club, and drove home in a brake from
football matches with a melancholy company that found in
barking cheers, a relief from weariness.

Yet, there is another type of working man, whose way of life
differs from that of the first, although his character is in essentials the
same:

This is one of the older type who seems to have adapted
himself more perfectly to the conditions of his existence and to
have acquiesced without protest. He does not need the excite-
ment for which the other craves, and so does not care for
football or whisky... his discussions are political and theological. He is a radical and Calvinist by inheritance and tradition,
and though his active interest in Calvinism may have abated,
its principles still control his conduct... .He is in the pink of
respectability from his parlour in Crown Street to his Sunday
blacks. He finds his occupations at home, in making model
yachts for his grandchildren, or in reading the *Weekly Mail*,
and he and the wife get on fine, with few words. He is the
backbone of the working classes... [3]

Significantly in itself, neither of these scions of the Scottish
working class are depicted as Orangemen, but representatives of
such general characteristics were surely present in the movement.
Probably too the rough and respectable elements in the LOI were
even distinguished in terms of their actual activities, with the
'respectable' adhering more closely to the quasi-Masonic Royal
Black Preceptory as opposed to the populist Orange. Even within
the Orange Institution a significant distinction is likely between
those who attended monthly lodge meetings throughout the year
and became officebearers, and those whose activity revolved around
the public and commemorative ceremonies of the LOI, particularly in
the marching season. If the proceedings of Campsie LOL No. 105 are
any indicator the former meetings were very routinized and not
particularly stimulating, save to the most stalwart and dutiful 'Sons
of William'.[4] Public outings in contrast offered the opportunity of
self-assertion, and of actual physical confrontation with 'the auld
enemy'.

One of the most interesting examples in this context is that of
'Orange' bands and their music. Most of these held a semi-autono-

mous position to the actual lodges, but again the rough/respectable distinction is prominent.[5]

On the one hand, for example, were those bands affiliated to the Scottish Flute Band Association, whose aim was to ensure that bands played a good quality of music from light opera to traditional Scottish airs and melodies. Band discipline was strict and controlled by a band conductor, band sergeant, and corporal after a military style. On the other hand, were the 'Billy Bands', which seem to have predominated in the nineteenth century, designed not so much for musical quality as for the production of maximum volume to provoke Roman Catholic onlookers. To this end 12-16 flutes played the melody lines only of party tunes, with little variation in intonation. These were usually preceded by 4-8 side drums, and the Bass drum or 'Ballywalter' with the band name printed on the drum hides: 'The Albion',[6] 'Sons of William',[7] or 'Blue Bells'.[8] Not surprisingly these bands, as previously, were at the root of most of the sectarian disturbances in Glasgow and surrounding districts, thus incurring the displeasure of the legal establishment.[9] Kinning Park was particularly effected from the late 1870s, and again provoked *The Bailie* into verse:

> 'The Protestants of Kinning Park,
> Though being but a hand full.
> Just for a lark, have made their mark,
> For of Party Songs they're bang full.
> They played their tunes through every street,
> While the crowd it followed after,
> Till one was caught, fourteen days he got,
> For the playing of Boyne Water'.[10]

Party songs themselves provide the most tangible survivals of the rough/respectable contrasts of the nineteenth century Order. There are, for instance, 'mild', 'establishment' songs such as 'Sons Whose Sires for William Bled', 'The Relief of Derry' or 'The South Down Militia'; the latter written in the early 1900s by Col. the Right Honourable R H Wallace, Grand Master of Belfast County Grand Lodge and Imperial President. Law describes this as 'the sort of song that is printed in catholic anthologies when an attempt is made not to offend Roman Catholic readers' … with 'a slightly spurious whimsical quality, not so much a party song as a party piece for a stage Irish Protestant'.[11] The chorus:

> Och talk about your King's Guard
> Scots Greys and a'.

> Sing about your kilties and your gallant Forty twa,
> And of every regiment in the King's command,
> But the South Down milishey is the terror of the land.

To this one can contrast 'No. 1 in the Orange Hymnbook', 'Kick the Pope', which could never be described as 'whimsical' and was a great favourite of the Billy Bands:

> Tooral – ooral Kick the Pope,
> Tooral – ooral Kick the Pope,
> Tooral – ooral Kick the Pope,
> We'll kick him intae candie.

Moreover, even the establishment songs were liable to corruption or 'rat-rhyming'. The official version of 'Boyne Water' runs (performing miracles of scansion):

> When that King William did observe the brave Duke
>   Schomberg falling,
> He reined his horse with a heavy heart,
> On his Enniskilliners calling.
> He said 'Brave Boys fear no dismay
> At the losing of one commander.
> For God shall be your King this day,
> And I'll be gineral under.'[12]

Compare this with the more robust version:

> Dae ye mind yon day, the bonnie day,
> The day of a' the slaughter,
> The wee bulldog put on his clugs
> And paddled in 'Boyne Water',
> Up to his knees in Fenian blood,'
> Up to his knees in slaughter.
> The wee bulldog put on his clugs
> And paddled in 'Boyne Water'.

The very language of the unofficial version captures particularly well the quality of that phenomenon of 'combative sectarianism' within the LOI's rank and file. For this was in essence a commitment to pugnacious Protestantism, a vigorous assertion of ascendancy and violent confrontation, actual or projected, with the Roman Catholic community which had its highest ritual expression in the practices surrounding the 12th of July. In these circumstances the Grand Lodge's leadership was above all legitimated by *action*; by its ability to maintain a vigorous public profile in the face of restrictions imposed through statute and by-law.

This general situation, however, placed the Grand Lodge in a compelling dilemma, for to be seen to encourage violence and the infringement of the law by the more unruly rank and file members would be invidious to the standing it sought for the LOI in Scotland. Yet an equally portentous risk of schism and discipline problems were presented by inactivity. The discontent of plebeian Orangemen in Belfast in similar circumstances, as Patterson indicates, was even translated into class terminology.[13] This also seems the case in Liverpool where Pastor Wise demanded a rejuvenated Orange Order 'free from aristocratic shackles and advancing progressive policies and Protestant rights'.[14] In these examples a militant populism could be asserted which cast the rank and file as the real repository of 'true blue' Protestantism, and found in the effete 'milk and water' Protestantism of the Grand Lodge, patrician betrayal of the cause in its reluctance to press it home in politics or on the streets.

THE GRAND LODGE'S COMPOSITION IN SCOTLAND

To some extent the predominantly petty bourgeois and artisan composition of this body placed it in better stead to face such difficulties than the Irish Grand Lodge. Although almost certainly it would not have appeared to Orange contemporaries in this light, to whom the lack of a significant aristocracy, gentry or even industrial bourgeois participation must have seemed a grievous handicap, and a further sad indicator of the movement's relative weakness in Scotland.

Again in this context fact has to be separated from the official accounts, which stress the involvement of notables from the 1870s, as Cloughley expresses it, 'a better class of candidate from the 1890s'.[15]

Thus, Johnstone of Ballykillbeg enthused at the November *soirée* of 1876 that:

> He was glad to find now in Scotland such men as the Grand Master, Chalmers I Paton, coming forward manfully and boldly to vindicate the principles of the Order, but he could not forget many a time when he had been present at Orange *soirées* in the City Hall, how loyal and true men in the artisan and labouring classes so long and resolutely held up the Orange banner when the gentry were few in their midst.[16]

The accession of C I Paton to the leadership in 1875 was clearly seen as a great coup. A lineal descendant of that 'famous Captain Paton of the Covenanting army',[17] he reviewed his troops on horseback at the 12th parades 'encouraging them to order and regular-ity'.[18] Beneath the gloss of rhetoric, however, the contrast should not be overstressed between the situation in the latter part of the century and the 1840s-50s. Paton had an estate at Belstane, but his gentry status was funded by his fine-art firm in Edinburgh, which he apparently inherited from his father, who had been a carver and guilder by Royal Warrant. Of the other leading Grand Lodge personalities of the 1870s and 80s, George McLeod, Past MWGM, was a tartan merchant; Thomas Macklin, GS, was Professor of Latin and Greek (not at Glasgow University but at the less prestigious Anderson's College); and Thomas Wetherall, DGM, was proprietor of a cutler's firm having 'risen from the ranks'.[20]

One of the few full listings of the Grand Lodge in 1875 at a special meeting commemorating the Battle of the Diamond, breaks down similarly, showing a strong petty bourgeois or professional predominance. Of 26 names the 15 which could be located fitted this description. As well as McLeod, Macklin and Wetherall, they included: an accountant, a clerk, two shopkeepers, a steamship agent, a plumber, a teacher, an insurance agent, two clergymen and a plasterer. The others may have been recent arrivals in the West of Scotland and not included in directories or electoral registers, or representatives from more outlying Orange areas.[19]

With Paton's death in October 1889 Edward Saunderson, MP for South Down became Grand Master, but again no overall change in class basis is evident. Till his death in 1906 Saunderson remained as much a figurehead as the Earl of Enniskillen had been in the 1830s, and indeed, whether through genuine ill health or by design, hardly attended any public celebrations in Scotland.[20] His duties fell by default to his deputy William Young , a tailor, who eventually became MWGM; James Rice GS, a housepainter; and James McManus, an insurance collector.

This is not to suggest that the Grand Lodge made no active attempts to attract a similar gentry affiliation as Ireland. Such attempts crystallised around the formation of Lodge No. 690 'Beaconfield's Purple Guards' in 1880. This was apparently intended to function along similar lines to the 'The Royal Gordon' Gentlemen's Lodge as a more viable incentive to upper class membership than the usual plebeian lodges, as well as a device to strengthen Orange and Tory links. Certainly at a meeting and dinner held in connection with it in 1881 the Grand Lodge had been ambitious in its platform invitations and had gathered a brace of Unionist luminaries. Paton chaired the meeting, supported, for example, by Col. Archibald Campbell, later Lord Blythswood; Sir William and Lady Baillie of Polkemmet; Mr. Ashmead Bartlett MP;

Col. Lloyd MP, Co. Monaghan; W E McCartney MP, Co. Tyrone; E
S D Cobaine, County Grand Master, Belfast – with apologies from
the Duke of Manchester, the Duke of Munster and the Duke of
Enniskillen.[21] At its first *soirée* the chairman, Allan Gilmour, heir to
an estate at Eaglesham, proclaimed:

> Whether we call ourselves Tories or Conservatives Orange-
> men or Loyalists let us be found side by side and fighting
> against one common foe... and under one common banner –
> the banner of loyalty, and in defence of our common cause the
> Crown, which we adore, the Church which we venerate, and
> the Constitution which we are determined to defend.[22]

At last in November of 1881, an 'extraordinary and special'
meeting was held to initiate 'two prominent gentlemen', at which
the lodges Worthy Master Samuel Geddes was able to rejoice:

> The time was... when to be an Orangeman was to be every-
> thing low and disgraceful. He was looked down upon by all
> persons and associations... but now we are entered into a
> better and brighter era. How so? Simply because we are getting
> men into our ranks, who are able to lead us, men of education,
> principle and ability.[23]

Such developments must be viewed soberly, however. Two
prominent recruits in over a year's existence, when Ireland was again
becoming a major issue in British politics is not particularly impressive. Geddes, moreover, who continued as Master of the Lodge and
became an Honorary Deputy Grand Master (HDGM) in 1883 was
himself of fairly lowly origin, working as a commercial traveller in the
Partick area. We are not informed who the two gentlemen were. One
possible recruit was Gilmour who was certainly listed as an HDGM at
the *soirée* of 1884, and was active in chairing meetings on the Irish
question under Orange auspices. His public links with the Order
seem to have lapsed swiftly with his adoption as parliamentary
candidate for East Renfrewshire in 1885.

Another possible recruit, though, may have been Col. Campbell
of Blythswood, President of Glasgow Conservative Association, Lord
Lieutenant of Renfrewshire and ADC to Queen Victoria, who was a
prominent figure at Orange *soirées*, regularly chairing the event in
Paisley from the 1870s onwards. Yet while it is probable that he took
the step of actually becoming an Orangeman, and while it is his
involvement which approximates most closely to aristocratic patronage of the Order, even here this 'patronage' is qualitatively
different from that, for example, of the Duke of Gordon, who was at
least willing to become titular head of the Scottish movement in the
1830s or from that of the Irish magnates such as Roden and

Enniskillen, who had a more open and unreserved role in the promotion of the LOI. Apart from guesting at the November *soirées* Col. Campbell was not apparently involved in the counsels of the Grand Lodge or even the Paisley District Lodge, nor did he appear on 12th platforms. If indeed he had been cast in the Irish mould, it would not have been at all surprising for him to adopt the MWGM position on C I Paton's demise, thus avoiding the need to import Col. Saunderson as a figurehead.

Disappointment over the Scottish gentry's failure to affiliate to the cause also served to compound a very basic problem for the movement. The simple fact was, as previously suggested, that the migration of Protestants from Ireland had been to pre-arranged skilled and semi-skilled work in the Scottish labour market, thus filling only rank and file positions in the LOI. Some 'middle ranking' Orangemen, District Master and Secretaries, for example, and Orange clergymen like the Rev. Robert Gault, were also included, and like Thomas Wetherall rapidly assured pivotal status in the Scottish Grand Lodge. Crucially, however, the class structure of Ulster was not fully reproduced, for the Irish gentry who had been the traditional patrons of the Institution were not part of the migration. Indeed, the Grand Lodge in Scotland had more in common in its petty bourgeois class composition with the dissident and populist Orange and Protestant Workers' Association, led by William Johnstone of Ballykillbeg, than with the Irish Grand Lodge, which the OPWA berated for its distaste of violence and of the 'True Blue' defence of Protestant rights.[24]

The lesser disjuncture between the class basis of the Scottish leadership and the Scottish rank and file did not completely solve the dilemma between physical confrontation and social and political advance. Internal tensions although rather muted were still in evidence, and it seems that the Scottish Grand Lodge could still assume 'patrician' airs with a fastidious concern for the conduct of some of its rank and file.

In general, the tensions and actual conflicts which did arise were waged, firstly, around the rough/respectable axis and, secondly, over the Grand Lodge's strategy in the political area. Nor were they always reducible in a simple sense to explicit class positions. Class antagonisms did at times occur, but it would be wrong to assume that they followed the form of a petty bourgeois, artisan (hence respectable) Grand Lodge against an unskilled (hence rough) rank and file. This would besides contradict the empirical evidence of the class basis of the mass of the LOI's membership. The truth was apparently a great deal more complex, probably with tensions over conduct *within* the rank and file. There may even have been tacit support for 'combative sectarianism' from some members of the Grand Lodge.

To distinguish why struggle was waged around the rough/respectable division, we must again return to the negative reputation which the LOI had acquired by the 1860s. Another *Glasgow News* editorial, this time of 1878, convincingly captures, for example, the problem presented by bourgeois opinion of the 12th celebrations:

> They disgrace society and originate evils of a particularly far reaching kind. They pander to ignorance and intolerance and excite political animosity and sectarian hate.
>
> They are at best a mischievous anachronism alike degrading and disgraceful – a splendid testimony to our perfect freedom but a sad example of the way even freedom can be abused.[25]

To this must again be coupled a more general feature of nineteenth century Scottish society, a certain ethos of 'respectability' which animated both bourgeoisie and some members of the working class. This had definite historical roots in the development of the Scottish proto-state, and the special position of the Scottish religious establishment. In short, an immense challenge was posed to the Grand Lodge in tailoring the LOI to such conditions, and in remonstrating to this effect with the 'rough' element of its mass membership.

POLICY: 'EACH DAY AN ORANGEMAN'[26]

For analytic convenience here, we can distinguish between concrete actions taken by the Grand Lodge, and the more general injunctions and exhortations issuing from various Orange platforms. Throughout attempts to combat the triple pitfalls of 'Irishness', drunkenness and violence are prominently intertwined.

Definite measures ranged from the awarding of 'Orange essay prizes' in schools for the best writers on the subject of Protestantism, to developing control over public activities, and the establishment of boards of enquiry over alleged Orange rowdyism.[27]

As regards the 12th parades, in the 1860s these had been restricted in many areas including Glasgow by legal prohibitions for fear of violent outbreaks. Significantly the Grand Lodge had also participated in this respect. In Glasgow in 1869, for instance, it 'discouraged processions and outward manifestations on the eventful day so that none of the brethren might come into contact with their hereditary enemies or break the law regarding party processions'.[28] The Lodge gave instructions along these lines on the understanding that the Sheriff should not issue any prohibitory proclamation.

Clearly some areas seem to have suffered under this regime – 'a very feeble attempt' being reported at Maybole, a previous stronghold, to resuscitate the defunct Orange Movement in the locality.[29] In 1867 even the normally ebullient Airdrie Orangemen were forced to hold their 12th celebrations indoors.[30]

Some alternative, though, was provided by the *soirées* held on or around the 5th of November in lodge rooms and public halls to commemorate the failure of the Gunpowder Plot. Earlier versions had apparently been extremely convivial, but from the late 1860s temperance principles operated. As Sir James Bain commented at the 1879 event, 'This is not the first Orange meeting I have been at. I was at an Orange supper thirty years ago. But how different a supper is our gathering tonight. Then the drink was hot punch – now it is the cup that cheers but not inebriates, now wives and sweethearts are present and children too – the Orange infantry... '.[31] Conservative notables and church ministers are more frequently found on the platform here than at the traditional 12th walks.

The circumstances surrounding the resumption of walks in 1872 at Glasgow provide a further good indicator of the leadership's eagerness for co-operation with the authorities and their desire to accord with accepted standards of legitimate and responsible behaviour. As the *Glasgow Herald* pointed out:

> Arrangements made by the Heads of the Orange Party evidenced so strong a desire to observe order that the authorities deemed it inadvisable to interfere and they only stipulated that the route of march should be kept strictly private and there be no party tunes in the street. All of which was strictly adhered to.[32]

T H Stewart, secretary of the committee of the Orange Procession, for his part wrote 'to tender our sincere thanks to Mr. McCall, Chief Constable, for the impartial and faithful manner in which he followed his official duties along the route of the procession'. In conclusion, he stated 'Whilst we as a body of loyal patriotic men asserted our right yesterday to walk in public procession on William's day, our chief desire was to give offence to none and be slow to take it'.[33]

Where, however, events passed less peaceably, such as the rioting which surrounded the celebration of the Irish Nationalist Daniel O'Connell's birthday anniversary in Partick in 1875, speedy action was taken to vindicate the character of the lodges. A week after the incident the Partick Orangemen met to discuss Provost Thompson and the Liberal press's allegations about their role in the disorder. Bro. Alex. McAllister in the chair affirmed that the individual who had pulled down the Home Rule flag was not an Orangeman, nor were onlookers who came into contact with the Roman Catholic processionists. He claimed rather that the Orangemen had been asked by the police to render them assistance and only marshalled themselves into military formation to distinguish themselves from the lawless mob. He went on to rail at 'the public press who were attempting to raise general feeling against a brotherhood of men whose only crime is that they are ardently loyal to Reformation principles and law and order... '.[34]

The Grand Lodge also seems to have been much concerned over this incident and instigated a commission of enquiry chaired by C I Paton. This reported the following month, determining to its own satisfaction that 'no Orangeman had anything to do with the inciting of the Partick riots', and repeated its demand to Provost Thompson and the press to make good or retract their statements.[35] Similarly, in 1876 following disturbances in Springburn, an Orange meeting, with T H Stewart presiding, demanded a retraction and even threatened legal proceeding against the *Evening Citizen* which claimed that Orangemen had originated the trouble. 'They considered that the character of the Springburn Orangemen had been slandered' [sic].[36]

Such initiatives are complemented by recurrent themes in Grand Lodge 'speechifying'. Most importantly these indicate the adeptness of the Scottish leadership in maintaining a delicate balance between the desire for respectable status, and the pressing need to slake the most violent anti-Roman Catholic sentiments of the rank and file. Unlike many of their aristocratic Irish counterparts, men like McLeod and Macklin displayed little well-bred disdain for the traditional 'No Popery' concern of the Order, but indeed communicated it with a passionate commitment, dear to the hearts of their listeners.

At the November soiree of 1867, for example, the Rev. Gault delivered a stirring speech which the *Glasgow Herald* termed as 'offensive', moving it to criticise the whole event as 'unworthy of the name of religion under whose banner it was held and liable to excite the bitterest and worst feelings of other sections of the community'.[37]

> Declaring his vigorous support for Garibaldi and Victor Emmanuel he thought that when he read the intelligence the Pope was very much like an old fox (boos and hisses from the crowd). That day he declared is not far off when Papist Rome would fall and the banner of the Lord Jesus Christ wave over the Eternal City, and we will be able to march on Rome and

strangle the old serpent in his den. His audience were not to suppose from his language that he had any hostility for the priests and people of the Church of Rome...

He concluded in the usual style:

I would stand tomorrow and fight for the liberties of my native land, stand as my fathers have done on the walls of 'Derry and do battle rather than Cardinal Cullen and Archbishop Manning (more boos and hisses) or any of the serpent brood of the Pope should have my beloved country and render that land, a land of darkness and spiritual destitution.[38]

Yet interwoven with such traditional tub-thumping oratory was a more pragmatic concern, increasingly embraced by the Grand Lodge in its attempts to improve the movement's standing from the 1860s, namely that of mitigating the LOI's impression as an 'alien' movement in the Scottish context.

Thus Gault was also anxious to stress:

The statue of William III at Glasgow Cross was erected in 1735, a year before the Boyne Monument so that at that time Scotland was in advance of Ireland. Now the heart of Scotland is in a great measure solid for this people suffered more than any other in the United Kingdom from the consequences of Popery... a man was not worthy to be called a Scotsman, nor woman, a Scotswoman who did not commemorate in some form the Battle of the Boyne (cheers). Scotland stands forever for the Protestant Ascendancy.[39]

This concern continued through the 1870s and 80s and beyond, being particularly prominent in orators' attempts to emphasise the anti-papal element in Scottish history and link this to events in Irish history and the Glorious Revolution. C I Paton, for instance, as befitted his distinguished forebear, frequently invoked the Covenanters in this respect. He proclaimed on the 1879 12th platform:

It was for no insignificant question that they struggled, they contended and they suffered, but for the right to worship God according to their own conscience and to the commandments given in His Word. They contended for the right of freely hearing and preaching the true Gospel.....If they had failed the British Isles would have been mere vassal Kingdoms of the Pope. The struggle ending in the battle of the Boyne, however, secured to them, who had been persecuted by Claverhouse and his troopers in the wild moors in which they sought refuge, as truly as it was the crowning victory of the brave defenders of Innskillen and Londonderry.[40]

Even more than the reinterpretation of Scottish history, it was the personal conduct of the rank and file Orangemen which was of consummate interest to the leadership. The purpose of the 1877 12th display was explicitly stated by McLeod, 'We wish to make recruits. We wish people to take note of Orangeism and our demonstrations draw attention to it... and through that we will receive accessions to our numbers (Applause and a voice: and you will get them)'. Accordingly, HDGM Wetherall entreated them to end the day in a peaceable and orderly manner and to do nothing which would injure their cause. 'In the factory and in the mine, in the workshop, in the country house, behind their counters in every capacity and relationship of life, they should never forget their principles but show they recognised the duties devolving on them'. They were further advised on leaving Glasgow Green to roll up their flags and take off their colours 'so in no way to offer provocation to their opponents'.[41]

Particularly worrying to the Grand Lodge on such public occasions was, of course, the prospect of drunkenness among their membership. Thus Johnstone of Ballykillbeg in 1884 strongly advocated for members the advisability of joining the Blue Ribbon temperance movement. 'They would not be worse Orangemen on account of total abstinence from intoxicating drinks'.[42]

The optimistic vision of Orangeism as an agent of actual moral improvement had been most powerfully expressed in Paton's speech at the regular Grand Lodge meeting the same year. The Institution he hoped:

> ... exercises a beneficial influence on its members and through them on their families... and fulfills its great purpose of promoting the interests of Protestantism... in the land – in other words the cause of truth spiritual enlightenment and moral improvement, of peace, order and good government, of the true liberty of all that tends to God's glory and man's welfare.

> Our lodges do not serve their proper purpose if wives at home have any cause to regret our attendance at Lodge meetings and if they do not find that their home is the happier because of it and every duty of home life is more perfectly discharged. Such ought to be the effect of the instructions received in the Lodges and of intercourse with brethren; such will certainly always be the effect of the principles of Orangeism really embraced.[43]

He had, moreover, a clear conception of how this should be accomplished in the lower ranks:

> Worshipful Masters of Lodges will allow me to remind them that the prosperity and usefulness of Lodges depend on them,

on their sedulous attention to duty and their constant care that the Lodge shall always be well employed during the whole time of their meeting, that nothing shall be allowed which is contrary to our laws and constitution but that these shall be faithfully observed to the utmost degree possible in every particular. District Masters also have it in their power to do much for the general good of our body, by visiting the Lodges of their district in a kindly and brotherly way – to stimulate and encourage them, to correct any irregularities and errors which might have crept in and to make suggestions for improvement and here let me entreat every brother... *to be regular in attending at public worship and in the observance of all religious duties and especially to be strict and careful in the sanctification of the sabbath and diligent in the reading of the Bible.*[44] (Author's emphasis)

With some business acumen he directed that his own 'Catechism of the Principles of Protestantism' was to be 'put into the hands of every new member and candidates shall not advance to the Purple without a thorough knowledge of it'.[45]

Characteristically, however, this message was made palatable for the ordinary Orangeman by the usual strictures on the great danger of the power of the papacy, with dark and ominous signs of its continuing encroachments being discovered in ritualism in the Church of England.

From the 1870s additional motivation for an improvement in conduct came from increasing involvement with the Scottish Conservatives. It is fitting then to conclude this section with the speech of the Tory partisan, Col. Campbell, in 1879 to the Orangemen of Paisley. The gallant Colonel's advice must have struck home eloquently to the Grand Lodge, if not to all of his audience:

Their principles being based on a sound foundation, they would do more to draw others towards them *by moderation than any other way* and they would in that way strengthen the Order. It might be hard for some of the fiery spirits to do as he advised, he admonished such men, they did as well as they possibly could. But from experience he could say that exuberance of spirits might better be shown *by moderation than by an ostentatious display of their principles in public,* and I he trusted that the reproaches which had occasionally been thrown at Protestants would be withdrawn on account of the moderation shown in following the principles which Protestants subscribed to on becoming members of the great Orange society.[46]

POLICY SUCCESS?

It is difficult to give a balanced assessment of the success of Grand Lodge policy from the late 1860s. In seeking to reduce the alien quality of the Order its effects seem limited by the simple fact that by and large it was an *Irish* movement. Many of its members and officebearers were from Ulster, it was above all built around events in Irish history, and as the 1880s progressed it increasingly identified itself with issues surrounding Irish Home Rule. The RBP indeed continued to be under the direct jurisdiction of the Grand Black Chapter of Ireland.[47]

The policy was probably more successful in muting the Institution's reputation for collective lawlessness. Sectarian outbursts did certainly persist, particularly when Orange bands invaded Roman Catholic 'territory', but apart from the Partick riot in 1875 (the last time the Riot Act was read in Scotland), large scale clashes were mostly absent. One might compare Liverpool where such incidents were common throughout the late nineteenth century and where as late as 1902, for example, thousands of Orange marchers joined battle with Irish Roman Catholics at Seaforth.[48]

Yet while in the Scottish case the Grand Lodge was able to secure a remission from large scale violent activity, it was particularly the conduct of the individual Orangemen which remained a problem and a source of internal friction.

It is interesting to note, for instance, that at the 1877 celebrations when Wetherall had made his pleas for his audience to hold true to their principles, already, 'some of them were observed slipping away from the ranks and making tracks, early in the day as it was for convenient public houses, while a few others demonstrated by their hilarious conduct that they had already been imbibing even earlier'.[49]

Indeed, the very frequency of such pleas throughout the period of study is perhaps the most eloquent testimony to their efficacy. The newspapers often with great relish noted that only 200 or 300 out of several thousand marchers actually gathered round the platform to listen to Grand Lodge speakers. In 1874 'the vast majority preferred other enjoyment, mainly dancing'.[50] In 1877 at Patna 3–4,000 mustered and the CGM for Ayrshire delivered an uplifting address on the history and principles of Orangeism. There were competing attractions, however, for 'a tent for the sale of intoxicating liquor had been erected and judging by the appearance of many of the brethren on the homeward journey it had been well patronised'.[51]

Compared with Belfast and Liverpool, such dissent from Grand Lodge policy in Scotland clearly assumed a less organised and institutional form. In analysing the extent to which tensions over conduct also contained an element of class conflict, as witnessed in Belfast, considerable caution is necessary. For the danger here is of extracting evidence to fit some preconceived notion of what form and extent class conflict within the Order *should* take, and perhaps too readily mould Scottish experience to fit Patterson's analysis.

More sustained instances of conflict stemmed from dissatisfaction with the Grand Lodge's internal structure and its attempts to champion 'Protestant issues' in politics. Tensions in the 1870s focus around the person of William Yuille, a Glasgow storeman, and then himself a member of the Grand Lodge of the Orange Association.

His public criticism of the LOI leadership began at the annual *soirée* of LOL No. 110 Enniskillen in 1874. Anticipating a revised constitution by over a year he advocated 'frequent periodic changes specially in masterships as more likely to ensure strength and enthusiasm in subordinate lodges'.[52] He suggested this should also be the case in the Districts and Grand Lodge. He was, moreover, discontented with the Order's efficiency as a political weapon for the Grand Lodge had been content at the 1874 election as it was for most of the nineteenth century and early twentieth century to work behind existing political forces in a rather deferential manner, rather than assert itself as an independent political power.

As opposed to this lukewarm defence of Protestantism Yuille felt the Order should be radically reconstructed ... 'to make its influence felt throughout the length and breadth of the land. The organisation should be developed so as to tell heavily on the elections of the city and compel Romanist and infidel sections of the community to feel the strength of Orangeism in defence of the Protestant cause'.[53]

At the next *soirée* be continued his critique of the Grand Lodge:

> ... at least during the preceding year progress had been made and the Grand Lodge were beginning to consider what means would benefit the Order in Scotland... .For some time past, however, they had almost thought their laws unalterable and infallible. They were perfect so far as the Word of God was concerned, but there were other things apart from that.[54]

Again it may be tempting to draw some similarities between Yuille's initiatives and those of populist Orangeism in Belfast in the same period, with its view of action as the legitimating function of the Grand Lodge. Yet again, the absence of easily assailable aristocratic and gentry targets mean that the language of class conflict is absent in Yuille's attack. This instead takes a more undifferentiated form which focuses on a fear of betrayal of the rank and file by the leadership's lack of commitment and their failure to develop independent election initiatives.

At the School Board elections of 1876, for example, the Orange Association of Scotland's Grand Lodge again avoided running an independent 'Orange' candidate and threw their weight behind the 'Establishment' candidates, including many Conservative notables such as J N Cuthbertson and the Rev. Dodds, and behind the general 'Protestant' candidate, H A Long. Yuille, however, dissented and actually chaired the election committee of the rival Orange Institution of Great Britain candidate, Robert Mitchell, who was eventually defeated.[55] At a subsequent meeting which Yuille chaired, a large part of Mitchell's defeat was attributed to the *Glasgow News* 'a paper which had no other object in view... than the maintaining of the aristocratic people of the city... No matter what subject they take up whether it is the labour question or the temperance question, it is always answered as, Is this on the side of the aristocracy or democracy'.[56] With this Parthian shot Yuille drops out of top level Orange activity.

Following this episode, conflicts are again isolated and sporadic. In Greenock, where Johnstone of Ballykillbeg was a most popular guest, anti-aristocratic sentiment could be displayed, but crucially this was directed towards the *Irish* aristocracy. At the 1880 *soirée* Mr. John Fergusson, for example, commented:

> If the aristocracy dealt with the Protestant yeomanry of Ireland... as providence and justice demanded, their descendants in the South and West would now be surrounded by a phalanx of loyal hearts instead of being a proscribed race and targets for the bullets of the lurking assassin. Like other people in high places they have been too timeserving in their generation.[57]

Perhaps the best aid, however, to conceptualise subsequent internal politics in Scotland, is to note the reception given to the Independent Orange Order (IOO) in the early twentieth century. Whereas in the Ulster case this is often treated as one of the clearest instances of class conflict in the Protestant bloc, in Scotland we find the need for independent Protestant defence spearheaded by the Grand Lodge itself. The contrast with its predecessor the Royal Gordon Lodge in the 1830s is also striking.

Similar sentiments to those which animated the IOO. do seem to have been present in Scotland at the turn of the century. The *Irish Protestant*, for example, the IOO paper, was sold at a number of outlets,[58] and carried such news as the founding of the Springburn Protestant Association and the discovery of 'ritualist rats' in the Church of Scotland.[59]

In 1904 it carried a sympathetic letter from one S M McConkey, which well expresses an average Orangeman's discontent. An Irish-

man, a sound Protestant, and for over twenty years a member of the
LOI, it seemed to him that:

> The whole energy of members of the Order is spent on
> contentions among themselves for place and power in the
> Order and when men get into place and power they simply
> become dumb ornaments... .The rank and file on the other
> hand do not, on pain of expulsion, make public attempt to
> defeat the principles of Orangeism. Intelligence, especially in
> Scotland seems to be a crime, as no man can move without
> permission of the Grand Lodge which meets only twice a year.
> It would be well for the Order at large if we could copy the
> actions of our independent brethren in Ulster whose actions
> are worthy of praise.[60]

Yet, such discontent in Scotland was still not expressed in
institutional terms, for the example of the 100 was *not* copied. Its
founder Thomas Sloan, for example, boasted of 100 outposts in
England and America but without a mention of Scotland, and Col.
Wallace, CGM Belfast, was able to congratulate the official LOI
accordingly:

> The outposts of the loyalists of Ireland are the members of the
> Orange Institution and it does us good to see how our Scottish
> brethren are right in front of the fighting line... I say the men
> who propound such a doctrine [Independent Orangeism] are
> lundies* pure and simple and as such demand the contempt of
> all Orangemen. Orangemen will shake them off as a dog shakes
> his ears when he leaps from water to the land... .When the 100
> started in 1903 Scottish Orangemen repudiated them root and
> branch. Your Grand Lodge refused to acknowledge them. We
> owe you a vote of thanks.[61]

It is surely significant that at the very time when the challenge of the
100 was being met, the Grand Lodge in Scotland was also pursuing its
strongest line of 'Protestantism before Party'. At the July anniversary
of 1904, for example, they sponsored the following resolution:

> That believing the time has come when every real Protestant
> must act independently of either of the great political parties,
> we hereby pledge to support in every possible way our Grand
> Lodge officers in the task they have undertaken, viz, the
> forming and working of an independent Protestant organisa-
> tion unfettered by Party ties and to act either with or against
> either party, in the interests of free Protestants.

In his speech in support, J G Hodgekinson, Grand Chaplain, ex-

---

*Traitors. The term refers to Lundie, Governor of Londonderry who attempted to
betray the city to James II.

plained they were not, however, deserting the Unionist cause, 'They were and must be unionists... ' and he was happy to say 'the Orange Order did not intend to desert their colours (cheers). But there was a sense in which the leaders of both the great parties had been weighed in the balance and found wanting... .Protestantism must be at the fore front and everything else was secondary (hear, hear)'.[62]

This concern for the familiar religions emphasis of the Order, and the general conduct of rank and file regulation raises a set of important theoretical issues.

Clearly, for example, the existence of internal tensions over competing definitions of respectability and unruliness and over political strategy, undermine the LOI's depiction in functional and conspiratorial interpretations, as a monolithic body of singular integrative significance.

In particular, the nature of leadership/rank and file relations indicates, firstly, how the most successful transmission of a dominant ideology can come from the most complex and indirect agencies, where fragments of this ideology on issues such as Irish Home Rule or National Religion, are 'spontaneously' reproduced. It would appear from this instance that the most viable forms of 'hegemony' are those which are also able to take account of the working class's situation and aspirations. Too insistent control by the Orange leadership would have jeopardised the basis of the Order's legitimacy. Instead a subtle process of negotiation and definition ensued where the conditional independence of the organisation had to be preserved. In this context it is useful to re-emphasise finally the existence of the large democratic component in the Institution's structure, with all major offices secured by annual election. Introducing the revised constitution of 1875, Col. Paton astutely observed. 'The interests of the brotherhood were thus better attended to if the management of its affairs does not fall exclusively into the hands of a few'.[63]

These points are equally relevant in turning to relations with external political agencies.

NOTES

1. Patterson, *op. cit.* (1981), p. 85.
2. H F Moorhouse, *op. cit.* (1981).
3. J Hamilton Muir (i.e. James Bone), *Glasgow in 1901* (1901), pp. 188-199.
4. GN, 6/11/73.
5. Members would usually be Orangemen and Lodges would hire bands to accompany them on processions. They were often associated with a particular Lodge or District Lodge. 'Orange Bands' Interview, J.McF, 8/10/1984.

6. GN, 29/7/78.
7. GN, 15/7/79.
8. GN, 9/5/81.
9. The matter finally reached the High Court in Edinburgh with the Gartness Band Case in 1906. *Glasgow Herald,* 20-21/6/1906. D Carson, a miner, had been arrested when marching with the Gartness Flute Band on the 12th at Shotts in 1905. (They had marched through Holytown playing 'Kick the Pope' and 'The Protestant Boys'.) He sued police for wrongful arrest, claiming their action arose from an arbitrary determination to stop Orange processions, the question at stake being the right of the public to form a procession so long as they were not endangering public safety. The Court found in favour of the defendants (the police).
10. *The Bailie,* 5/6/78. GN, 17/10/77 provides a classic incident of the type in Kinning Park.
11. W Low, 'Orange Songs', *New Edinburgh Review,* No. 17, 1972.
12. *The Orange Songster,* Neil Graham. Printed in Glasgow (n.d.). In Linen Hall, Belfast. Also *Orange Songs* compiled by W. Peake, Belfast, (n.d.), and for an academic treatment, G D Zimmerman, *Irish Political Street Ballads and Rebel Songs 1780-1900,* Ph.D University of Geneva (No 180) 1966.
13. Patterson (1981), *loc. cit.*
14. P J. Waller, *op. cit.* (1981).
15. BWN, 28/11/1929.
16. GN, 4/11/76.
17. GN, 13/7/75.
18. GN, 13/7/78.
19. GN, 23/9/1875. Glasgow, Paisley and Greenock Directories and Registers were consulted. See also bibliographical index for occupations of leading Grand Lodge officebearers throughout the period of study.
20. Letter of apology for inability to attend 12th in first year as MWGM 1890, also 1891, 92 and 93. GH, 14/7/1896, 11/7/91, 13/7/93. He does, however, manage to attend the more sedate November *soirées* in 1892, 93 and 94.
21. GN, 22/10/81.
22. GN, 4/11/81.
23. GN, 29/1/82.
24. Patterson, *op. cit.* (1981), Chapter 4, 'Origins of Populist Orangeism 1868-85', passim.
25. GN, 27/7/78.
26. Thomas Wetherall's plea for respectability at the 12th display of 1880. They were to live each day as Orangemen, i.e. live up to their laws and principles. For 'they could not expect the Institution to have an influence on society unless the members of the Institution were such as the laws of the Institution declared they must be'. GN, 12/7/80.
27. Rev. McNaught was voted £5 annually for 6 years to be distributed as prizes. GN, 4/11/76.
28. *North British Daily Mail,* 14/7/70.
29. NBDM, 14/7/70.
30. NBDM, 13/7/66, 13/7/67.
31. GN, 8/11/79. Col. Saunderson was less impressed by the *soirée* of November 7, 1890. 'We have had a great meeting, the largest they have ever had in Glasgow, Crichton [the Earl of Erne] was much pleased with my speech – I was not. It was a difficult audience to speak

to, owing to women and babies; the latter caterwauled at the wrong
time which is trying to an orator'. R Lucas, *Col. Saunderson MP: A
Memoir* (1908), p. 169. Joyce *op. cit.* (1980), p. 257, notes the presence
of Orange 'wives and sweethearts' in the Order's convivial functions in
England.

32. GH, 14/7/72.
33. GH, 16/7/72.
34. GN, 10/8/75, 11/8/75. Trial of rioters 11/8/75. Orange meeting 17/8/
    75.
35. GN, 8/9/75.
36. GN, 12/8/76, 16/8/76.
37. GH, 5/11/67.
38. *Ibid.*
39. GH, 6/11/69.
40. GN, 13/7/79.
41. GN, 13/7/77.
42. GN, 4/11/82.
43. GN, 13/6/85.
44. *Ibid.*
45. *Ibid.*
46. GN, 8/11/79.
47. A McClelland, 'The Origin of the Imperial Black Chapter of the
    British Commonwealth', *Journal of Royal Society of Antiquaries of
    Ireland*, Vol. 98, Pt. 2 (1968).
48. Waller, *op. cit.* (1981), p. 192.
49. GH, 13/7/77.
50. GN, 13/7/74.
51. GH, 13/7/77.
52. GN, 5/1/75.
53. *Ibid.*
54. GN, 4/1/76.
55. He got 2374 votes, a close runner up. GN, 30/3/76.
56. GN, 3/4/76.
57. *Greenock Telegraph*, 8/11/80.
58. W Love, 22 Argyll Street, Glasgow; T Kerr, Eastfield House, Dum-
    barton; D McIntosh, Edinburgh and W Ramsay, Edinburgh. Source
    The Irish Protestant.
59. *The Irish Protestant* (IP), Vol. III, March 1903, 26/12/1903.
60. IP, 10/9/1904.
61. IP, 25/11/1905.
62. IP, 16/7/1904.
63. GN, 18/12/75. C I Paton was re-elected in the June of that year. At the
    September Grand Lodge meeting he received his seals of office and
    was presented with a medal, incorporating an equilateral triangle –
    'the three sides representing Order, Truth and Love'. GN, 23/9/75.

9
The Mainspring of Conservatism? 1865–85

Given its distinctive version of the period's 'ruling ideas', Orangeism appeared as an incomprehensible and even threatening phenomenon to most sections of the Scottish ruling class. From the late 1860s, however, the historical bloc of gentry and commercial and industrial bourgeois, who dominated the Conservative and Liberal Unionist parties, became much less squeamish over Orange links than their 1830s counterparts. How genuine was this acceleration in the LOI's political fortunes?

Conservative commonsense functions through traditional definitions and pre-conceived concepts usually attached to emotive images. In the nineteenth century the string of associations came easily: 'Crown', 'Constitution' and 'Civil and Religious Liberty'. Yet while the LOI shared this 'True Blue' frame of reference, the alliance between the Order and the Conservatives was far from natural or inevitable.

In the first place, Conservatism itself was not fixed and monolithic. One vital development during the period of study was precisely the evolution of Conservatism from its status as the old 'Country Party', as it was caricatured after the Free Trade debate of 1846, to the 'Patriotic Party' of the 1880s and 90s, with urban bourgeois support.

Even more revealing for the inevitability of an Orange alliance is the Party's ancestry. In fact, the term 'Tory' itself had originally meant an Irish Papist outlaw and was applied to those who supported James II, despite his adherence to Rome. It was the Whigs, Liberals and Protestants, who brought over William of Orange to Britain in 1688. Hill indeed suggests that although Tory loyalty to the House of Stewart was insufficient to raise the English countryside in 1745, the taint of Jacobitism and Catholicism was long felt in the Party into the 1830s, when the great Catholic influence of the North was apparently placed on the side of the Conservatives.[1]

The paradox of LOI allegiance to the Conservative Party was not lost on contemporaries. The moderate Liberal *Glasgow Herald* gleefully commented in 1880:

Orangemen turning their coats towards the Tories is a whimsical comedy. If the Orangemen had any political and historical raison d' etre it must be sought for its pure Whiggism – i.e. the revolutionary principles of 1688. Orangemen should be pure Whigs and Liberals rather than Tories. The latter party in the old days persecuted Protestants and especially Scottish presbyterians... Orangemen we suppose resent the Liberal policy which gave justice to Ireland, militated a long period of religious monopoly and sectarian despotism and dealt out equal rights to all.[2]

Grand Master McLeod's response to these taunts is particularly revealing, 'Orangemen have nothing to do with the Whiggery or Toryism of William III they have to do only with the platform he established in 1690 and they will at all times support the political party who defended that platform, *whatever name they may be known as politicians.*' He went on to explain, 'it is because the Conservatives as a party occupy this platform and have done so for many years past, the Orangemen claim to be their natural allies'.[3]

Such pragmatic and contingent motives for seeking Conservative links point to the fundamentally *conditional* nature of the relationship which resulted. In other words, the LOI loyally supported the Conservative party as long as it was recognised to be the true party of Protestantism. The Rev. Gault characteristically underlined the point:

> We must be on alert, and Protestants of every denomination must sink their peculiar differences that long may put in sound Protestant representatives for Glasgow. I don't care one farthing it be for Benjamin Disraeli or William Gladstone provided he is a sound Protestant. I don't care – and I call myself a progressive Conservative – unless the Conservative party conserves and strengthens sound Protestantism.[4]

As regards the Conservatives, their own interest in the Order was similarly dependent on a range of factors, including the class composition of the lodges in particular localities, the extent of their 'respectable' status, and even the position of the Catholic Irish vote. Continuities with the 'Royal Gordon' episode were in fact still in evidence. For, as we shall see, the party patronised the political potential of the LOI, both from sympathy and expediency, while still neglecting the central religious dimension.

In short, far from being a natural one, the Orange-Conservative alliance in Scotland had to be sought out, actively constructed, defined and redefined on both sides in accordance with definite historical circumstances.

CONTOURS OF POLITICAL RELATIONSHIPS : THREE CASES

In tracing the extent and dynamics of relations it is important to recognise the decisive realignment of political forces in 1885 with the division of the Liberal Party over Home Rule. Accordingly, the 1885-1900 period will be dealt with separately.

Given the scanty nature of secondary material on the LOI in Scotland it is surprising to find a semblance of debate for the 1865-85 period, although from commentators whose focus of interest is considerably wider than the Institution itself. Joan Smith, focusing on class consciousness in late nineteenth century Glasgow, suggests that, 'Conservatism did not develop an Orange base...'[5] and attributes this to Glasgow's expanding economy from the 1880s; labour aristocrats' self perceptions; the predominance of friendly societies; and finally an overwhelming 'liberal commonsense' for whom the enemy was 'the landlord and the despot and not the Irish'.

In contrast, Hutchinson in his encyclopaedic work on politics and society in nineteenth century Glasgow suggests that the Conservatives put little emphasis on such social and economic issues as tariff reform, but appealed to the strong ultra-Protestant sentiment in the city, a strategy typified in a semi-official alliance with the LOI. Indeed by the early 1880s, he argues, fusion between the two bodies grew apace so that 'the process of integration seemed complete on the occasion of Lord Salisbury's visit to Glasgow in 1884, when he was presented with an address from the Grand Lodge of Scotland immediately after the GCA's one and before any other body'.[6] The considerable power enjoyed in party circles by the Order, he further suggests, affected the Party's appeals to the electorate in a very decided manner, since, 'the stridently Protestant tone carried over into the Party's utterances – meant the virtual jettisoning of the hopes entertained by some local Tories of winning over Whiggish Liberals, as evidence mounted that wild radicals controlled the Party'.[7] The result for the Tories was, in short, an 'electoral cul de sac' from which they were saved only by the emergence of the Liberal Unionists.

Empirically, for Glasgow, Hutchinson errs more on the side of truth than Smith. Conceptually, though, there are difficulties, for he neglects the reciprocally conditional element in the Orange-Tory relationship. It is precisely this which prevented the LOI's 'fusion' or 'integration' into the party machine, and ensured that the Orangemen were regarded as reliable but not ultimately indispensable allies.

Nor can the Glasgow case be extended unproblematically to give a comprehensive picture of relation in Scotland as a whole, since

Orangeism had geographically variable membership levels and class composition, both likely to influence Conservative links. Again then it is also worth including Greenock and Paisley when considering Orange strength at local organisational level and in electoral activity.

Greenock: It is, in fact, this instance which most closely matches Smith's comments on the absence of an Orange-Tory Caucus.

The Greenock Conservatives had not made it their practice to contest parliamentary elections till the by-election of 1878. This had been immediately accompanied by the formation of the Greenock Constitutional Association – an event which fits neatly a contemporary description of a typical Conservative inaugural meeting with 'the worthy gentlemen passing round positions along with the snuff box'.[8] Despite the Liberal Greenock Telegraph's anxiety to implicate the new Association with an Orange taint, these worthy gentlemen were drawn from the professional, commercial and manufacturing bourgeoisie rather than the LOI.

A similar distance was maintained during the actual by-election campaign, although this was in the midst of the Disestablishment controversy and the restoration of the papal hierarchy in Scotland. Orangemen were apparently active in local wards and providing vote support for the candidate James Ferguson,[9] but they are not prominent on his public election platforms, though they occasionally appear like William York as token 'working men'.[10] Ferguson was unsuccessful but recognising that the Orange lodges could prove a useful auxiliary rather than a positive input into the Constitutional Association itself, there is a Conservative turnout at the next Orange *soirée*.[11]

While some progress in Orange-Tory links occurred in the 1880 general election, with the Tories at least prepared to give local Orangemen greater public recognition on their platforms, there is no apparent increase in influence in the Constitutional Association.[12] The keynote issues of the campaign, moreover, dwelt on the local effects of economic depression and imperial taxation rather than Disestablishment and 'Protestantism in danger'. Thus at the one meeting when an Orangeman does speak at length for the new Tory candidate, J Scott, it is to give an account of Scott's position on 'stagnation in the sugar trade' rather than his 'No Popery' principles.[13]

Paisley: Orange-Conservative links here approximate more closely to the 'integration' posited by Hutchinson, though even here the integration is not total, and in the course of the 1880s the relationship grows increasingly to resemble a strong but informal alliance.

With a strong radical tradition, Paisley was an unpromising base for Conservative mobilisation and the LOI's membership in the town formed one of the few enclaves of potential support. Unlike its Greenock counterpart, the Paisley Conservative Association (PCA) from the outset was Orange dominated. Present at its inaugural meeting of March 1878 were Orangemen Thomas Fraser, J Kerr, A R Pollock, T Muir, Peter McCluskie, Thomas Graham, Hamilton Coats, J N Gardiner and Peter Burt. A R Pollock moved that the PCA be set up, Burt seconded, J N Gardiner submitted the rules of management and Fraser seconded. A R Pollock was appointed one of the two vice presidents, while Gardiner was treasurer and secretary. McCluskie, Fraser, Graham and Muir were elected to the management committee.[14] The Liberal *Express* was scathingly sarcastic 'A Live Tory in the streets of Paisley' – a real out and out True Blue' The thing is almost too delicious to realise, a rarity of rarities in our midst, a live walking biped'.[15]

This liaison had one of its most important tests at the Paisley by-election in 1884 when the Conservatives at last put up a candidate, the young aristocrat Lord Ernest Hamilton. Orangemen were prominent through his fairly lacklustre campaign, W J Bell seconding the usual 'fit and proper person' motion at his first meeting and Burt and McKimmon appearing on subsequent platforms.[16] Hamilton was eventually soundly defeated.

Already by the general election of 1885, however, some dislocation can be identified. Orangemen do figure notably on election platforms of the new Conservative candidate Robert McKerrel of Hillhouse, but somewhat fewer and in less prominent positions than in 1884.[17]

Potentially even more significant are McKerrel's comments after the election while chairing the Orange *soirée*. Eschewing any formal connection with the Institution he spoke warmly of its 'unflinching loyalty and devotion to the Crown', and remained 'deeply conscious of what he owed to their generous support and cordial assistance during the political contest... they had just accorded him such personal kindness that he could always regard the Orange body of the town with feelings of personal affection'.[18] In contrast with the Orangemen's intimate involvement with the early PCA, there is an impression amid McKerrel's blandishments of 'the Orange body' now being regarded as a *separate* interest in alliance with the Conservatives. Nor would his warm comments on another source of electoral support be well received by the Orange audience.

One significant feature of the election was that the Irish were united in a body supporting the candidates who supported the Constitution. Not only did the Orangemen come forward as they had always done to support the good cause but Roman Catholics also joined hand in hand and stood shoulder to shoulder for maintaining Constitution and Empire... He was under deep obligation to the leaders of the Irish party generally and the Roman Catholic clergy of Paisley for the support they gave, and he trusted the support would continue.[19]

Glasgow: Glasgow presents a more complex case than the two preceding locations, but the general pattern here is one of substantial development in Orange-Tory links at a local ward level, with less impressive and less unilinear progress in the Party's directing bodies.

The construction of a viable electoral framework for Conservatism in the 1865-85 period received a substantial impetus from the foundation of the Glasgow Working Men's Conservative Association (GWMCA). Like the PCA this initially had significant Orange involvement. The organisation, for example, seems to have originated from a newspaper advert in November 1868 from a Mr W Cadman, who had presided at an Orange meeting at Johnstone in 1871 to commemorate the relief of Londonderry.[20] Other prominent Orangemen were certainly represented in the new GWMCA, James Wyllie DGM[21] and Rev. Gault GC[22] and in turn at the Orange and Protestant *soirée* of 1868 GWMCA luminaries, J Paul and James Frazier, can be identified on the platform.

The organisation's early activities are also revealing. Leading Grand Lodge figures like George McLeod featured prominently among the Association's publicists on topics such as secular education.[23] Rev. Gault and Wyllie were also popular lecturers to the Association, the former on 'Martin Luther', the latter in a more practical vein on 'The function of the skin in reference to cleanliness'.[24]

Developments in this situation are soon apparent as the Association began to expand from its fairly humble beginnings around the mid 1870s. Gilbert Heron presiding in 1875 reported that the previous year 'pecuniary support, especially from the middle and upper classes, has exceeded that of any former year...'[25] and it is now indeed that this group begins to take a more active managing role in the Association. It had dropped the 'Working Men's' from its title in 1873 to become the Glasgow Conservative Association (GCA). Never again, in fact, do Orangemen quite recapture that intimately influential position they held in the pioneering days of the GWMCA.

Perhaps an indicator of this is the lecture committee's decision in 1875 that 'lecturers should as much as possible be confined to *subjects bearing upon politics*, and that just a few decidedly good ones were preferable to many on less important though popular subjects'. One of the lecturers in the previous year, for example, had been given by Sir Andrew Burry on 'Impressions of America from a Conservative point of view in relation to free trade and commerce' – in some contrast to Wyllie's contribution of only two years earlier.[26]

Early marginalisation had also been indicated in the 1874 parliamentary election in Glasgow. Six prominent members of the Orange Association of Scotland, and the Orange Institution of Great Britain, sat on the candidates' Whitelaw's and Hunter's general committees, as well as around a dozen Orange office bearers on eight of the local ward election committees.[27] Yet this must be set against the fact that the Conservative electoral machinery of 1874 was much expanded and more efficient than in the preceding election, and that this Orange group is in a very small minority, even in general committee and ward election committees which involve several hundred Conservative supporters *in toto*. Interestingly also, Orangemen did not number among either candidates, vice presidents, ward agents or ward conveners,[28] nor apart from the seasoned performer H A Long were they prominent on public platforms. This was despite the lodges' considerable efforts at canvassing and public work, particularly in the working class wards of the East End.[29]

The next potentially galvanising event for Orange political involvement was the General Election of 1880. This is worth examining in detail, since for Hutchinson this is 'the most apparent evidence of the weight of Orangeism... when the Order was able to trust its chosen candidate on the party, in the face of the manifest reluctance of the GCA to accept their nominee'.[30] The candidate in question was Sir James Bain, ironmaster and ex-Glasgow Lord Provost.

In fact, this interpretation poses serious difficulties. First Bain was in no simple sense 'the Orange choice', though he seems to have courted the Order in view of the oncoming election. At the November *soirée* of 1879, for example, he had appeared 'arrayed in an Orange sash', despite having much more active links with Freemasonry,[31] and delivered a rather unusual speech in which he seems to have culled every available Orange maxim and aphorism. (It contains three references to 'religious and civil liberty', four to 'glorious forefathers' in addition to a liberal sprinkling of 'Williams' and 'great principles').[32]

Despite this display, Bain's conduct at the actual election failed to fully satisfy the LOI. The *Glasgow News* noted at the time that 'The Orangemen find no one has yet presented himself who has unquestionably subscribed to the crown and constitution and rejected absolutely the pretensions of the Home Rulers'.[33] The point here is that Bain, who was represented in a contemporary cartoon as a weathervane, was widely perceived as 'the type of candidate who superciliously tries to impose upon electors by promising everything to everybody...'.[34] His address, described as a 'model of tergiversation' attempted to appeal both to Orangemen *and* Home Rulers.[35]

The Orangemen were eventually reconciled to Bain, but their representation on his committees seems actually less marked than on his eventual running mate's, a more orthodox Tory the shipbuilder William Pearce. Bain did have George McLeod as his vice chairman but Pearce's central committee had Orange Grand Secretary Thomas Macklin and Thomas Wetherall DGM. As for the ward election committees, Pearce's has at least eighteen identifiable Orangemen of whom nine are not on Bain's committees, while Bain has twelve, at least four of whom are not on Pearce's committees.[36]

Not surprisingly then, official Conservative resentment of Bain did not, as Hutchinson suggests, stem largely from his Orange links. In fact this had a wide variety of sources. For one thing, Bain seems to have been an eccentric character. He had dabbled in spiritualism and produced a pamphlet on the subject and, even more culpably in the eyes of the local party establishment, he had shown an unseemly enthusiasm to become Lord Provost, even chartering the Buchanan steamer *Eagle* and taking an 'influential party' on a cruise down the Clyde to further his cause.[37] At the parliamentary election, as Hutchinson notes, Bain also proved an extremely inept and unorthodox candidate. His views on the Eastern Question, the Local Option and the Franchise Question were hardly Party policy and he seems to have been a very poor public speaker, his meetings often degenerating into beargardens.[38] He had also forced himself on the GCA as candidate without due attention to the official channels of selection.[39]

Yet Hutchinson's argument is plausible that Bain's campaign with its populist overtones drew in a number of 'working men' to the Conservative fold. These need not have been Orangemen but some of them were, like T H Stewart who becomes prominent in the GCA after 1880. Certainly, 1880 marks a clear upswing in Orange electoral involvement compared with 1874, though again it is strongest at the level of local grassroots campaigning.[40]

For the next few years progress in Orange-Tory links persisted. For Hutchinson, as noted above, this signifies the extent of 'fusion' or 'integration' between the two bodies.

At first acquaintance again there does seem persuasive evidence up to 1885 for Hutchinson's case. Following Bain and Pearce's not unexpected defeat at the polls and after an initial spell of depression in which a winding up of the GCA was considered, the Glasgow Conservatives in 1881 again began to remould the organisation's structure. Most important was 'the reorganisation of the organisation on a wider basis' since it was felt, according to Col. Campbell that the GCA 'had not been sufficiently in rapport with the great masses of working men' and the new structure would 'place themselves more in a position to assist them in an organisation which would be worthy of their numbers and make them a power at the time they were required'.[41]

Accordingly the city wards were to be grouped into five districts. East: wards 1, 2, 4; North East: wards 3, 5, 6; West: wards 10, 11, 12, 13; South: wards 14, 15,16; Central: wards 7, 8, 9. Members of the Association in each ward were to meet in January to appoint ward committees of ten to fifteen, a chairman, vice-chairman and secretary, who would represent the ward in the committees of the district in which it was situated.[42] (See Fig. 5 for ward distribution.)

In so far as this promoted working class involvement and increased the strength of the wards, it promoted the Orange political presence. Thus in 1882 six Orangemen became ward officials including Wetherall and T H Stewart, six also were represented the following year, including Peter Morrison who became chairman of the 15th Lauriston/Gorbals ward. In 1884 their numbers increased to seven, with another Orange chairman, J E Fairlie, of No. 2 Camlachie ward.[43]

Also apparently supporting the 'integration' thesis are closer Orange-Conservative links on public platforms, particularly from 1881 and the revival of the Home Rule issue.[44] At these meeting. the language of integration is at times overt. Wetherall, for example, at a distinguished political meeting under the auspices of the LOI suggested:

> They were met that night to endeavour to consolidate the parties belonging to the Conservative interest and bring them together in a firm and compact body in spite of all opposition. He need not remind Orangemen, although it might be necessary to remind other Conservative gentlemen that Orange-ism was based on the Bible and the Crown.[45]

William Johnstone of Ballykillbeg reminded his listeners at the

1884 *soirée* that:

> They had taught all men that the Orangemen of Glasgow and
> of Scotland were a power in the state; they had shown that the
> Conservatives could not do without Orangemen; that
> Orangeism was a *motive power – the mainspring of Conservatism*
> – and must be so throughout the British Empire.[46]

Yet Orange rhetoric here did not equate with political reality. In
the first place, one can set against it the statement of a leading
Conservative, Gilbert Heron, which has a quite different stress:

> You are an organised army of industrious loyal subjects of the
> British Crown and as such eager and prepared to *co-operate
> when invited* with Conservative associations against the
> machinations and open assaults of misguided enthusiasts – of
> radical republicans and atheists... I am here to say for myself,
> and I may venture on behalf of my Conservative friends in
> Glasgow, who like myself have come to know your political
> principles and influence at the polling booth that we fully
> appreciate the services Orangemen have rendered to the cause
> of Conservatism in Glasgow and the West of Scotland and we
> will look to you *as allies we can count on, on the day of battle.*[47]

To return to the reorganisation after 1880, this should also be
placed in perspective Thus in an expanding GCA, almost doubling
from 1880-4, the Orange presence is still very much localised in the
working class eastern wards, No. 2 Camlachie being a particular
growth point with an Orange chairman and vice-chairman in 1884,
and in the Southern wards 15 and particularly 16. No Orange
representatives can be identified for the bourgeois residential and
commercial wards (No 11 and Nos.7-9).

Perhaps most decisive against Hutchinson's case is the LOI's own
desperate campaign to rally Conservatives to its standard and tempt
them to become actual members of the Order. If 'fusion' had been
so pronounced, as he suggests, surely the establishment of a 'gentlemen's lodge', LOI No. 690 'Beaconsfield's Purple Guards' in 1881
would have met with notable success.[48] As it was, despite platform
declarations of common principles and mutual support, the episode
was largely an unhappy one for the Orange leadership, with few
'converts', who were willing to assume an active and sustained role.

The strengths and limitations of Orange political involvement are
finally indicated in the 1885 election. This contest had been preceded by the Franchise Reform Act of 1884 and Redistribution Act
of 1885, resulting in an enlarged electorate and a redistribution of
parliamentary seats which divided Glasgow into seven constituencies.[49]

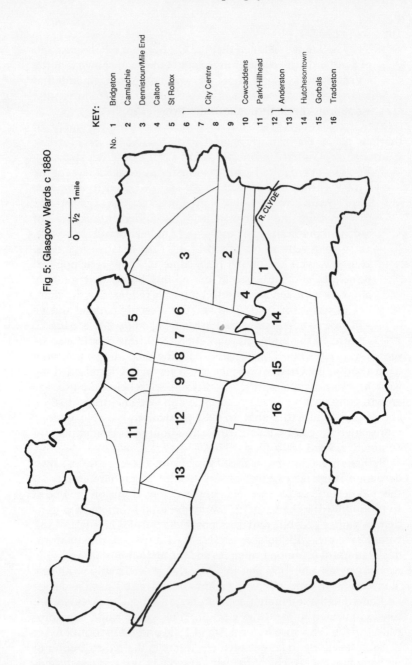

Fig 5: Glasgow Wards c 1880

0   ½   1mile

KEY:

No.	
1	Bridgeton
2	Camlachie
3	Dennistoun/Mile End
4	Calton
5	St Rollox
6	
7	City Centre
8	
9	
10	Cowcaddens
11	Park/Hillhead
12	Anderston
13	
14	Hutchesontown
15	Gorbals
16	Tradeston

R. CLYDE

In turn the GCA had yet again reorganised[50] with a further increase in the Orange presence. Orangemen began to figure to some extent among vice presidents in the new constituencies, as well as more notably among the representatives to the GCA in areas where Tory-Orange links were traditionally strong, such as Camlachie and Tradeston, but increasingly now also Blackfriars and Hutcheson-town.[51] Crucially though the College and Central divisions still were immune.

This continuing pattern of highly localised involvement was reproduced in electoral activity. At Blackfriars, for example, Orangemen such as T H Stewart had been prominent in selecting the 'True Blue' W C Maugham as candidate.[52] They continued to chair election meetings for him throughout the campaign.[53] Similarly J E Fairlie frequently presided at Camlachie meetings assisted by various other Orange worthies, H F Loundes and William Martin, and Grand Lodge member Peter Morrison was influential at Tradeston Conservative Association when Somervell of Sorn had been eventually adopted as candidate.[54]

Even in these divisions there is evidence that less than a unanimity of purpose prevailed between the Tories and their Orange supporters. Despite his attachment to 'the Blue Banner of the Covenant', frequently invoked in his speeches, Arnot Reid, the Camlachie candidate, displayed views on monastery and convent inspection which were highly disturbing to the Order. In answer to a question whether he would support such a measure he replied:

> I understand the whole of the Roman Catholic party are bitterly opposed to the inspection of convents, and I think that in these days when secularism and infidelity are making progress it would be a wrong and injudicious thing to irritate the feeling of a great body of men who are followers of Christ with ourselves.[55]

Summing up these case studies what emerges is an unofficial Orange-Tory liaison ranging along a continuum, with Paisley and Greenock at opposite poles. Moreover as the 1865-85 period progresses, whatever 'interpenetration' did occur in fledgling Conservative Associations, is largely supplanted by 'alliance', as 'the Orange vote' becomes a dependant variable in the electoral calculations of the mature Conservative Party. To explain this transition we must re-examine the motivations of both parties in the relationship.

DYNAMICS OF MUTUAL DISTANCE AND SUPPORT:
THE CONSERVATIVES

Predisposing factors to an Orange alliance existed in the staunch Protestantism of many Scottish Conservatives, and in the Ulster descent of key figures such as W C Maugham.[56] Yet these are best viewed as a supplement to a more basic and pragmatic impetus. This was provided by the historically weak position of Conservatism in Scotland.

The feeble organisation that had existed in the West of Scotland in the early century had evaporated by the 1840s with splits over Free Trade and the Scottish Church. No Glasgow election was contested till 1868 and even in 1874 the Party carried only nineteen out of sixty seats in Scotland despite substantial victories in England. The debility of Scottish Conservatism led to a variety of diagnoses and remedies, ranging from the cautious reports of Party workers in 1885, detailed by Crapster, to Disraeli's injunction to the Scots to 'leave off mumbling the dry bones of political economy and munching the remainder biscuit of effete Liberalism'.[57] In particular, additional pressures were imposed by Disraeli's 1867 Reform Bill, which for the first time potentially enfranchised sections of the working class.

The consequent need for organisational reform, to promote working class mobilisation, seems well recognised in the West. Considerable effort was required, for example, simply to secure registration among the new electorate, to enable them to secure their votes. Hutchinson suggests there was no confidence that they would actually vote Tory, but the major industrial bourgeoisie, rapidly assuming a directive role in the GWMCA, certainly did not shrink from explicit working class links.[58]

Such general developments promoted Orange involvement in two ways. First as detailed in the preceding section, 'democratisations' of the GCA such as occurred in 1880 and 1885 were beneficial in an indirect sense, in so far as they promoted involvement at local level from working men, who also composed the largest part of the LOI's membership. Secondly, and more directly, the proletarian LOI must have impressed the Conservatives as itself a useful source of working class votes – and one which, if the 12th of July demonstrations were any indicator, had been visibly expanding from mid-century. More than that, it was in its own right a valuable organisational mechanism, already well developed for the actual canvassing and delivery of such votes. Even with the introduction of the secret ballot in 1872, the local weight of Orange officebearers could still be considerable. A useful insight into how this might operate was given at a GCA meeting in 1882 when the Orangeman, T H Stewart, secretary of the No.14 (Hutchesontown) Conservative Ward Committee, confided they had adopted the Liverpool system of 'captains' and 'sub-captains' for each street, assigned 'to pull every man to the poll'.[59]

The situation of the founding and early development of the Paisley Association seems to follow fairly similar lines. Though here, as indicated, the Party was even more marginalised by the radical tradition of the town and consequently in need of working class support. Moreover in this respect the Orange lodges in the town may well have proved more palatable to local Tories, given their significant skilled artisan as well as petty bourgeois elements.[60]

Conversely this link between mass electorate demands and use of the lodges may go some way initially to explain the seemingly anomalous case of Greenock, where from the outset the Constitutional Association was bourgeois dominated and 'working men' frequently had to form their own committee at election time. A real 'point of entry' to the selection and control of candidates was thus not available to the Orangemen. In addition, the LOI's membership in the town was residentially concentrated, and reflected most strongly the casual and unskilled nature of much of the local working population.[61]

This, overlaid with the fact that many had been fairly recent arrivals from Ulster, may have given rise to doubts among local Conservatives over the ability of this rather disreputable group to even qualify for the franchise.[62] Even those working men who were involved in the Conservatives' organisation were anxious to distance themselves from an 'Orange' cast, a member of the Working Man's Committee in 1877 protesting indignantly that there were 'Working men as well as Orangemen who are Conservatives'.[63]

Yet this is only a partial explanation for the negative moments of the Tory-Orange relationship. One should also be aware of a countervailing tendency to the democratisation of Conservative associations which had promoted grassroots Orange involvement. This took the form of a broader structural realignment and absolute expansion of the basis of Tory support from the 1870s with the increasing presence of the urban bourgeoisie in the party, perceiving it as the true representative of their class interests. This group, as emphasised in previous chapters, had little favourable inclination towards Orangeism and was unlikely to be enthusiastic for Tory organs which were perceived as being dominated by an 'uncontrollable' populist movement.

Even if the exact extent and composition of bourgeois involvement is open to doubt, more certain is its potential to build a new Conservative heartland, as the 'aristocratic' era of politics drew to a close, and as the controversies of Scottish Disestablishment and Home Rule challenged existing class alignments behind the political parties. These points could not have been lost on the more perceptive sections of the local leadership.

Their fears for the LOI driving off this potential support were fastidiously expressed in a letter to the *Glasgow News* under the pseudo-nym of 'Kilmailing'.

> Orangeism is the prevailing sentiment on some of these [ward] committees. Now none will deny that the patriotism of Orangeism is admirable, their devotion to the Empire praiseworthy, their love of Her Majesty deserving of hearty approbation... But they are sworn to opinions which must at times be harmful to the Conservative cause, especially among Scotchmen. Orange is believed by many men, good and true Conservatives to be the fanaticism of a religious party, not the fundiment of a political one. It would only be fair then, on behalf of all supporters, that less Orangeism prevail on the committees. *It is hurtful to the association numerically and hurtful to the Party politically.* It grieves one again who feels a deep interest in the Party to find men in the committees whose perception does not allow them to judge between candid controversy and slanderous imputation – who mistake calumny for invective and rashness for enthusiasm. Why not have more *discreet and influential* men on ward committees[64] *(Author's emphasis).*

Indeed it is this development which increasingly exercises a determining role in Tory counsels, marginalising the Orangemen from their earlier 'organic' relationship.

A further indicator of the perceived importance of bourgeois support is found in Conservative overtures to disgruntled right-wing Liberals. Contrary to some suggestions, by no means had these overtures ceased by 1880.[65]

As McCaffrey noted, for example, by the 1885 election Liberal unity was still severely tested, from a long standing rivalry between radicals and right wingers over policy.[66] This had been brought to a head by the redistribution in seats prior to the election, which meant that candidates from contending camps were no longer being run in tandem.Accordingly, each side strove frantically to control constituency Liberal associations and influence the selection of candidates.[67] Whiggish Liberals were upset both by plans to abolish the House of Lords and to promote land nationalisation, but in particular in Glasgow they resisted policies to disestablish the Church of Scotland, repairing to Church Defence Associations which rapidly expanded as the election loomed.

These circumstances were most opportune for Conservative exploitation, raising the standard of 'The Church in Danger', as widely perceived in the campaign.[68] Although the *Glasgow News* protested stridently to the contrary, this seems to have met with some success, with abstentions and votes cast for the Tories by the Liberal churchmen contributing to the narrowness of Liberal majorities in Bridgeton and St. Rollox, and the size of the overall Conservative vote as against the Liberals.[69]

It is not possible to specify exactly how much this affected Orange links in the Glasgow case, since the predominantly bourgeois constituencies where Church Defence was most at a premium, like Central and College, had little Orange involvement from the outset in ward committees. Certainly, as indicated above, Orange support was not automatically dropped, and a feature of the Conservative campaign on disestablishment is, as McCaffrey notes, its popular nature, stressing the dangers for Scotland's Protestant heritage.[70]

Yet these developments do suggest the error of the electoral 'cul de sac' interpretation which views the LOI was the only potential Tory ally. In fact something of a practical dilemma presented itself for the Glasgow Tories, with on the one hand the tested support of the plebeian Orange lodges and on the other welcome tactical votes of the right-wing bourgeois Liberals. The latter might be converted into a more permanent presence but crucially could also evaporate if the Orange input to the campaign seemed too intrusive. In this rather fluid situation the Orange-Tory links which did exist, though considerable, could never be unproblematic or unchallenged within the Party.

The effects of the Liberal wooing can be more positively assessed in the case of Paisley. Here, as noted, the originally marked LOI penetration of the Conservatives began to suffer some decline also around the 1885 election. Significantly the new candidate, McKerrel was of a traditional background, a local landowner and major in the Ayrshire Volunteers, but a 'moderate' Conservative whom the *Paisley Daily Express* stated explicitly was brought in 'to influence the weak-kneed Liberals'.[71]

Similarly in Greenock hopes for rapprochement with right-wing Liberals may be cited as a further contributory factor in the weakness of the Orange-Tory alliance. Here such hopes predated the 1885 election, for Liberalism in the town seems to have been particularly prone to fissiparous tendencies, as a result of which

Conservatism became less precariously based.[72]

The 'cul de sac' interpretation encounters even more serious problems from a surprising source. For it appears that not only did some Conservatives realise the potential of dissident Liberal votes but also, at certain points, those of Irish Roman Catholics.

Three factors were at work here. First the Conservatives and the Roman Catholic clergy were in harmony over the evils of 'free education'. In order to maintain their denominational schools Roman Catholics had kept out of the state system and hence did not benefit from the school fund set up in the 1872 (Scottish) Education Act. The burden of maintenance, therefore, was heavy but would be even heavier with 'free education' through indirect tax. In addition there would be the difficulty of countering the attractions of the new state system.

Secondly, Tory policy on Ireland at this stage was more subtle than the downright opposition to Home Rule which prevailed after 1886. As McDowell notes, some Conservatives from the 1870s had begun to consider transforming the Irish agrarian system.[73] Eventually in 1887 Salisbury's second government passed a Land Act providing for the revision of judicially fixed fair rents, thus raising the wrath of Irish Tories. There was even a hint before the 1885 general election that some Conservative leaders might have been tentatively considering an imaginative solution for the Irish question, involving the creation of a local legislature, thus best protecting the interests of property and at the same time 'dishing' Gladstone and the Liberals. Randolph Churchill claimed he 'had not educated the Party as yet' along these lines.[74]

Thirdly, by 1885 Parnell and the leaders of the Irish party had become disillusioned with the failure of their traditional allies, the Liberals, to deliver significant concessions in the direction of Home Rule. According to their manifesto of 1st November they were prepared to direct their party's vote tactically for the Conservatives, hoping for Tory support in return for the Irish vote. This bound the Irish in Glasgow, for previously at an Irish National League meeting in Glasgow, addressed by T P O'Connor, motions had been passed supporting Parnell and pledging to vote as directed by the league's executive.[75] This was an awkward position and nowhere more so than Blackfriars and Hutchesonstown where the Tory candidate was the familiar figure of W C Maugham who placed convent inspection at the heart of his election address. The local INL branch sent a telegram begging an exception from its directing body, but none was granted.[77]

In these circumstances the Conservatives obviously had to exercise considerable caution over their Orange links. Such links in the GCA or local associations could not in practice be broken or denied during the 1885 campaign. However, it was crucial that all candidates, and particularly those in constituencies with the highest Irish settlement were not perceived by Roman Catholic voters as 'under Orange control'. In consequence, diplomacy and the desire not to offend the Roman Catholic Irish community were frequently the characteristics of Tory addresses and public utterances.

In Camlachie, with 13% Irish born (in 1881) Arnot Reid for example proved highly circumspect. When asked at a public meeting by an Orangeman, H Hannay, if he was in a position to do away with Roman Catholic schools he stated, 'I am thoroughly in favour of voluntary schools and think that all schools that follow the government inspector's requirements should get the same grant as board schools'.[78] Even J N Cuthbertson, a frequent visitor to Orange *soirées*, was forced to tread carefully in his constituency of St. Rollox which had the highest percentage of Irish born of any Glasgow division, 14.5%. Asked whether he would approve of the inspection of nunneries he was deliberately ambiguous, 'That would depend on the circumstances, if it were to annoy the Roman Catholic Church I would be the last man to do it. At the same time I have my own private opinion that all Institutions of the country should be on the same footing and open to inspection.'[79]

A similar situation prevailed in Paisley where, of course, McKerrel had fully acknowledged support from the Roman Catholic clergy at an Orange *soirée*, but an even clearer example is offered in Greenock which, of course, had a particularly large percentage of its population Irish born, 19.1% in the period 1876-1901.[80]

Again the alignment of the Irish vote behind the Tories in this case predated the 1885 election. As early as the 1878 by-election the *Bailie* had reported that, 'the Orange lion and Catholic lamb were found lying down together at the recent election' and that 'the Tory platform showed how forcibly extremes meet in political warfare'.[81] The Tory candidate Ferguson who had previously got into parliament on a 'No Popery' ticket had to moderate his views and assert his independence of Orange influence. Thus on the question of the restoration of the papal hierarchy in Scotland he explained, 'I am not at all jealous of seeing the Roman Catholics have their bishops in Scotland. I think it would tend to better government of a religious community and anything that tends to better government of the church must be good for the state'.[82]

A similar if more confused situation also accompanied the 1884 by-election. A deputation from the Irish district of Cartsdyke were dissatisfied with the Liberal Sutherland's refusal to sign a document against free education and instead pledged themselves for the Tory Scott, who notwithstanding his attendance at an Orange *soiree* earlier the same month, 'had pledged himself to do his best endeavours to get Catholics a fair share of the school rates'. There followed, according to the *Telegraph*, 'a regimented march of the Irish to the Tory side'.[83]

THE ORANGEMEN

What motivated the Orange party to persist in this shifting alliance? Again this had less to do with 'natural predispositions' than practical exigencies. In the first place, the existence of potential mechanisms for control, both internal and external to the Order, must be noted. The system of 'captains' and 'sub captains' for each street which the Tradeston Conservatives had pioneered under T H Stewart, and which probably mirrored the authority structure of officebearers/ rank and file in the Lodges themselves, is surely significant in this respect.

Pressure may also have been placed on the Orangemen in their capacity as industrial workers to vote Conservative. The leading Glasgow Tories, as suggested, were frequently major employers of labour, like Pearce, Beardmore and Whitelaw, and the radical *North British Daily Mail* was replete at election time with reports of threats and blandishments employed on their workforces. At the Govan by-election of 1889, for instance, foremen of the Liberal Unionist candidate Sir John Pender, a local shipbuilder, were said to be canvassing for him and putting a cross against men refusing support.[84] Conservative meetings, moreover, were frequently held with employers' blessings at factory gates. On polling day 1885 at Camlachie forty men were dispatched from Duke Street tannery marching four abreast with a blue flag and 'Vote for Arnot Reid' placards.[85]

Such coercive factors must not be overstressed. Something of a limit on electoral manipulation was, of course, set by the 1872 Ballot Act. Moreover, judging from events of the 1830s, naked attempts at the coercion of unwilling Orangemen from their Grand Lodge would have incurred considerable resentment and probably publicly expressed opposition.

It is essential to grasp that the relevance of strategies like the 'street captain' system was as mechanisms for the efficient organisation of already existing support for the Conservatives. Two factors underpinned this support, as neatly expounded by T H Gilmour in 1892 in opening the new Coatbridge Orange Hall. 'Why vote for the Conservative Party? It is beneficial to the working classes, it got one-third less tax for them, and moreover because it is Protestant in its character, and got Protestant legislation for them'.[86]

In other words, the distinctive version of the dominant ideology contained in 'Conservative principles' from the 1870s and 80s was able to take adequate account of many Orangemen's real social experience. This was as wage labourers in a system of capitalist production which from mid-century had assumed the character of a relatively fixed environment. Secondly, and more importantly, Conservatism could accord with their world view as Orangemen, presenting a 'True Blue' bulwark of evangelical Protestantism against the papal encroachments the LOI increasingly identified from the 1860s. This second factor, however, was always rather precarious and could be seriously undermined when a Conservative government in office was perceived, for example, to have cynically exploited the lodges' political resources at the expense of their fundamental religious motivation.

To return to the Tories as employers of labour, one can now see that this could have a double edged effect. Orangemen employed by Pearce or Beardmore might well believe that their best interests lay with the personal prosperity of such industrialists and further that such prestigious figures were best suited to the efficient management of Britain's fortunes. Thomas Wetherall's explanations of why his audience should support Pearce in 1880 are instructive here:

> Mr Pearce is the very gentleman to represent us in Parliament... I am addressing working men, a great body of working men and allow me to tell you that Mr. Pearce has increased the great credit that has always accrued to Clyde-built ships. A short time ago he constructed here two of the quickest going ships in the world, the *Arizona* and the *Orient* and for having done that he deserves your good support.[87]

The 1885 election, fought amid a severe economic depression, is also revealing. Here, amid the campaign to save the Church of Scotland and 'the Protestant character of the state' from Disestablishment, Tory candidates in most Orange areas and their Orange supporters on election platforms had to focus strongly on the Liberals as a 'bad trade government', and the need for protective tariffs. This stood at the head of Arnot Reid's address in Camlachie and in his first speech to the working men of the division.[88] Even Maugham displayed some economic pre-occupations in Blackfriars. Thus at a meeting chaired by T H Stewart at which he pursued his more familiar theme of opposing government grants to Roman Catholic institutions, he also felt compelled to state that:

> Conservatives were the real and true friends of the working man, ever alive to ameliorating the conditions of the working

man... .could point to a large number of measures... by the Party to which he belonged which had raised the social status of the working man, which had increased wages, diminished the dangers to life and limb in daily work and Conservatives were also alive to the need to provide proper housing.[89]

However, factors such as Conservative attempts to present themselves as 'working men's friends', operate on a very general level. They are not in themselves sufficient to explain the specific alignment of the Orangemen behind the Conservative party, as opposed to any other 'working men'.

For this we must return to the second set of factors, a series of politico-ecclesiastical issues which arose from the late 1860s, dramatically convincing Orangemen that their 'Protestant faith' and 'the Protestant nature of the British Constitution' were seriously in danger.[90]

Firstly, increasingly 'Ultramontane' tendencies had become apparent in the Roman Catholic church, during the reign of Pius IX. This movement towards papal monarchism was particularly well represented in one of the Order's favourite *bêtes noires*, Paul Cullen, who became Ireland's first Cardinal in 1866, a champion of triumphalist ceremonial and religious absolutism, which until then had not distinguished the Irish Catholic church.[91]

Such tendencies, the Orangemen and many other Protestants genuinely believed, set native Roman Catholics on the offensive, removed the Papacy from the domain of mere religion, and threatened 'civil and religious liberty'.[92] 'They were two parties', explained H A Long, 'Protestants and Catholics and they could not be put on an equality – that thing was impossible. The Roman Catholics must rule the Protestants or the Protestants the Roman Catholics... '.[93]

For them such fears received confirmation both from Fenian activities (which were actually condemned by Cullen) and from what was seen as an alliance between Gladstone and the Liberals, and the Ultramontanes. 'Mr. Gladstone had sold himself to that party [the Ultramontanes] to obtain power' stated Long, 'he obtained power by a compromise with the papal party and he was bound to continue a line of policy favourable to the papal party'.[94]

The issue which held the key to this alliance was the Disestablishment and Disendowment of the Church of Ireland. For the policy had already been adopted by the more advanced sections of the Party in the 1830s but finally became the major issue at the 1868 election. After a Liberal victory an appropriate Bill was introduced in March 1869 and eventually passed.[95]

The LOI was outraged and organised various protest meetings

'pledging to maintain and assist our Irish Protestant brethren in maintaining Protestantism in Ireland against papal aggression...'.[96] The Order was also most vociferous in its support of Conservative candidates at the 1868 election who, although vacillating over the specific case of Ireland, nevertheless in principle supported the church and state connection as a foundation of national religion.

Therefore at this very juncture when working class votes seemed particularly at a premium following the 1867 Reform Bill, Orangemen, both ordinary members of the proletarian Order and their leaders, were experiencing what they saw as a threat to the very heart of the Protestant faith in Ireland, as constitutionally guaranteed. This was felt all the more deeply since many Orangemen were of Irish origin and often former communicants of the Established Church.

The sense of threat from papal encroachment, and its favourable effects for the Conservative connection, received a further impetus in the early 1870s, this time located firmly in the Scottish context, from the question of religious education in state schools. For many Protestants the 1872 Education Act, again introduced by the Liberals, gravely undermined the 'godly upbringing' of the young, or more specifically the existing practice in Scotland (Use and Wont, as it was termed by contemporaries) whereby Bible reading and the Shorter Catechism had a pivotal role in educating pupils. For in establishing a national system of democratically elected school boards it removed control of curriculum and staffing from the hands of the Established Church.

For the Orangemen, the dangers had a more definite emphasis. How much the Ulstermen among the rank and file could empathise with 'Auld Scotia's Use and Wont' is open to doubt. More certainly they feared in the schools controversy 'Romanists on the vigil as ever to their religious interests' promoting the 'effete Italian superstition' to undermine their children's moral training.[97]

In these circumstances the first School Board elections of 1873 were important in various ways. First, being based on an extremely low franchise qualification of £4 ratepayers they allowed the LOI a particularly useful opportunity to feel the extent of its electoral potential. The Orangemen's votes (and probably their wives', since women made up one-fifth of the School Board's electorate) played a vital role in returning H A Long to the top of the Glasgow poll with over 600,000 cumulative votes, though both the Orangemen and Long himself pointed out he had the support not only of the LOI but 'the sound Protestants of Glasgow'.[98] Secondly, since the Roman Catholic vote was also well marshalled and three of their candidates were returned second, third and fourth the threat of Papal involvement was hardly eclipsed.[99] Thirdly and most importantly, though, for the future direction of increased Orange self-confidence, it could hardly escape the attention of the average Orange voter in these elections that many of the candidates who stood on the 'Use and Wont' platform, such as J N Cuthbertson, William Kidston, and Alex Whitelaw, were also Conservative stalwarts. The 'Use and Wont' position subsequently headed the election addresses of Whitelaw and Hunter in 1874, when Orangemen were explicitly asked by their Grand Lodges to vote only for those pledging to uphold 'the Bible in the School'.[100]

The confluence of Orange and Tory inclinations was not so pronounced over the next 'Ultramontane challenge' with the restoration in 1878 of the papal hierarchy in Scotland,[101] but another ecclesiastical crisis in the early 1880s again promoted alliance. This was provoked by the attempts of radical Liberals to disestablish the Church of Scotland. For the Orange Grand Lodge these 'Liberationists' were quite clearly 'the allies of papists' intent on dismantling the foundation of the nation's Protestantism. 'The best way to oppose their activities... was to do all they could in the parliamentary elections to return not Liberal members but those candidates who were opposed to and would vote against the disestablishment of the church'.[102] In effect these were, the *Conservative* candidates such as J G A Baird or Arnot Reid who to a man supported the Establishment in Scotland with much less reserve than they had in the case of the Irish Church in the 1860s. For J N Cuthbertson, for example, it was 'the one link which connects us to the days of the Old Kirk and the Covenant... defended by your fathers and by my fathers at Loudoun Muir and Bothwell Brig.'[103]

AN ORANGEMAN'S POLITICAL DUTY

The Orange response on ecclesiastical and educational controversies illustrates the continuing relevance of 'No Popery' for the Order, the basis of its traditional 'religious' emphasis. Indeed, the appeal of the old warcry is underlined by the fact that in political contests and debates where it is not appropriate or in abeyance, LOI involvement becomes at best peripheral in the School Board elections, for example, interest wanes to a great extent after 'the Bible in the School' controversy had yielded in the 1880s to questions of teachers salaries and the cost of textbooks.[104] Local and municipal elections were similarly regarded as unsuitable for sectarian disquisition, though one exception to this role is itself revealing. Thus in Greenock in 1874 the municipal elections had run their usual placid course, but a storm arose over the election of police commissioners when Skivington, a local publican and Roman Catholic, was put up as candidate against the ratepayers' list. The Orangemen were duly outraged – as if their sense of 'territory' had been invaded by *local* papal incursions. Holding 'that as a Protestant country Protestants ought to have the direction of Protestant affairs' they threw their weight behind another candidate who was also an Orangeman and he eventually headed the poll.[105]

As suggested above, this concern for 'Protestant Defence' on the part of the average Orangeman was now amply echoed by the Grand Lodge, a feature which tended to mitigate internal conflicts. This also ensured that any support given to the Conservatives was of a contingent sort, dependant on the latter's promotion of Protestant principles. Reducing the Order to a simple political adjunct would have in turn threatened the Grand Lodge's legitimacy. We can now look at this in more detail.

It is true that the elements of conditionality and distance are not always easily apparent. The Orange-Tory relationship involved close personal links and provoked characteristically sweeping declarations of loyalty. George McLeod, for example, in 1874 stated, that, 'All Orangemen are Conservatives, or if men in our ranks profess radicalism, they are what Luther called honest Italians – black swans – and are very rare indeed'.[106]

Yet away from the perorations of 12th platforms, in Grand Lodge counsels sentiments over political allegiances in the Grand Lodge were by no means unanimous. In Liverpool the *Protestant Standard* identified two types of Orangemen: 'Christian Protestant Orangemen' and 'Nominal Protestant Political Orangemen', the former embracing independent representation on class and sectarian grounds, the latter waiving everything for political ends such as the legislative union.[107] In Scotland, tensions were not made so explicit but it is possible to distinguish differing emphasis in the various fulminations of C I Paton, Rev. Robert Gault, H A Long (religious) and George McLeod, T Macklin and Wetherall (political).

Although during the 1865-85 period it is the latter which dominates the stance of many of the Orange leadership's day-to-day dealings with the Tories, the conception of Orangemen as 'Protestants First' before Party remained the *official* policy of the Scottish Grand Lodge.

An important text here is C I Paton's inaugural address as Grand Master. Delivered in January 1875 it offers a most sustained exposition of the 'Christian Orangemen' position in its quite precise prescription for the Institution's correct role in politics. He opens by denying the LOI to be the fodder of party political machinations by its very superiority.

It is no political participation which is the bond of our union. The principles which animate us belong to a higher and nobler sphere. Political parties are always fluctuating and changing, their watchwords and battlecries are soon forgotten but our principles are not changeable and our course of action must be the same till victory crowns our efforts and till the cry arises 'Babylon is fallen, fallen...'[108]

As a religious organisation, above all the LOI was nevertheless reluctantly called into the political arena because its deadly foe 'Popery' was essentially a political beast. In these circumstances the course of action Paton recommended was to exercise pressure working behind existing political forces and institutions and mobilising them in support of 'Protestant issues' and 'Protestant rights'. This was to be a persistent feature throughout the period of study and beyond, and was moreover wholly in accord with the Grand Lodge's desire for respectable status in Scotland.

Thus we shall make our influence felt most powerfully and increase it every day, and gain the co-operation of those who have not joined the brotherhood but have the cause at heart. How? One, by petitions from each Lodge signed by the WM and members; two, laying wishes and views before parliamentary representatives. Those who are already decided in favour of the course which a true regard for Protestant interests requires will thus be encouraged; the hesitating may be led to decide in the right way and those inclined the opposite way may be induced to change their course or at best,, if they will not vote as we would wish, to abstain from voting.[109]

The Home Rule issue finally illustrates how this conception of Orange support functioned on a practical level. Far from a unity of interest and expression on this, the Lodges offered a distinct articulation of elements of the prevailing Conservative ideology. In that this articulation came most frequently from McLeod, Macklin and the more 'politically' orientated Grand Lodge figures, the Home Rule case also indicates that even here incorporation in Conservatism could not be total.

The flexible attitude towards Ireland displayed by the more intelligent sections of the Tory party was eclipsed by Gladstone's public commitment to Home Rule at the end of 1885. Henceforth opposition was total and entrenched. As in the case of the Ultra-Tories of the early 1830s, the Conservatives' understanding of the Protestant ascendancy in Ireland had profound political rather than religious overtones and was very clearly rooted along class lines. The behaviour of Irish Nationalists and Land Leaguers, and Liberal remedial measures, were thus seen not only to undermine the rights of property in Ireland but to threaten these rights in the whole of the United Kingdom. As Somervell of Sorn stated, 'it is not a question of religions, it is a question of measures...'.[110] Irish Nationalist opinions also ran contrary to the growing sense of British national pride and urge for imperial consolidation, fostered by the Conservatives from the 1870s. Here Ireland was viewed as merely an integral part of a great nation, as Somervell again expressed it 'the brightest jewel in the imperial crown'. Nationalism, then, could be dismissed often with strongly racist overtones as the artificial agitation by ambitious politicians among an ignorant peasantry. 'The Celtic people had no senses', explained Mr. Keown Boyd, High Sheriff of County Down, 'the way to treat them was by the strong arm of patient government'.[111]

For the Orangemen, however, while opposition to Home Rule was equally intense, the interpretation underlying it had the familiar religious emphasis. This was now given a certain sense of immediacy and desperation from the fact that the site of the struggle with the old enemy had again shifted to Ireland, where many expatriate Orangemen had left friends and relations. Their fears were neatly captured in the speech of Col. Waring, DGM of Ireland, who evoked, 'the smoke of burning homesteads... seen from Galloway to Kintyre'.[112]

The leadership ably echoed these fears and resulting frustrations. For the Orangemen the real root of Ireland's crisis was in the Roman Catholicism of the mass of her people and the hold over them enjoyed by the 'popish priesthood', rather than political agitators. Roman Catholic priests, the Rev. Dr. Kane a Belfast Orangeman believed, stood behind the agitators in the belief 'any old stick will do to beat a dog with, using the Land League to knock the Protestant church.'[113] For the Rev. Thomson, priests were 'the curse of Ireland' and would do well 'to take and marry some farmers' daughters and emigrate to the far west of America.'[114]

Similarly, Paton demanded of his audience, 'What is the cause of the evils that affect Ireland? – Popery! If the Bible were better known and read there, there would be fewer outrages'.[115] Elsewhere he elaborated, specifying the list of concessions that had been made to the Irish Catholics, Emancipation, Disestablishment, Maynooth, and the Land Acts:

> ... each concession made in the hope that... it would satisfy the papists and make Ireland peaceful. And what had been the

result? (Murder). Peacefulness, loyalty, contentment? No! but
louder and still louder the cry of the daughters of the
horseleech 'Give, Give'. The truth must be spoken the British
government and legislature had not been faithful to the Protestant Constitution of Britain... It behoved all true Protestants
to set themselves with all their might to the resistance of further
popish aggressions'.[116]

These differing political and religious analyses did not produce
open conflict between the LOI and Conservatives at this point, and
could even be combined in a single resolution.[117] Yet they do emphasise that the Conservative worldview had still to co-exist with
another picture of reality based on uncompromising 'Anti Popish
Principles', and formed by the ordinary Orangeman's perception of
increasing 'Popish machinations' from the late 1860s. This in turn
suggests the potential for disjuncture which was present, again
negating the 'natural' or 'fixed' quality of their relations.

While threatening Liberal governments were in power and especially when Home Rule was on the horizon this potential was unful-
filled and Orange-Tory links were relatively prosperous. When,
however, the Conservatives formed a government and the Irish crisis
temporarily subsided, Orange and Conservative demands might not
be so harmoniously combined. At this point, the Tories' record as
the party which 'upholds the Revolutionary settlement, prefers
nobility to nihilism, and goes in for a Protestant government and
constitution, a House of Lords and for the established national
religion', came under closer Orange scrutiny.[118]

NOTES

1. R Hill, *Toryism and the People, 1832-46*, p. 15
2. GH, 31/3/80. See also *Glasgow Telegraph* editorial 'Jacobites Turned
   Whigs', 25/2/77.
3. GN, 28/7/74.
4. GN, 12/11/73.
5. Smith, *op. cit.* (1982), p. 186.
6. Hutchinson, *op. cit.* (1975), p. 384.
7. *Ibid.*
8. W E Hodgeson, 'Why Conservatism Fails in Scotland', *National Review* 2, 1883-4, GN, 25/12/77, 28/12/77. Only one Orangeman
   appears on the platform and none of the Orange officebearers of the
   town are present.
9. GN, 25/1/79.
10. GN, 5/1/78.
11. J Alexander, Secretary of the GCA, is present, GT 16/11/68.
12. GN, 23/10/85, 7/11/85.
13. GN, 11/11/85.
14. *Paisley Express*, 29/3/78.
15. *Ibid.*

16. GN, 6/2/84, 14/2/84, 5/2/84.
17. GN, 9/11/85, 28/10/85, *Paisley and Renfrewshire Gazette*, 23/11/85.
18. GN, 12/12/85.
19. *Ibid.*
20. GT, 14/12/75, *Glasgow Working Men's Conservative Association* (GWMCA) *Annual Report* (GWMCAAR) 25/1/1870 Conservative Offices Edinburgh.
21. GH, 2/12/68.
22. GH, 5/4/68.
23. *GWMCAAR*, 9/1/72.
24. *GWMCAAR*, 9/1/72, 14/1/73 respectively.
25. *Glasgow Conservative Association Annual Report*, (GCAAR), 16/2/1875,
26. *Ibid.*
27. GN, 5/2/84. The six are: R Gault, H A Long, R G Loundes, D Lang, G McLeod, T Macklin. The others are: J Haddock, W Sloan, J Reid, J Rodger, A Thomson, P Hutchinson, R Steward, S Geddes, W Yuille, D Black, R Mitchell, J Wylie.
28. GN, 27/1/74 – 4/2/74.
29. GH, 2/2/74.
30. Hutchinson, *op. cit.* (1976), p. 384. For Bain see Appendix E and *The Bailie* 27/11/72 for portrait.
31. GN, 17/5/80. He became Provincial Grand Master of the Masonic Lodge for Glasgow.
32. GN, 18/9/79.
33. GN, 10/3/80.
34. *Ibid.*
35. GN, 15/3/80.
36. GN, 26/3/80.
    Pearce's Orangemen: *J Adamson, *W J Anderson, J Brown, *R Gault, *P Hutcheson, *J Haddock, *J Johnstone, H A Long, *R G Loundes, *T Macklin, G McLeod, W McHaffie, *W Orr, J Reid, C Summers, T H Stewart, W G Taylor, J Wyllie.
    * Not on Bain's committee.
    Bain's Orangemen: J Brown, *J Davidson, *S Geddes, H A Long, G McLeod, W McHaffie, T H Stewart, C Summers, W G Taylor, J Wyllie, *W Hunter, *H Kennedy.
    * Not on Pearce's committee.
37. *The Bailie*, 27/11/74.
38. GN, 18/3/80, 19/3/80.
39. GH, 15/3/80. The NBDM noted joyfully that Bain's candidature would be more accurately described if one were to say he adopted the Tories rather than they adopted him, 18/3/80.
40. GH, 3/4/80.
41. See *GCAAR* 17/3/81 and GN report of special meeting 10/11/80.
42. *Ibid.*
43. *GCAAR*, 13/2/82, 17/2/81, 13/2/84.
    The six ward officials in 1882: W Hutcheson (Ward 2), S Geddes, T H Steward (Ward 14), P Morrison (Ward 15), T Wetherall, H Houston (Ward 16).
    1883: W Hutcheson (Ward 2), G Phair (Ward 10), T H Stewart (Ward 14), P Morrison (Ward 15), T Wetherall, H Houston (Ward 16).
    1884: J W Fairlie, T H Gilmour (Ward 2), J Wyllie (Ward 11), T H Stewart (Ward 14), P Morrison (Ward 15), H Houston (Ward 16), J O'Hara (Ward 6).

44. GN, 19/11/81, 26/11/81. See also Orange meeting GN, 26/3/81 for platform packed with local Tory notables.
45. GN, 27/6/81.
46. GN, 4/11/84.
47. GN, 13/2/82.
48. GN, 9/6/81, 29/11/81.
49. Central, College, Bridgeton, Tradeston, Camlachie, St. Rollox, Blackfriars and Hutchesontown.
50. In each of these new constituencies, existing ward committees were fused into a single divisional association with its own set of vice presidents and sub committees. The seven divisional Conservative associations in turns sent representatives to the GCA's general committee.
51. See *GCAARs* 1884-6.
52. GN, 9/9/85.
53. GN, 14, 16, 17/11/85.
54. GN, 17/10/85, 7/11/85. For Morrison 20/8/85, 3/9/85.
55. GN, 23/11/85.
56. Maugham had only arrived in Scotland in 1874. For Protestant character of Toryism see GN editorials, 15/9/73, 13/6/74, 6/3/75, 4/1/78, 30/7/79, 3/7/80.
57. B Crapster, 'Scotland and the Conservative Party in 1876', *Journal of Modern History*, xxix 1987, p. 357. GN, 27/11/73.
58. See C Levy, *Conservatism and Liberal Unionism in Glasgow 1874-1912*, Ph.D University of Dundee 1983.
59. GN, 16/2/84.
60. See Appendix D.
61. See Appendix B and C.
62. See J McCaffrey, 'The Irish Vote in Glasgow in the Later 19th Century', *Innes Review*, XXI, 1970 on the predominantly Roman Catholic Irish and the Franchise.
63. GT, 21/12/77.
64. GN, 25/7/84.
65. Hutchinson *op. cit.* (1975), p. 384. See GN Editorials 24/4/80, 5/9/80, 23/4/80 using the Bradlaugh controversy to win over Liberal support.
66. J McCaffrey, *Political Reactions in the Glasgow Constituencies at the General Elections of 1885 and 86*, Ph.D University of Glasgow, 1970, Chapter 2. Also his 'Origins of Liberal Unionism in the West of Scotland', *Scottish Historical Review* 50, 1971, pp. 47-71.
67. *Ibid.*
68. NBDM, 27/10/85, GH, 17/10/85.
69. GN, 30/11/85; called the claim 'preposterous', but contrast GH 2/12/85 and NBDM 2/12/85.
70. McCaffrey, *op. cit.* (1970).
71. *Paisley Daily Express*, 9/11/85.
72. GT, 12/11/77 for 1877 by-election splits.
73. R B McDowell, *British Conservatism 1832-1914* (1959), p. 112ff.
74. W S Churchill, *Life of Lord Randolph Churchill* (1906).
75. GH, 12/10/85.
76. GN, 28/11/85.
77. *Glasgow Observer*, 28/11/85.
78. GN, 23/11/85. McCaffrey, *op. cit.* (1970), Chapter 1 for useful discussion of Irish populations in the Glasgow constituencies.
79. GN, 20/11/85.
80. Lobban, *op. cit.* (1971), p. 272.

81. *The Bailie*, 6/2/78.
82. GT, 5/1/78, 8/1/78.
83. GT, 18/11/84.
84. NSDM, 11/1/89.
85. GN, 25/11/85, 3/12/85.
86. McDonagh, *op. cit.* (197?).
87. GN, 26/3/80.
88. GN, 17/10/85.
89. GN, 16/10/85.
90. This was also felt in a physical sense. Election day gave the opportunity for rougher elements to exercise their combative zeal. For an example See NBDM, 3/8/87.
91 *Irish Times*, 22/10/1983.
92. GN, 6/10/75.
93. GN, 2/2/74.
94. GN, 8/10/74. There were even suggestions that Gladstone himself was a Jesuit. The Rev. Potter and Johnstone of Ballykillbeg nearly came to blows on the issue on a public 12th platform, GH 16/7/73.
95. GH, 12/10/68, 14/10/68.
96. GH, 29/10/68.
97. GN, 29/11/74. See J H Roxburgh, *The Glasgow School Board Elections 1873-1919*, M Litt, University of Glasgow, 1968, for general background.
98. H A Long, *The Glasgow School Board Elections* (n.d.), p. 11.
99. Result GH, 31/3/73.
100. GN, 19/1/74.
101. GN, 25/12/77, for Orange memorandum to Lord Beaconsfield.
102. GN, 30/10/78.
103. GN, 23/10/85.
104. GT, 26/11/85.
105. GT, 11/11/74, 14/11/74.
106. GH, 3/7/74.
107. Waller, *op. cit.* (1981), p. 96.
108. GN, 23/1/75.
109. *Ibid.*
110. GN, 6/11/84.
111. GN, 22/10/81. Racist imagery is much less common in Orange opposition to Home Rule. Anti-Irish sentiments were perhaps rather too close to home for Ulstermen in its ranks.
112. GN, 8/11/84.
113. GN, 12/3/81.
114. GH, 13/7/81.
115. *Ibid.*
116. GH, 13/7/84.
117. GN, 8/11/84.
118. GN, 28/7/84.

10
Truckling to Popery (1886-1900)

The Liberal party's fragile unity was shattered by its more advanced sections' commitment to Home Rule for Ireland, and attempts to introduce a Bill to this effect in 1886. This also ended Conservative overtures for the Irish Nationalist vote and Salisbury's parliamentary alliance with the Parnellites. In these circumstances the Tory press rapidly urged an electoral pact with the new 'Liberal Unionists'.[1] Co-operation, as Levy details, proceeded fruitfully albeit with 'some currents of mutual tension and suspicion'.[2]

In Scotland these developments resulted in a more distinct polarisation in political ideologies and a more explicit class basis for party politics. The business and professional fraction of the bourgeoisie, whose support the Conservatives in Glasgow had courted from the mid-1870s, now formed the backbone of the new party. For their part, the Conservatives benefited from the Liberal schism, as LU votes promoted their political ascendancy for the next sixteen years till 1902, and buttressed their resultant status as the 'great national party of rational and moderate progress at home and a patriotic foreign policy'.

This chapter will now examine how Orange political involvement responded to these immediate political contingencies. Again we begin by sketching electoral activity and involvement in the parties' internal structures.

POLITICAL RELATIONSHIPS

Electoral Activity: The first test of LU strength at the polls was, of course, the 1886 election. In this highly charged campaign Orange fortunes were mixed. Many former areas of Orange political strength such as Blackfriars, Camlachie, Tradeston and Paisley now had the new party at the helm.[3] While it is probable that Orangemen provided vote support for the LUS, the level of public activity on the part of the LOI is much diminished, both in terms of platform appearances and electoral work around polling day.[4] This is in some contrast with Bridgeton, where a Conservative candidate, Mackenzie was selected, and where local Orange worthies W McKinnon, J

and C Summers and William Young, later Grand Master, had a very
high profile.[5]

Regardless of the extent of the LOI's public participation, the
strength of anti-Home Rule and anti-Irish feeling in Glasgow and
the West of Scotland generally, ensured a Unionist victory. Opportunities to supplement this were presented by a series of by-elections
later in the year. These again indicate the distance between Orangemen and the LU, though this is not immediately clear from contemporary press coverage

The first by-election was Bridgeton in 1887, now contested by an
LU, the Hon. Evelyn Ashley. The *Mail* was in no doubt of the centrality of Orange participation here, with 'Orange rowdyism'
seemingly directing the tactics of the Unionist side. They furnished
an example.

> Arrangements of T P O'Connor and Parnell to get the full Irish
> vote out has disturbed the peace of mind of the Orangemen,
> and some member of the pious brotherhood has safely deliv-
> ered after suffering the pains of parturition the following 'To
> the Irish electors of Bridgeton and fellow countrymen, you
> cannot vote for Trevelyan [the Liberal] who has proved our
> bitter enemy in the past' ending 'God save Ireland'. This is the
> product of the capricious febrile brain of some Orangeman
> inspired by the Conservatives and it is posted all over the
> district. The electors should not forget the Orangeman has no
> politics in the ordinary sense of the word. The religious
> element is the motive which colours and underlies all his
> actions. Persecution of the Catholic i.e. the glorious prospect
> of hearing their bones 'crunch' in the sack is *the* one aim of the
> Orangeman's religious and political existence.[6]

Yet caution is needed here, for as a radical organ the *Mail* regarded the LUS as traitors to the Liberal cause, and one of the most
effective tactics to belittle their candidate was not only to refer to his
'catwitted' address but to brand him as the *Orangemen's* candidate.
In looking more soberly at the *Mail*'s strident accusations one finds
firstly that the term 'Orange' is used indiscriminately to refer, for
example, to the impromptu Protestant orators of Glasgow Green,
like W Alexander Godwin, who had no connection with the official
LOI.[7] In fact, it becomes apparent that the involvement of the Lodges
was marginalised, when compared with previous contests.

The *Mail* is more accurate when it describes the backbone of
Ashley's public support as 'those minor satellites... the peripatetic
band of Grahame, Jackson, Cross and Co. (limited)', in other words
the prominent LUS of the city who were successful at the 1886

election. For Orangemen figure on his platforms only when and where they are calculated to be of the maximum benefit and minimum embarrassment. In Dalmarnock, for example, a working class section of the division and territory of No. 44 district of the LOI, James McManus then secretary of the Orange district is present at a Unionist meeting in the local parish churches.[8] When George McLeod is invited on the platform at the Bridgeton Temperance Hall his presence is balanced by the presence of prominent ex-Liberals.[9]

A rather similar situation prevailed when Ashley, again unsuccessfully, contested the Ayr Burghs seat the following year. Orange District Master William McCormick then had an important role at Irvine where the Order had some weight but in the rest of the constituency Ashley seems more comfortable in the support of 'the peripatetic band' and of notable Ulster Orange figures such as Col. Saunderson and Mr. Hillsmore rather than local LOI luminaries.[10]

The momentum of developing Orange-Conservative links was promoted more surely in the 1892 and 95 General Elections. In Bridgeton, for example, the Conservative candidate in 1892 was the ubiquitous W C Maugham who had 'offered himself spontaneously' for the contest.[11] James McManus, now a Grand Lodge official, was again particularly active in the Unionist interest, but occupying a more central place in this campaign than in 1887.

Particularly significant is the public recognition that such co-operation now receives from many Tories, although this strongly gives the impression that the lodges now increasingly constituted a formidable interest bloc in their own right whose support was not automatically guaranteed. Thus J S Maxwell, Conservative candidate for College division willingly addressed a meeting of Cowcaddens district of the LOI, apparently the first time a parliamentary candidate had done such a thing in Scotland. His speech, moreover, was highly flattering.

> He was glad to recognise in the quality of their enthusiasm, something different from that meeting in the theatre over the way. [A Liberal meeting addressed by Gladstone]. There was spontaneous enthusiasm. The chairman had said it was not usual for a candidate to address an Orange lodge. (Why not?). He agreed with the gentleman – why not? (Cheers). It had certainly never occurred to him to refuse the invitation. (Cheers). There might have been in the past some neglect of the Orangemen by the Conservatives, but he thought that probably arose from the fact that the Conservatives were sure of the Orange vote.[12]

Conservatives now also shrunk less from acknowledging Orange support on 12 July platforms. In the aftermath of the 1892 election C Bine Renshaw, successful Conservative candidate for West Renfrewshire, who was unable to attend an Oranges celebration, sent a warm letter of apology stating that he 'would have been glad to have had the opportunity of thanking them for the loyal and hearty way he had been supported at the poll (loud cheers)..., he wished to carry grateful thanks for the manner they had all worked.'[13] A precedent for this had already been set in Ayrshire in 1890 when the Conservative agents for the north and south of the county, had appeared in person on the 12th July in Kilmarnock.[14]

The 1892 election also gave the LOI its first 'Orange' MP in the person of William Whitelaw, who had been extremely lucky to win Perth after a split Liberal vote. He did not dissemble over his Orange credentials but said 'he had the honour to belong to the body of Scotch Orangemen and there was no better organisation on the Unionist side'.[15]

While failing to form a parliamentary majority in 1892, the Unionist coalition prospered in Glasgow and the West. Success continued in 1895, again contested on the Home Rule issue, but now local gains reflected an impressive national victory. Here too public Orange-Conservative rapport was maintained.

This is again particularly noticeable in Bridgeton where the Conservative Scott Dickson was candidate, and Young and McManus were frequent platform visitors.[16] The closest Orange links though are with the Conservative candidate for Blackfriars, Alex Stuart of Blairhill, Stirling. Stuart appears at the 12th celebrations at Falkirk eagerly courting the Orange vote, and has T H Stewart and Peter Morrison as well as speakers from Ulster in attendance at his meetings. One of these, Rev. Thomson, proved particularly unsuitable and 'when the meeting was not taking Mr. Thomson's Orange harangue seriously, Mr. Stuart deemed it necessary to pull the orator's coat-tails.'[17]

In fact, it is not until the 'Khaki election' of 1900, fought over the emotive issue of the Boer War, that it is possible to trace some faltering in Orange involvement with the Conservatives.[18] The Orange presence is still significant at Bridgeton where Dickson is again candidate with Young and McManus in support.[19] At Blackfriars, though, although the veteran T H Stewart is prominent, presiding over one of Bonar Law's meetings, the candidate does not make a comparable effort to his predecessor, Stuart, to woo the Orange electorate, even publicly stating his support for a Catholic University of Ireland 'under proper conditions'.[20] In College, J S Maxwell, who at the previous contest, as noted, had addressed local Orangemen, now responded negatively to the perennial question of Convent Inspection.[21] In the LU seats Tradeston, Camlachie and St. Rollox the reserve over Orange links which had characterised the Party from its outset was maintained.

Committees & Councils: Not surprisingly, in the case of the Liberal Unionists no prominent Orangemen are found either in the original West of Scotland branch of the Liberal Committee for the Maintenance of the Legislative Union between Great Britain and Ireland, or in the later West of Scotland Liberal Unionist Association, or the Glasgow Liberal Unionist Council.[22]

Significantly, as in the Conservative case, low representation at committee level balances to some extent the Orangemen's high public profile at election time. In Glasgow, for example, the strongly localised pattern of Orange-Tory links noted for the 1865-85 period, persists. Bridgeton boasted the most significant Orange involvement with as many as five known Orange vice presidents.[23] In this division Orangemen also manage to achieve more influential executive positions. McManus is vice chairmen in 1888, Heriot Longmuir and William Young delegates to the central body, the GCA, in 1889. In Camlachie the pattern is similar. Here the HDMG, J E Fairlie, was particularly active in representing the Division in the GCA in 1887, and in 1899 an Orangeman, T H Gilmour, actually became paid organising secretary for the area.[24] In Tradeston and in Blackfriars three to four Orange vice presidents are also regularly found.

Yet even in these 'working men's divisions', by no means did Orangemen numerically dominate their committees. The Bridgeton vice presidents were 5 out of a total of 49. In the more prosperous constituencies of Central and College their representation was even less significant, though College's greatly extended list of Vice Presidents in the early 1890s does allow some of the Cowcaddens Orangemen to appear.[25]

This varying strength at constituency level was further reproduced in the new Western Divisional Council, created in 1893 to manage all central work for the divisions in its area. While formal co-opting of Orange officials took place early in the twentieth century, at this stage the only Orangeman who can be identified is William Young in his capacity as delegate for Bridgeton in 1893-4. Much more numerous among delegates were local Conservative notables and sitting MPs and it was certainly these figures who dominated the WDC's representation to the Conservative party's Central Council.[26]

DETERMINANTS OF POLITICAL RELATIONSHIPS: THE LIBERAL UNIONISTS

The maintenance of a 'public distance' between the LUs and the Orangemen can be explained to a large extent by the former's ideological antecedents, and the circumstances of their foundation.

In the first place, the major leaders and supporters of the LUs were largely drawn from the business and professional sections of the Scottish bourgeoisie, alarmed by the threat to imperial unity and the access to foreign markets on which much of their prosperity depended. As such, they were liable to the long standing prejudices of that class against the 'ignorant' and populist overtones of the LOI.

Unlike their Tory allies, whose Orange links were now fairly well established, their recent experience as Liberals in successive elections had by no means mitigated such impressions and may have prompted some to give credence to a typical anecdote, circulating around the LU constituency of Partick in the 1890s, of an illiterate Orangeman who was said to have mistaken the polling booth, with curtain, for a photographic studio.[27]

More pragmatic considerations also intervened. At the time of their succession, as Hutchinson suggests, the permanency of this manoeuvre was not immediately obvious to the actual participants. In the very fluid situation around 1886 it was imperative for the LUs not to fuse with the Tories but to maintain a separate identity and oppose Home Rule as *Liberals* – a particularly valid position in Scotland given the Tories' historically poor performance since 1832. An independent 'Liberal' stance, however, would hardly be assisted by a high profile on LU platforms from leading Orangemen, who were perceived by the Liberal press as the most extreme adjuncts of 'True Blue' conservatism. Even in their absence the *Mail* pointed to 'Whig-Tory-Orange' dirty tricks.[28]

The LUs faced two further initial imperatives namely to win over Gladstonian Liberals uneasy over Home Rule and, as Levy suggests, to persuade wavering LUs to leap the psychological barrier not only to vote against Gladstone, but in some divisions to vote *for* a Conservative candidate.[29] Here again, given the delicacy of the situation, the public assistance of their Conservative allies, not to mention forceful Orange participation was unwelcome to many LU candidates. The Conservative *Scottish News* was tactfully aware of this and suggested that Ashley, the Bridgeton candidate in 1887, 'might if he had chosen had his platforms filled with the leaders of Glasgow Toryism... but he has not desired these aids. He holds, we presume, that such aid might tarnish his reputation as a Liberal and might prevent weak-kneed Liberals from supporting one who seemed too intimate with the Tories'.[30]

Advice along similar lines directed at Orange involvement was given to the Partick by-election candidate Parker Smith from a sitting LU member of Parliament, H T Anstruther.

I should advise you not to have the Irish Loyalist lectures; they mean very well by their offers and... might keep your Orangemen in good heart; but if... it is to be an electors' battle make it so, and call in everyone to your aid who will give a little time and trouble amongst them personally and 'influence' them[31]

Parker Smith seems to have accepted this advice, and the contest placed little emphasis on Irish issues or personalities. He also diplomatically declined an invitation from the Orange partisan, the Rev. Quintin Johnstone of Whiteinch, to visit his church. Johnstone, though, was most understanding on the matter. 'I think the fact that you will not come to our church in the present circumstances only furnishes an additional proof of your struggle to represent the Partick division of Lanarkshire. When you can write 'MP' at your name we shall be glad to see you in church any day you see fit to come'.[32]

There were exceptions to this pattern. In the 1895 election, for example, a deputation of Orangemen was brought over from Belfast in support of the LU candidate, Fergusson, in the Govan division.[33] Here local factors come into place. In Govan then, attempts were also made to win the Rechabite vote and the candidate may have favourably calculated the viability of a Temperance/Orange/Working Man-type coalition against a wavering Liberal/Gladstonian Liberal/Irish Nationalist one.

Generally speaking, strong and lasting links between the LUS and LOI could not be secured until the formers' pre-occupation with a distinctive identity was in abeyance and the 'Unionist' vote had become a more solid reality. Such developments do not take place until after 1900 when the LU position begins to be eroded by doubts over the 1902 South African Peace Settlement and over Tariff Reform, and as the Conservatives increasingly became senior partners in the alliance. A drift towards Conservative-LU fusion then began in the constituencies and was eventually effected in 1912, with the formation of the Scottish Conservative and Unionist Party.[34]

THE CONSERVATIVES

It has already been emphasised that the picture of the Conservatives confined in an electoral 'cul de sac' prior to 1885, greatly underestimates the range of political alliances open to them. In particular it was argued that projected links with right-wing Liberals and Irish Nationalists were vital in conditioning the level of Tory involvement with the LOI.

Now, far from simply providing an escape route from a circumscribing Orange liaison, the emergence of the LU grouping meant the die was cast regarding both sets of alternative alliances. First, there was no longer any prospect of an electoral agreement with the Irish Nationalists and this situation was bound to prevail as long as the Liberals remained committed to Home Rule, and as long as issues deemed important by their ecclesiastical authorities did not cleave the Irish from Liberal support by appealing to their Roman Catholicism. Secondly, of course, by 1886 Whiggish Liberal assistance for the Conservatives was already established, not by direct participation in the party, but through the electoral coalition with the LUs.

Orange-Conservative links were also helped by the fact that a new generation of Conservatives was coming to prominence from the late 1880s and early 90s. They identified less with the pejorative reputation of Orangeism, and more with its increasingly important role in the period as an effective popular bulwark in Ireland for the maintenance of the Unionist establishment.[35] The Whitelaw family prove an excellent example. Alex Whitelaw, MP for Glasgow in 1874, was a staunch Protestant, a supporter of the Established Church and 'Use and Wont'. Yet he never publicly courted the LOI much less appeared on a 12th platform. Of his sons, as indicated, William, MP for Perth, was actually a member, while Grahame and Alexander had close practical links, granting the Order use of their land for demonstrations and at times themselves speaking in support of resolutions prepared by the Grand Lodge.[36]

While these general developments promoted intensified local Orange involvement in Conservative associations such as Bridgeton, they were not sufficient to extend links significantly into new areas like Glasgow Central or Greenock.[37] Nor did they alter the real extent of the LOI's influence on decision making or policy formulation. Here again it is important to remember that the higher public visibility the Tories granted their Orange connections took place in the context of the party's general expansion and growth in confidence. Thus, objectively, the very size and success of the party now moderated the extent and importance of Orange influence, a quite different situation from the late 1860s when the West of Scotland Tories had been a most downcast and peripheral group among whom an energetic and vociferous Orange presence was bound to bulk large.

More specific factors finally lay behind the lower profile enjoyed
by Orangemen in the 1900 Tory election campaign. We return here
to a familiar pattern in Orange-Tory relations. For, most important
here was the renewed hope held out to the Conservatives of Irish
Roman Catholic electoral support, on this occasion over educational issues, with A J Balfour's scheme for establishing a Catholic
University in Ireland and debates over the position of denominational schools.

In the latter case the Conservative government had already
pledged to relieve the position of these establishments which were
ineligible for aid from the local rates. While this was most germane
to English Nonconformists, in Scotland it was also seen to be of
particular benefit to Roman Catholic schools and the Bishops accordingly instructed their flocks to support the Conservatives as 'clerical'
candidates. The *Glasgow Observer* resisted this advice and continued
to support Liberal candidates, but given the general situation the
local Tories had to proceed cautiously not to alienate the Irish vote.

They were accordingly compelled, even C S Dickson in Bridgeton, to support government policy on the voluntary schools,[38]
though the Catholic University idea provoked a wider range of
response. J S Maxwell gave 'unqualified dissent... having considered the idea without prejudice he felt perfectly certain that there
was no obligation upon a Protestant country to endow a Roman
Catholic University.'[39] Rather more adroit was Bonar Law:

> He had no hesitation in saying that this was one of those
> questions which he had just as soon it had not been necessary
> to face because he might possibly lose votes which would
> otherwise have been given him. He was in favour of granting a
> Catholic University under proper conditions. These were first
> that the Bill would seem to hold out a good promise of
> providing a University which could compare favourably with
> other Universities of the country, and another condition it
> would be taken advantage of by Roman Catholics and Prot-
> estants, then he believed it would no more be a Catholic
> University than Glasgow was a Presbyterian one.[40]

The effect of the education issue on the Roman Catholic Irish
vote, and the contribution of this to the seven Unionist victories in
Glasgow in 1900, is difficult to assess. The 'Boer or Briton' appeal
was also vital in winning widespread national support for the
Unionists. At least in Blackfriars though, the Irish Liberal vote
crumbled and Bonar Law was returned.[41]

Such developments, however, also profoundly jaundiced the
Orangemen's perceptions of their Conservative allies.

THE ORANGEMEN

The official Orange attitude to the LU-Conservative electoral pact was one of approval.[42] This approval, moreover, overrode minor irritations such as the adherence of some LUs like Patrick Sellars to the Disestablishment cause. The next ten years witnessed a flowering of spirited resolutions, 'declaring... unabashed confidence in the Unionist policy of Her Majesty's ministers and... determination in supporting them in refusing Irish Nationalists a separate parliament'.[43]

The dynamics for this support were still found in Orangemen's perceptions of the Tories as best guardians of their economic interests and in their fears for 'the Protestant religion in danger'. Indeed these conditions had intensified after 1886.

First, the Unionist grouping, with an impetus from the LUs, developed more constructive elements in their programme focusing on social and labour questions. The 'True Blue' W C Maugham, for example, declared his 'support for measures tending to elevate the working classes', pledging his vote, 'in aid of objects for promoting temperance, thrift and prosperity at home and abroad' and for 'any well devised plan for affording support to the deserving poor in old age'.[44] Sir John Pender followed a similar tack: '... he was one of themselves. He had been a working man. He served an apprenticeship on the Clyde and by his own industry and perseverance had raised himself to the position he now occupied.'[45]

Secondly, the threat of Irish Home Rule, which the Orangemen regarded with almost apocalyptic dread, had by no means subsided. On the contrary it received further emphasis with the return of a Liberal government in 1892, and the introduction of a second Home Rule Bill. In these circumstances the spectre increasingly conjured up by the LOI from 1886 is one of an armed struggle in which the Scottish Orangemen would assist their Irish counterparts. Macklin, for example, pledged the 1893 twelfth demonstration:

> to assist by every means in its power, our brethren in Ireland in the campaign they are now waging against the forces of rapine, disorder and disloyalty... Should the traitors impose on the north the dire necessity of civil war, Ulster would muster his sons and the Orangemen of Scotland would join them and the watchword from rank to rank... would be 'No Surrender'.[46]

It is interesting that these warlike sentiments are voiced by the Grand Lodge leadership. Given their fastidious attitude towards Orange involvement in street violence, one might speculate how they would have reacted if several of their more robust and rowdy followers had actually heeded their call to arms. This call was most likely some judicious sabre-rattling, further indicating the Grand Lodge's increased responsiveness to rank and file sentiments. Reinforcing this in the 1890s, as in the Conservative case, was the emergence of a 'new guard' in the Grand Lodge, best represented by William Young, James McManus, and T H Gilmour. These figures were also more likely to countenance an independent attitude to their Unionist allies. For although closely involved in Conservative organisations, unlike Wetherall or McLeod in Glasgow or Farmer and Pollock in Paisley, they had not personally nursed Conservatism in its early stages of growth, but instead had come to politics when Orangemen had already become something of an autonomous pressure group in the Conservative camp. This attitude was expressed for example, in the publication of separate election manifestos in 1892 and 1895, albeit binding the Scottish Orangemen to 'throw themselves heart and soul into this momentous contest [1895] and place their active services at the disposal of Unionist candidates'.[47]

In practice, the Orangemen's capacity for autonomous action for the promotion of 'Protestant Issues' was increasingly tested from 1895 onwards. Now with a Unionist government returned to power with a resounding majority, and Irish constitutional change no longer on the agenda, the potential for disjuncture in Orange-Tory relations, noted in the preceding chapter, was at last realised.

Three issues gave rise to conflict. First, the Unionist administration from 1895 had continued to pursue a policy of conciliation in Ireland, 'killing Home Rule by kindness'. This had been Salisbury's policy in his first two administrations and was eagerly embraced by Chamberlain and the LUs who also advanced an extensive programme of public works. Typical here was the 1896 Land Act, and Balfour's 'Catholic University' plan. Secondly, as also indicated above, the Unionists promoted reform in the financing of voluntary schools, in effect providing rate support for Roman Catholic and Nonconformist establishments. Third was the vexed issue of ritualism in the Church of England. To extirpate such practices the Church Discipline Bill was introduced in 1897 banning the Mass and Confessional in the Anglican Church. This was enthusiastically advocated by the anti-ritualist Church Association and also received strong support from Sir William Harcourt, leader of the Liberals. Crucially though the Unionist government was not particularly energetic in its efforts to see the Bill passed and, put to a free vote, it was unsuccessful.[48]

For the Orangemen of Scotland, the government's initiatives, or lack of them in the case of ritualism, appeared both as a betrayal of the electoral support the Order had consistently offered them and as a running down of the Conservatives' traditional standard of 'True Blue Protestantism' on which this support had depended. Their wrath was swiftly and effectively voiced by the Grand Lodge leadership. Thus William Young presiding at the 1897 12th Celebrations now emphasised:

> Orangemen would only support a Conservative candidate where they supported Orange principles. In the last election Orangemen were the means in the West of Scotland of returning a great number of Unionist candidates and expected great things of a Unionist government. In the name of the Orangemen of Scotland he begged to inform the Unionist government that they would not receive their support if they attempted to pass a bill for the benefit of Roman Catholics in Ireland. If they tried to take money from the Emerson Smith Endowment*, left by a Protestant for the promotion of Protestant principles, the Orangemen would do all in their power to put them out and return a good Protestant government in their place.[49]

The following year protests were even more forceful. The Rev. Townsend drew his audiences' attention to the fact that the enemies of Protestantism were also at work in parliament.

> Where were the Glasgow MPs during the Benefices' Bill [an anti-High Church measure]. Their voices were not heard against sacerdotalism which was eating the vitals out of the Church of England... Glasgow MPs could come to their Orange *soirées* and talk a lot of amiable-nonsense but when Protestantism was at stake they sat like a lot of dumb dogs. Mr. Balfour and other Unionists were smiling now on rebels and traitors... while they insulted the Orangemen and those who placed them in power. Their thanks that day were due to Mr. William Harcourt and Mr. Smith as defenders of Protestantism. Let them as Orangemen be neither Conservatives or Liberals in the future but Protestants first and foremost.[50]

The next resolution of Bro. Yuill reinforced this, 'regretting that the Conservatives had for some time *truckled to Popery* and trifled with Protestant constitutional interests both in church and state and calling on MPs to make it clear to Lord Salisbury and the government that by their pro-Romanism policy they are alienating the Protestant vote in the country.'[51]

At this stage, however, the alienation of the Scottish Orangemen was only temporary, for by 1900 another general election loomed

*A projected source of finance for the new Irish University.

and with it the prospect of another Home Rule Bill if the Liberals were returned. The Boer war had also intervened, considerably boosting Unionist prestige as the National and Patriotic party, and moreover halting the Liberal anti-ritualist campaign. Now Harcourt and his associates whom the Orangemen had applauded in 1898, were firmly branded as 'Pro-Boer' opponents of British policy in South Africa, thus confirming the Institution's previous conceptions of the Liberal party as 'treasonable' and 'disloyal'.

In these extreme circumstances the Grand Lodge's position shifted. As Young again explained:

> Since last July there have been great events in the country... The people of the country should be grateful that in such a crisis they had a strong government in power (applause), a government which had the honour of the country at heart and was not like to make the mistakes of the government of 1881*... As they knew the Orangemen had always supported the Conservatives and were thankful they had supported that Party when they took account of South Africa. He counselled his audience therefore to support that Party which he was convinced had the best interests of the country at heart.[52]

Yet such sentiments do not indicate a general retreat from 'Protestant Issues' by the LOI, and at another large demonstration in 1900 resolutions were passed pledging 'loyal devotion to the Unionists', but also further condemning the Roman Catholic university project in Ireland.[53] For the ordinary Orangemen the 'National Threat' may not have completely driven from their minds the threat posed to the 'Protestant religion' by 'Pro-Romish' policy. Again evidence is scanty here. There does not seem to have been open conflict with the Orange leadership, but it is significant how frequently at public meetings in the 1900 election campaign, potentially embarrassing questions on the Catholic university, voluntary schools and ritualism are put to Unionist candidates 'from the back of the hall'. So unsatisfactory did Bonar Law's replies prove that the Orangemen were exhorted in an anonymous letter to '... see to it that Mr. Provand [the Liberal] gets their vote, as it would be contrary to the principles of Orangeism to support any candidate of whatever Party who acts contrary to Protestant sentiment and practice. Mr. Provand is sound on Imperial questions and has dropped Home Rule.'[54]

---

*A reference to the Liberals' handling of a previous South African campaign.

COMPARATIVE ISSUES

The Scottish Orangemen seem to have enjoyed a more positive impact in the political sphere than, for example, in their relations with the Scottish churches or the press. Yet in this final section it is important to widen the scope of the analysis to again include some comparative cases. This exercise illustrates that political progress was in fact relatively circumscribed in Scotland, and that although significant, the LOI's political independence was less practically implemented.

Ulster: Orangeism's political significance received a great impetus with the historic reorientation of the presbyterian bourgeoisie away from the lingering United Irishmen tradition of 1798 and towards a pro-Crown and Union stance. This can be traced from the 1860s and the Fenian rising, but developed more surely in the wake of the Home Rule crisis from the early 1880s.

From the outset the anti-Home Rule campaign and the Conservatism which underpinned it had Orangeism as a central binding factor. Its extraordinary impact on the political structure even received formal acknowledgement in the Order's right to 122 delegates or 10-20% of all delegates in the Ulster Unionist Council. James Craig, premier from 1921-40, was indeed able to proclaim, 'I am an Orangeman first and a politician and member of parliament afterwards... all that I boast is that we are a Protestant parliament and a Protestant state'.[55] Paradoxically it is not only in terms of its extraordinary weight in the political establishment that Ulster Orangeism differed from its Scottish offshoot, but also in the greater critique of oligarchic Tory leadership, voiced by dissident organisations like the OPWA and IOO. This promoted certain 'limited forms' of class consciousness from the proletarian Orangemen albeit ultimately contained within the Unionist ideological framework.

Canada: Turning to the less familiar example of Canada, rather similar contrasts with Scotland in the extent of Orange political impact and the degree of independence and self-assertion in the Institution's political alliances are evident.

The Order in Canada in the 1820s, introduced by Irish Orangemen who were then migrating to British America in large numbers, rapidly flourished, as Senior suggests: 'Because Orangeism was based on religion and monarchy rather than race and geography, it provided a patriotism eminently suited to the needs of a colonial society.'[56] By 1830, much earlier than in Scotland, it was already emerging as a political force.

The period between 1830-41 in Canada was dominated by the struggle between 'reformers' on one hand such as W L MacKenzie, and on the other the Tories and particularly the 'Family Compact' – the name coined by reformers to refer to the leading families who administered the affairs of the province by retaining the confidence of successive governors. They were drawn from the same class as the 'reform families', differing only in their control of government and political philosophy. The balance between these groups was upset by further massive immigration challenging both Reformers and Family Compact. The Order's political response in this situation further belies the 'naturalness' of an Orange alliance with Conservative groups.

There was a temporary liaison with the Family Compact in 1836, but the latter strongly distrusted popular movements of any kind and was unwilling to accept the Orange leaders as equal partners. Even more importantly, since the main political issue was reform not religion, there could not be a simple bloc Orange vote in favour of 'Protestant candidates'. Consequently, since Orangemen were politically divided, some *were* Tories but others, as in Britain in the 1832 reform crisis, were 'staunchest among the reformers'.[57]

Two developments did increasingly promote unity. First was the increasing direction and cohesion which the Grand Lodge received from the arrival of the prominent Irish Orangeman, Ogle R Gowan, an extremely able figure. From now, as in Scotland, it is this leading body which provides the main initiatives for the conduct of political alliances. Secondly the Reformers, mostly native-born Canadians, were becoming more committed to 'Jacksonian Democracy', which was hostile to all European connections and to those immigrants which upheld them. In this way a direct threat was posed to the Crown and the British links most prized by the Orangemen.

Again the Order's reaction here is complex and defies their reduction to adjuncts of the Tory/Family Compact grouping. They became instead an independent force and one, as Senior suggests, 'seeking a place' in the still rather malleable conditions of Canadian society and politics. This was achieved by combining the platform planks of 'reform' and 'loyalty', challenging the radical-liberal monopoly of the former and the Family Compact's hold on the latter.

Consequently, in one of the most 'progressive' episodes in Orange history, the lodges became champions of immigrant democracy, best summarised by Gowan himself as 'the protection of immigrant rights with loyalty to the old country'. This even involved alliances with Irish Catholic immigrants and the formation of 'Union Lodges' to include Catholics. In Hastings and Northumberland Orangemen also helped elect Catholic candidates and in Durham Catholics in turn supported Orangemen.[58] As the major force loyal to the British Crown in Canada, alliances also had to be renewed with the Tories, but excepting cases where their candidates were also Orangemen only very conditional backing was offered.

Such attempts to establish an immigrant party and broad loyalist alliance proved short-lived and rather over-ambitious. Nevertheless the independent spirit of the Canadian Orangemen in their political dealings persisted. The lodges began to secure a powerful influence in local politics in the 1840s attracting the younger sons of the Family Compact, including the rising Tory politician, John A Macdonald. The Grand Lodge subsequently formed an association with Macdonald, which was to keep the Orange vote tied to the 'Liberal-Conservative' party for the next forty years – with the party in turn usually including two Orangemen in its cabinet.

Yet even here the Orangemen were not Tory satellites, and were themselves again divided over various religious and educational. issues. It is perhaps best to describe their position as one of 'critical support'. At the time of Macdonald's death in 1891 moreover, as Senior notes, there was neither an outstanding Conservative leader who could capture the imagination of Orangemen nor an Orangeman who could effectively defend within the lodges the Tory policy of co-operation with the Catholic French Canadians.

Difficulties arose, for example, in the 1896 Election when the Conservative government under P M MacKenzie Bowell, himself Orange Grand Master, took oppositional measures against the decision of Manitoba Province to revoke the rights of Roman Catholic schools.

By this date the Grand Lodge had already become increasingly responsive to militant 'Protestants First' type sentiments at large among Canadian Orangemen. Orange/Conservative compromise ended accordingly and all Orangemen were reminded of their duty at the election to oppose candidates favouring remedial legislation on Manitoba. A 'de facto' withdrawal of support for the Conservative party resulted. Orangemen running on Conservative tickets had thus either to reject party policy or run as independents, while in some areas large numbers of the Order voted Liberal. This contributed rather ironically to the return of a Liberal administration under the French Roman Catholic, Laurier.[59]

Liverpool: As early as the 1830s in Liverpool, 'The Whigs apparent Irish Catholic sympathies', Waller suggests, 'inspired a Tory-Protestant alliance'.[60] Protestantism was subsequently to become an 'electoral charm' for the Tories assisting them to dominate both parliamentary and municipal elections.

The Orange lodges which had first formed in the city around

1807-8 probably did have an important role here, though their involvement is not at all well documented at this early stage. It is more certain though that the Conservatives fully played 'the Protestant card' at the 1868 election on Irish Disestablishment and ritualism, when the 'Orange element' was reckoned to be strong. By 1876 the Conservative leader, Edward Whitley, could thank the Orangemen for their support, 'without which no man could lead the Conservative party in Liverpool'. This is a much more unreserved compliment than the LOI ever received from the notables of Glasgow Conservatism.

This support was sustained at the next two elections and particularly in the midst of the Home Rule crisis. Yet also from this period Orange dissent becomes increasingly apparent, as the Tories were perceived to be patronising in an opportunistic manner the political potential of the lodges. Evidence for this was found, for instance, in Conservative leaders absence from the 12th July celebrations which followed the 1886 election, and more generally in their failure to maintain a true 'Protestant position' on the issues of sabbatarianism, temperance and in particular ritualism.

Dissent ripened into open revolt in 1888. Now Orangemen, as in Scotland, under their leadership's direction challenged the leading Tory body, the Liverpool Constitutional Association (LCA). Thus the Orange Provincial Grand Secretary, James Lincoln, formally intimated to the Conservatives that his members were withdrawing from the LCA and accused the Tory leaders, in familiar vein, of 'truckling to Catholics and Ritualists, failing to support an Orangeman, Harry Thomas, in the School Board elections, and ignoring the celebration of the tercentenary of the defeat of the Spanish Armada.' The following year they again asserted their independence by nominating Thomas for the Scotland electoral ward, against an official Conservative candidate. Thomas, came bottom of the poll, and his followers were left avowing that 'Conservatism is Popery of the deepest strain when it is "ritualistic" in the church'.[61]

Relations improved to some extent over the next few years. Yet while, as in Scotland, 'the Union in danger' provided the impetus for renewed links, it did not diminish the centrality of the ritualism issue or the general impression of Tory capitulation to Popery. Again in 1903 the Orangemen were apparently considering a withdrawal from the LCA in protest against the Education Act, the Prison Minister's Bill and the Duke of Norfolk.

THE SCOTTISH CONTEXT

Why was dissent more muted in Scotland? And why was Orange political involvement less impressive when compared not only to Ulster, but to other major transplantations of the Order?

As regards the capacity for independent action, one factor was that electoral conditions in Liverpool and elsewhere were more conducive to strains in Orange political allegiances than were conditions in Scotland. When provincial, local and municipal elections were contested along party lines, with sectarian issues considered appropriate, this simply offered more opportunities to test allies' practical commitment to 'Protestant issues'. The fortuitous timing of national elections could also intervene, as in Canada in 1896, to convert dissident rhetoric from the leadership into action. It is interesting to speculate how the Scottish Orangemen's discontent with the Tories and their threats of independent action over voluntary schools and ecclesiastical disputes would have been realised if a general election had fallen in Britain in 1896 or 1897.

A second contributory factor was precisely the availability and intensity of such issues in Scotland. As regards education, for example, the Canadian Orangemen were forced to defend 'Protestant legislation' already enacted by Manitoba Province from a Conservative administration, while for their Scottish counterparts the issues tended to be less clearly defined around threats of 'Rome on the rates' or a 'Popish University'.

Similarly, although the threat of ritualism was deeply felt by the Scottish Grand Lodge leadership it remained at one stage removed, being essentially a problem for the Church of England and without a real material basis in Scotland. It is useful to contrast this situation with Liverpool where the issue had a commanding presence. Ritualistic practices frequently outraged popular feeling in the city. At St. John's church in Toxteth, for example, services were fairly conventional but the vicar faced eastwards during the profession of the Apostles' Creed. In the face of this 'abomination', protesters either faced west or withdrew from the church. Early in 1887 a crisis was reached when churchwardens jostled the vicar and extinguished an altar candle to prevent the church becoming a 'house of Baal'.[62] Such scenes, as suggested in Chapter 7, were largely unknown in Scotland.

Thirdly, in considering the level of dissent, one must return to the relatively marginalised position of the Scottish Orangeism in the calculations of their Tory allies. For, despite bold claims to be 'the mainspring of Conservatism', the reality of their position was detrimental to that degree of self confidence, evident in Liverpool and

Canada, which was a prerequisite to a more consistently independent attitude.

We come finally, however, to the explanation of this more limited political role itself. Obviously important here were the familiar internal characteristics of the Scottish LOI. There was, for example, the Order's lesser numerical progress in Scotland. Around 25-30,000 members were estimated towards the turn of the century, while, of its other major transplantations Liverpool alone had 17,000 Orangemen around 1880, and in Canada the Order had made particularly rapid strides growing from 13,000 members in 1836 to 40,000 by 1850, and 100,000 by the 1870s.[63] Interacting with this was the unsavoury reputation Scottish Orangeism had gained for violence and general rowdiness, from as early as the 1820s. This it was suggested helped shape LU relations with the LOI and often lay behind Conservative perceptions of their allies.

Yet for a really satisfactory explanation here, as argued in dealing with the LOI's relative weakness generally in Scotland, some broader 'external' features of Scottish society must also be taken into account. After all the Liverpool Orangemen had suffered similar handicaps from unfavourable subjective judgements, and even in Ulster the rhetorical query 'Who would be an Orangemen?' still had currency into the 1870s and 80s.[64]

Two central points stand out. First it is important to stress that for a large part of the period under study the political force which the LOI chose to support – the Conservative party – was itself marginalised in most of Scotland. Alex Whitelaw, elected in 1874, was Glasgow's first Tory MP since the 1832 Reform Act, and it was not until the 1880s that the Tories begin to gain real prominence in the West of Scotland. This is in strong contrast to Liverpool where they were the dominant party in parliamentary and municipal elections from 1841 and also differs from Canada where the Tories held office from 1840-96.

Moreover, when the commercial sections of the Scottish bourgeoisie did decisively desert the Liberal standard after 1886, it was not to the Tories they turned, as in Ulster, but to their own Liberal Unionist party – on whose electoral co-operation the Tories were dependent for success until the closing years of the century.

As for the Scottish working class and petty bourgeoisie, the Liberals still remained the party of the majority even after 1886. Although in the 1890s links with the Liberals began to break down, as the party's ambivalent attitude towards its working class support became clearer and internal divisions over the direction of British imperialism grew, it was the need for independently-based working class representation which became increasingly recognised in Scotland, eventually finding expression notably in the ILP.

These points suggest an important but very indirect role of Smith's 'Liberal Commonsense' in checking Scottish Orangemen's advance – namely as a bulwark against full-blown working class Toryism which might have given the LOI access into the mainstream of Scottish political life. This seems more plausible than the notion of a Labour movement/Orange dichotomy, where the latter is won over by the transmission of the former's neutralising, progressive and anti-sectarian ideas.[65]

Finally, in analysing the LOI's political impact a suggestion of Gallagher's is also useful. Examining the lesser extent of 'inter-ethnic conflict' generally in Scotland, he suggests one possible reason may be that the scope of Scottish-based movements was limited, owing to the fact that most political decision making took place outside the country.[66]

In this way, even when the Scottish Orangemen did throw their weight behind parliamentary candidates like C B Renshaw and J G A Baird or where one of their own number stood like William Whitelaw, they had little subsequent control over them. For once returned to Westminster, these figures were bound by national party demands and the realities of these most frequently outweighed platform pledges to support convent inspection, the repeal of Catholic emancipation and other issues dear to Orange hearts. It is possible to capture some of the Orangemen's resulting frustration in the Rev. Townsend's remarks on Glasgow MPs as 'dumb dogs' in parliament.[67] Ulster Orangemen, too, may have shared this frustration at times, but their Scottish brethren did not even have the compensation of local and municipal elections at which such issues could be legitimately raised. In this situation there is something rather plaintive in the frequent memorials and petitions dispatched earnestly, but without effect, to Beaconsfield and other Conservative leaders at a safe distance in London.

NOTES

1. *Scottish News*, 12/5/86.
2. Levy Ph.D., *op. cit.* (1983), Chapter IV.
3. Levy, *loc. cit.* (1983).
4. GH and NBDM, 6/7/86, 24/6/86 for meetings. Blackfriars nominations 2/7/86.
5. GH, 3/7/86, for example.
6. NBDM, 2/8/87.
7. *Ibid.*
8. GH, 29/7/87.
9. GH, 1/8/87.

10. GH, McCormick meetings, 7/6/88, 13/6/88. Other meetings 6/6/88, 14/6/88. NBDM, 14/6/88. A similar pattern was evident in the Govan and Partick by-elections of 1889.
11. NBDM, 6/5/92.
12. NBDM, 4/7/92.
13. GH, 13/7/92.
14. GH, 14/7/90.
15. GH, 5/7/92, 6/7/92 for his victory.
16. GH, 3/7/95. NBDM, 3/7/95, 14/7/95.
17. GH, 18/7/95.
18. The Unionists milked the patriotic issue for all it was worth, even inviting a war-blinded Gordon Highlander's Officer on a Paisley platform. NBDM, 2/10/1900.
19. GH, 22/9/1900.
20. GH, 26/9/1900.
21. GH, 3/10/1900.
22. *West of Scotland Branch of the Liberal Committee for the Maintenance of the Legislative Union between Great Britain and Ireland* (WSLCMLU) *minute book* 1886. *West of Scotland Liberal Unionist Association* (WSLU) *minute book 1894-1912,* Conservative office, Edinburgh.
23. *GCA annual reports 1886-1900.* They are C and J Summers, J McManus, W Young and H B Wilson.
24. *GCAAR,* 1899.
25. *Ibid,* 1893.
26. *National Union of Conservative Associations for Scotland, 1893 Annual Report.* Miscellaneous material relating to National Union and Western Divisional Council, *Minute Book* 1893-1902.
27. *Partick Star,* 27/7/95.
28. NBDM, 28/7/87. The Bailie frequently referred to its rival as the 'North British Daily *Wail'.*
29. Levy *op. cit.* (1983), Chapter IV.
30. GN, 28/7/87.
31. HTA to PS 22/1/90. Parker Smith Correspondence, Strathclyde Regional Archives.
32. QJ to PS, 8/2/90, Strathclyde Regional Archives.
33. NBDM, 19/7/95.
34. See Levy for details, *op. cit.* (1983), Chapter IX.
35. *Ibid,* See Chapter III.
36. E.g. G H 3/7/93, 11/7/98. Grahame granted them use of his land at Belshill.
37. GCAAR, *loc. cit.,* for Glasgow constituencies. For Greenock, GT, July 1886, July 1892 and June/July 1895, September/October 1900. Especially 23/6/92, 3/7/95, 10/7/95, 25/9/1900. No Orangemen can be identified among nominators supporters or platform guests in this now strongly LU seat. No. 6 Ward, though, was reckoned to be strongly Orange, 5/7/85.
38. NBDM, 26/9/00.
39. ibid.
40. *Ibid.*
41. GO, 29/9/00. 'Clear him out' exhorted the *Observer.*
42. GH, 12/7/86.
43. GH, 15/7/88.
44. NBDM, 28/6/92.
45. GH, 5/1/89.
46. GH, 10/7/93.

47. GT, 29/6/92. Also indicative of greater self-reliance was McManus' decision to contest No. 1 Ward Bridgeton. He was unsuccessful. See GH, 14/10/96, 3/11/96. (He did few public meetings.) Result 4/11/96.
48. See Waller, op.cit. (1981).
49. GH, 12/7/97.
50. GH, 11/7/98.
51. *Ibid.*
52. GH, 9/7/1900.
53. GH, 13/7/1900.
54. *Daily Record,* 2/10/1900. See also letter from H A Long defending Provand 3/10/00.
55. J C Beckett, *The Making of Modern Ireland 1603-1923* (1962), p. 399.
56. H Senior, *Orangeism, the Canadian Phase* (n.d.) p. 92.
57. *Ibid,* p. 16.
58. *Ibid,* p. 21 and p. 29.
59. *Ibid,* pp. 88-90.
60. Waller, *op. cit.* (1981), p. 18.
61. *Ibid,* p. 183.
62. *Ibid,* p. 172.
63. Senior, *op. cit.* (n.d), p. 77.
64. Dewar *et al, op. cit.* (1967), p. 56.
65. Smith, *op. cit.* (1984). Discussed in chapters 2 and 5 above.
66. T Gallagher, *Glasgow : The Uneasy Peace* (1987), p. 35.
67. GH, 11/7/89.

Postscript
Orangeism in Modern Scotland

For an 'anachronism at birth' the Orange Order has survived remarkably well in modern Scotland. The main challenge has come from elements of broad structural change in the Scottish economy and society, which have reduced the scope for discretionary practices in the workplace and housing market, and promoted cross-sectarian ties. Yet explanations for the movement's survival are to be found less in adaptation to these changes, than in the preservation of key characteristics from its formative years in the nineteenth century. The most important continuities have been in the lodges' social and communal function, in their failure to be reduced to simply Tory adjuncts, and in the Grand Lodge's willingness, whether out of timidity or astuteness, to avoid potentially damaging tests of strength. In other words, as Gallagher suggests, the Order has shown an appropriate awareness of its own limitations in a Scottish setting.[1]

The new century had opened with the Orangemen in fairly good heart, albeit experiencing one of their periodic estrangements from the Scottish Unionists. Unwillingness to check ritualism and Mr Balfour's 'Popery Bills' on education, prompted Grand Lodge attempts in 1904 to organise an independent Protestant organisation 'unfettered by party ties'. The drive for independent Protestant representation was swiftly stemmed though, for the renewed Home Rule crisis in Ireland drove the Orange leadership back into the established political fold, and in 1913 Grand Master Rev. David Ness was co-opted by the Scottish Unionist whip onto the executive committee of the Western Divisional Council.[2] At last, this development was complemented by the willingness of leading Tories like Sir John Gilmour, Secretary of State for Scotland, to assume honourary positions in the Order.[3]

Yet beneath an apparently impressive rapprochement Orange relations with the Unionists reflected the Order's generally circumscribed progress in Scotland. While the Lodges continued to campaign in specific localities in Glasgow, Lanarkshire and Ayrshire, the 'Orange card' still had limited validity, especially in constituencies where ex-Liberals had joined in an anti-socialist alliance. It is also doubtful how much impact on policy-making the co-opted Orangemen were actually permitted.

Two factors prevented the Order in the 1920s and 1930s becoming simply a redoubt of Tory working class votes. First, the conditional nature of Orange support for the Unionists was reasserted, as the latter were perceived to be deserting the Protestant colours over the 1921 Anglo-Irish Treaty. On January 11 1922 the secretary of the wDC read a letter from the Grand Lodge of Scotland to the effect that they wished to discontinue their association with the Unionist party and that their representatives would cease attending wDC meetings.[4] Dissent culminated in a characteristically half-hearted political adventure. An Orange and Protestant Party was formed in 1923. Its one MP Hugh Ferguson, representing Motherwell, took the Tory whip in Parliament. Ferguson was defeated after a year, and although the fledgling party was reabsorbed by the Unionists, formal Orange-Tory relations did not subsequently prosper beyond the early 1930s.[5]

Secondly, once official ties had been broken, and as Ireland diminished as a political issue, the way seems to have opened for more 'progressive' sections of the Orange membership to turn, not to their old enemies the Liberals who were identified with Home Rule, but to a new political force in the 1920s – the emerging ILP. This seems to have been the case in the Lanarkshire villages of Harthill and Larkhall.[6] Allegiances here were not, of course, unqualified and Labour selection of Roman Catholic candidates and sympathy with the new Dublin government were sources of friction, but in this way the LOI was at last confronted with multiple loyalties among its rank and file. This in turn rendered impractical the united political front which had characterised much of the nineteenth century. Increasingly then from the 1930s onwards a 'no politics' rule at many lodges seems to have operated.[7]

In the volatile inter-war decades the Order had further threats to face, from a rather novel source. As detailed by Bruce and Gallagher, the loss of national self-confidence and the economic slump in Scotland provided appropriate conditions for the emergence of local militant Protestant parties, dedicated to replacing 'secular politics by the politics of religious identity and religious principle'.[8]

The Scottish Protestant League, led by Alexander Ratcliffe, not only castigated Orangeism for its 'milk and water' defence of Protestantism, but enjoyed a short-lived local election success in Glasgow to which the Order could hardly have aspired. Potentially more problematic was the Edinburgh-based Protestant Action

movement. Its leader John Cormack made direct attempts to trans-
form Orangeism from the inside into a vigorous, independent
political force. The Order's decisive rejection of these overtures
resembled its response to the populist 100 at the turn of the century,
but received even greater impetus from Protestant Action's 'street
politics' which ran contrary to the Grand Lodge's longstanding
quest for respectability. Its unwillingness to commit its mass
membership to Protestant Action apparently speeded this dubious
fringe party's demise, leaving its own position as the largest institutionalised form of militant Protestantism intact.

While outpacing its more politicised rivals in the 1930s, the Order
found the altered conditions of post-war Scotland more difficult to
confront. A series of long term socio-economic shifts threatened its
level of support.

The heavy industries, steel and shipbuilding where the LOI had
traditionally drawn a large section of its membership, entered a
phase of radical decline, so that by 1971 they provided only 7.9% of
jobs in the economy.[9] Mining too began a long run-down, threatening the viability of villages in Ayrshire and Lanarkshire which had
also been the bases of membership. This process was compounded
by programmes of slum clearance which transplanted populations
from the key Orange areas of Bridgeton, Blackfriars and Camlachie,
although some Orangemen did regroup in the peripheral estates and
New Towns.[10]

More indirectly, industries were increasingly either nationalised
or owned and controlled from outside Scotland - in 1973 58% of
employees in manufacturing had to deal with employers in the
United States or London.[11] With standardised personnel proce-
dures, multi-plant companies were less likely to implement selective
recruitment along religious lines than the old ironmasters and
shipbuilders.

Furthermore, most sections of industry were now reliant on some
form of state aid in line with regional development policy. The
intrusion of Central Government values further tended to mitigate
the potential for sectarian employment practices, while on the local
level professionalised administration in housing and local government undermined Orange claims, however justified they were in the
first place, to advance the interests of the 'brethren'.

A final, less tangible process had further negative implications.
With roots in nineteenth century urbanisation, the process of
seeularisation intensified in Scotland after 1945, evident in the
institutionalised decline in religous participation and affiliation.
While the precise impact on Orange membership levels is doubtful,

since the Order had from the outset drawn a large number of adherents from 'the unchurched', this development did reinforce the Lodges' peripheral position in a modern society where religious issues in general, not just 'Protestant' ones had become increasingly displaced. Nor did shared adversity promote closer links with the churches. On the contrary, a by-product of secularisation in the Church of Scotland was greater enthusiasm for ecumenicalism, involving co-operation with other churches, including the Roman Catholics, rather than the Orangemen.

Given these unfavourable circumstances, the Order entered a period of retrenchment in the 1950s, its survival dependant on its traditional strengths - public processions and the lodges' convivial role. Licenced social clubs flourished, recognised in the formation of a Union of Social Clubs in association with the LOI.[12] While benefitting the Order materially, these did little to counter its reputation for paying lipservice to temperance and sabbatarianism. In particular, perceptions of the lodges as drink-orientated were to alienate independent evangelical ministers such as David Cassells and Jack Glass, who might otherwise have been allies.

Tensions developed within the movement. In 1958 the colourful figure of Rev. Alan Hassan was elected as Grand Master. Leading parades from horseback, like C I Paton eighty years before, he also attempted single-handedly to reform the Order along similar lines to the nineteenth century Grand Lodge. Hassan's primary aim was to evangelise the membership using the Orange newspaper *Vigilant*. Again this was sweetened for the rank and file by an uncompromising critique of 'papal aggression'. Secondly, he hoped to use the subsequently transformed Order as an independent force to promote Protestantism in the political arena.

In both of these respects Hassan was disappointed. The Orangemen's personal conduct still proved difficult to redeem, while personality conflicts in the Grand Lodge seem to have contributed to his ignominious downfall.[13]

Following this rather embarrassing period, with charges of fraud and counter-charges of 'time-serving', Orangeism entered another quiescent phase. Although the religious emphasis was maintained, the Grand Lodge showed less interest in a politically assertive role. From the late 1960s though, the Order's passivity was challenged by the re-emergence of conflict in Ulster.

The immediate effect of 'the Troubles' was to boost membership, as indeed had been the case with successive Home Rule crises. In the longer term though, they reasserted a familiar dilemma. On the one hand, the Grand Lodge was 'legitimated by action', especially over the issue of Ulster where many members had close fraternal ties, yet to be identified with violence and unlawful activity would produce conflict with the authorities in Scotland. This was pragmatically resolved by combining spirited resolutions from Twelfth July platforms, with considerable reserve towards Protestant paramilitaries like the UDA and UVF. To some extent the latter attitude altered with the escalation of sectarian attacks against fellow Orangemen in Ulster in the mid-1970s. An Orange distress fund was established to help Loyalist prisoners and their families, but the Grand Lodge was still adamant in utterly rejecting, 'all support be it active or tacit, of terrorist organisations, where actions contravene the laws of the land.[14]

This muted position proved wise, given the manner in which the Ulster crisis was received in Scotland. Despite superficial similarities with Ulster and a well-established tradition of labour migration, the Scottish setting, as stressed throughout this account, remained quite distinct. As Bruce indicates, the majority of the population have interpreted the crisis not as 'Catholic aggression', but as, 'what happens if you mix religion and politics'.[15] A more insistent stance by the LOI would have thus incurred the charge of importing sectarian conflict. Besides, without a real physical threat to Protestants in Scotland, paramilitaries here have been more isolated and less well resourced. Consequently, they have also been less well able to challenge the Order over its relative moderation than their Ulster counterparts.

Such then have been the oscillating fortunes of Orangeism in the twentieth century; but how does the modern movement compare with that of the nineteenth century? The impression is above all that conspicuous numerical strength in the marching season is still balanced by the Order's position on the margins of Scottish society. The zeal of the Grand Lodge to reform the average Orangeman points, for example, to the persistence of the Order's reputation for intemperance and rowdiness in press and public opinion. When a number of violent incidents attended the 1986 Twelfth July parade in Glasgow, the *Sunday Post* responded in character. Apart from the standards of journalism, its editorial 'Time to Call a Halt?' could have come from the *Glasgow Herald* or *Glasgow News* in 1870s.

> Many feel that, at a time when Glasgow is making a successful effort to present a revitalised image of itself to the world, the appalling behaviour witnessed last Saturday will only reinforce visitors' impressions of Glasgow as a city populated by drunks and neds.[16]

The Order's determination to remain relatively aloof from the

Ulster crisis has probably mitigated impressions of 'Irishness', though whether the label of 'home-grown bigotry' is preferable to one of 'imported bigotry' is open to question.

It is in the area of politics that most change is evident. Links with the Conservatives have considerably weakened with the party coming under heavy criticism for its handling of the Ulster situation when in government in the 1970s and 80s. It has been suggested that the majority of Orangemen are now Labour voters, though a number may have been attracted to the Scottish National Party from the 1970s, like the ILP an emergent and 'neutral' political force.[17] More enduring has been the Order's political timidity and distrust of high-profile developments beyond its control. Conservative support for the Anglo-Irish Agreement in 1986 did prompt the Order into sponsoring a new party, the Scottish Unionist Party (SUP), commited to fight nine Tory-held seats, but in practice this challenge melted away at the General Election and no candidates were actually fielded.

The LOI is also anxious to distance itself from the taint of illegality. A recent trial of Scottish UDA members for would-be terrorist activity revealed that the five convicted men were members of a Perth Orange lodge. Orange Grand Secretary, David Bryce, pointed out that LOL St Andrew's True Blues was, in fact, a rogue lodge which had frequently been censored for 'behaviour below normal standards'.[18]

As for the future of Orangeism in Scotland, there are three possible lines of development. The first and least realistic is an alliance with fascist groups like the British Movement, which in the 1980s have added the Ulster issue to their more familiar racist agenda. Their 'Ulster is British' stance might appeal to some rank and file members - possibly to the younger element who have already been drawn to the Scottish Loyalists, a ginger group formed in 1979 with aspirations towards 'street politics'.[19] For the Grand Lodge, though, to respond to fascist overtures and mobilise its mass membership in this direction would be to take a fundamental departure from the movement's history over the past century. It is difficult to see why the Orange Order should give official support to groups with a minimal presence in Scotland, simply because they have chosen to cynically exploit the Ulster crisis, when in the past it has rejected genuine Protestant parties at the height of their popularity. There are also ideological objections. Pointing to the Roman Catholic origins of leading Fascists in history, Hitler, Mussolini, Franco, and of many British Fascists, such as Martin Webster, Fascism itself is dismissed by some Orangemen as a Jesuit-inspired plot. This is reinforced by reference to the historical instances of clerical support for Fascism in Italy and Spain, or to the 'Blueshirt' movement in the Irish Free State in the 1930s. The LOI's present periodical *The Orange Torch* has various examples. The following passage is characteristic:

> ... in the BBC's programme on Martin Luther slick attempts were made to equate Luther's anti-semitism – a product of his Romanist upbringing... – with Protestantism and German Protestantism with Nazism' That the programme's producers reckoned they could get away with this, shows how ignorant the public are about *the Papist origins of Fascism (including Nazism) everywhere.*[20]

So all-embracing is the Orange conspiracy theory that Fascism's anti-Semitic version appears stunted in comparison.[21]

The second possibility is a more political Order. This is a lingering ambition for some sections of the leadership though the exact form is rather vague.[22] Certainly, in common with the Scottish churches, the Order has shown greater concern for 'social issues' in the 1980s, reflected, for example, in the emergency resolution, moved by Grand Master Magnus Bain, calling all Orangemen to support the fight for the Ravenscraig Steel Plant.[23] Yet it does not seem feasible for Orangeism to move beyond generalised sentiments, given the variety of political alignments that now exist among its members. The prospects for greater overt political involvement as a campaigning body for the preservation of 'civil and religious liberty' are similarly limited. The salience of politics has been declining in the Order over the last three decades. The abortive SUP venture was an exception, but one unlikely to encourage Orangemen further in a political direction.

A more likely development is for the lodges to place a greater reliance on their welfare and charitable functions. This route has been increasingly followed in North America where Orangeism is now viewed as primarily an 'ethnic' or 'cultural' organisation. In Scotland it offers particular advantages. Welfare provision for its own members is important, since many lodges function in economically depressed areas. Relief work for prisoners and fundraising and other Loyalist causes helps forstall criticism from more militant members over the Order's inactivity in the Ulster crisis, though the Grand Lodge is careful to stress it does not raise money for arms. In addition, it is no doubt hoped that donations made to independent charities will go a little way to rehabilitate the Order's reputation with the broader public. In response to recent criticism this was one aspect of the Order's activity which was emphatically stressed, with fundraising for the Save the Children Fund forming an important part of its celebrations of the 300th anniversary of the Glorious Revolution.[23]

Despite the constraints of a Scottish setting, if this 'low risk' philanthropic option is coupled with maintenance of the traditional public processions, and a concern for the social and recreational potential of local lodges, there seems little reason why Orangeism should not continue well into the next century. For the key to its existence, as argued throughout in this account, lies not in 'deviance' or 'conspiracy', but in the movement's continued grounding in the daily conditions of life of its predominantly working class membership.

NOTES

1. Gallagher, *op.cit.* (1987), p.175.
2. D W Urwin, The Development of the Conservative Party in Scotland till 1912, *Scottish Historical Review*, Vol 41, 1965.
3. Gallagher, *op.cit.* (1987), p.144.
4. WDC Minute Book, 11/1/1922.
5. Gallagher, *op.cit.* (1987), p.149.
6. McDonagh, *op.cit.* (197?).
7. Interview JMcF.
8. Bruce, *op.cit.* (1985), p.54; See also T Gallagher, *Edinburgh Divided* (1988).
9. J Foster and C Woolfson, *The Politics of the UCS Work-In* (1986), Chapter 1, 'Clydeside Capital and the Regional Question' for an excellent introduction to the post-war period.
10. Bruce, *op.cit.* (1985), p.255. The Order also seems to have followed the pattern of labour migration to the North East with the development of the oil industry.
11. Foster and Woolfson, *op.cit.* (1986), p.22.
12. Bruce, *op.cit.* (1985), pp.201-2.
13. *ibid.* Chapter 6 for a detailed account.
14. *ibid.* p.169.
15. *ibid.* p.296.
16. *Sunday Post*, 19/7/1985.
17. For Labour, see Gallagher, *op.cit.* (1987), p.330.
18. *The Scotsman*, 7/8/1989.
19. Gallagher, *op.cit.* (1987), p.297.
20. *Orange Torch* n.d. (Probably 1983.)
21. Alexander Ratcliffe of the SPL did develop fascist links. Indicating the Byzantine potential of conspiracy theory, he saw the Jesuits as a group of Jews who had taken over the Catholic Church and used it as a Zionist Front. Bruce *op.cit.* (1985), p.75.
22. Gallagher, *op.cit.* (1987), p.331.
23. *The Scotsman*, 13/7/1986.
24. *The Evening Times*, 8/12/1988.

Appendix A

District Lodges' Numbers and Locations *c.* 1878

No.	Location	No.	Location
1	Airdrie	28	Thornliebank
2	Glasgow	29	Kilmarnock
3	Glasgow	30	Greenock
4	Maybole	31	Bridgeton
5	Greenock/Port Glasgow	32	Slammannan
6	Paisley	33	*
7	Unknown (hereafter indicated by *)	34	Greenock
		35	*
8	Bellshill	36	Falkirk
9	Kilwinning, North Ayrshire	37	Glasgow, Calton
10	*	38	Glasgow, Cowcaddens
11	Irvine	39	*
12	*	40	Cumnock
13	Renfrew	41	Glasgow, Anderston (Later Greenock)
14	Irvine and Dalry	42	Glasgow, Govan
15	Partick	43	Dalry and Glengarnock, North Ayrshire
16	Wishaw		
17	Glasgow, Calton	44	Glasgow, Bridgeton/Dalmarnock
18	Johnstone, Renfrew	45	Glasgow
19	Port Glasgow	46	Partick/Whiteinch
20	Rutherglen	47	*
21	Glasgow, Parkhead	48	West Lothian
22	Coatbridge (founded 1863)	49	Motherwell
23	Stevenston (founded 1864)	50	Glasgow, Gorbals (founded 1880)
24	Glasgow, Candleriggs		
25	*	51	Glasgow, Anderston.
26	Airdrie		
27	*		

Compiled chiefly from *The Glasgow News, The Glasgow Herald, The Greenock Telegraph, The Glasgow Sentinal.*

The districts which could not be positively identified were probably in South Ayrshire, Wigtown, Dumfries and West Lothian.

Appendix B
Greenock Orangemen: Occupational Breakdown 1879-86

Name	*Occupation*	*Address*
James Barclay	Joiner	Ingleston Street
J Boden	Pansman	Trafalgar Street
Alex Bradley	Seaman	Drumfrochar Road
Johnathan Burns	Labourer	Cathcart Street
Joseph Campbell	Ironworker	Crescent Street
William Chambers	Labourer	John Street
William Chapman	Seaman	Cathcart Street
Robert Chestnut	Wine & Spirit Merchant	Cathcart Street
Andrew Craig	Baker	Sir Michael Street
Thomas Currie	Labourer	Drumfrochar Road
R H Dignum	Clergyman	*
J. Dobbin	Labourer	Prospecthill Road
Robert Farrel	Grocer	Main Street
H Forbes	Engineer	Cathcart Street
J Fulton	Trunkmaker	Market Street
Robert Gamble	Labourer	Belleville Street
R Gemmel	Labourer	Holmscroft Street
P Gordon	Labourer	Ingleston Street
James Gray	Joiner	Prospecthill Road
R Halliday	Gatekeeper	Crescent Street
Adam Hunter	Engineer	Ingleston Street
Robert Hutcheson	Labourer	Ann Street
William Hutcheson	Labourer	Roxburgh Street
William Hyde	Labourer	Drumfrochar Road
J Jackson	Moulder	Crescent Street
R Johnston	Labourer	Drumfrochar Road
William Lee	Labourer	Drumfrochar Road
James Leslie	Boilermaker	John Street
James Lynn	Tenter	Drumfrochar Road
John Lyon	Brass Founder	Baker Street
Robert Madill	Coal and Wood Merchant	Captain Street
Alex Martin	Labourer	Bruce Street
S H Miller	Wine & Spirit Merchant	Nelson Street
William Miller	Fitter	East Crawford Street
A J Moleseed	Painter	West Blackhall Street
John Mories	Salesman	Nicholson Street
R M McCauchy	Sugar Sampler	Ann Street

Name	*Occupation*	*Address*
Arthur Macfarlane	Veterinary Surgeon	Kelly Street
A McGowan	Broker	Shaw Street
William McInnes	Cooper	Kelly Street
W J Mackenzie	Ironmonger	Shaw Street
H McMaugh	Labourer	West Blackhall Street
Archibald McNeil	Woolsorter	Prospecthill Road
William McQuoid	Cartwright	Mount Pleasant Road
James Nixon	Joiner	Market Street
James Rattray	Missionary (formerly Boilermaker)	Dempster Street
T Ross	Yardsman	West Blackhall Street
W Ross	Labourer	Baker Street
Alex Steel	Foreman, J. Poynter, Manufacturing Chemists	Dellingburn Street
S Sloan	Labourer	Wellington Street
Andrew Swan	Slater	Finnart Street
William Swan	Sailmaker	Regent Street

Compiled from *Greenock Telegraph*, Greenock *Post Office Directory*, Fowler's *Greenock Directory*

Appendix C
Greenock Orangemen: Occupational Breakdown 1892

Name	Occupation	Address
R J Allan	Labourer	Wemyss Bay Street
James Ballantyne	Labourer	Serpentine Walk
W Barnes	Labourer	Crescent Street
R Bell	Watchman	Ingleston Street
Samuel Bell	Grocer	St. Lawrence Street
R Berryman	Labourer	Bearhope Street
Henry Braine	Labourer	Dempster Street
A Brymer	Blacksmith	Mount Pleasant Street
William Carson	Fireman	Dempster Street
J T Clark	Carter	Drumfrochar Road
J Craig	Smith	Ann Street
R Gamble[†]	Labourer	Belleville Street
William Gillanders	Mashman	Inverkip Street
P Gordon	Labourer	Belleville Street
William Halliday	Labourer	Drumfrochar Road
W Hill	Policeman	Wellington Street
W Hyde[†]	Labourer	Drumfrochar Road
Robert Johnstone	Labourer	Drumfrochar Road
W Kerr	Plumber	Drumfrochar Road
T Kyle	Joiner	Belleville Street
James Leith	Grocer	Mearns Street
James Lynn[†]	Tenter	Drumfrochar Road
James Magee	Engineer	Carwood Street
J Marshall	Patternmaker	Ingelston Street
Alex Martin	Joiner	Wellington Street
W Martin	Woolsorter	Dempster Street
Hugh Matheson	Fitter	Old Hillend
J. Mountford	Curator, Mechanics Institute	*
R Murphy	Marine Store Dealer	*
D McAllister	Janitor, Glebe Public School	Crawfurd Street
James McEachran	Spirit Dealer	Lawrence Street
Malcolm McLean	Joiner	Holmscroft Street
W Ross[†]	Labourer	Baker Street
W Ross	Grocer	Drumfrochar Road
James Spense	Rivetter	Hill Street
Alex Steel[†]	Foreman	Dellingburn Street

Name	*Occupation*	*Address*
Henry Walker	Insurance Agent	Belleville Street
T Wilton	Carpenter	John Street

Compiled from *Greenock Telegraph* and Fowler's Directory 'Loyal Orange Institution' entry, pp.99-100.
† Also in 1870-86 list.

Appendix D
Paisley Orangemen: Occupational Breakdown 1866–86

Name	*Occupation*	*Address*
Henry Archer	Thatcher	High Street
William Barbour	Clerk, Bank of Scotland	Causeyside
W J Bell	Ham Curer and Provision	Calside Merchant
Robert Blair	Tailor	George Street
A Brisbane	Cowfeeder	Cotton Street
James Browne	Clerk, Joint Lines Railway	Underwood Road
P Burt	Draper	Calside
Jas Burton	Labourer	*
J Clark	Shuttlemaker	Causeyside
Hamilton Coats	Church Officer	Cotton Street
W Cockburn	Clerk, Caledonian Railway	Wardrop Street
H Enterkin	Cutter	Gauze Street
Robert Farmer	Coal Merchant	Westmarch
J Fair	Labourer	*
R Fisher	Draper	New Street
Alex Fraser	Tenter	Water Brae
T Fraser	Wine & Spirit Merchant	New Sneddon Street
R Galbraith	Chemist	Gauze Street
A N Gardner	Printer	East Greenlaw
T Graham	Doctor	Garthland Place
J Hair	Boot and Shoe Makers	Canal Street
G Hair	as above	
J Johnstone	Fishmonger	George Street
T. Muir	Insurance Agent	Castlehead
David Macbryde	Patternmaker	Barclay Street
P McCluskie	Sawyer	*
James Quinn	Labourer	Thread Street
A Parlane	Printer	Gilmour Street
R Patterson	Grocer	George Street
A R Pollock	Drysalters Firm (Proprietor)	Greenhill
W Robinson	Minister, Primitive Methodist Church	Abbey Close
E Schollan	Spirit Merchant	Moss Street
Mr Smellie	Gentleman	Gallowhill

| D Sloan | Feuar | Queen Street |
| Hugh Thomson | Brewery Worker | High Street |

Appendix E
Biographical Index

John Adamson: Billposter, treasurer of LOL. No. 442, Maryhill.

James Allen: Deputy Master, LOL. No. 340, Greenock 1880-4.

Archibald Allison: Tory Sheriff of Lanarkshire 1830s. Prominent freemason but hostile to Orangemen. Antiquary and author of 'Some Account of My Life and Writings'. Obituary, *Blackwood's Magazine*, May 1867.

W J Anderson: Joiner and cabinet maker. Glasgow Orange official 1870s on, GPM, LOL No. 239, HSGM.

William Angus: Moulder, PM, LOL No. 442, Maryhill. Active in Maryhill Conservative Association from its inception in 1885. Died 1913.

James Bain: Ironmaster, Lord Provost of Glasgow, Conservative candidate 1880 Glasgow election. An ambitious politician, eventually MP for Whitehaven. See *Bailie* No. 6 and 387 for portrait and *The Lord Provosts of Glasgow 1833-83*.

R Baxter: Engineer, Secretary of No. 44 Partick District, 1881.

Edmund Bell: Officebearer, Orange Institution of Great Britain 1860s and 70s in Partick District. Agent for Scottish and District Railway Company.

James Browne: District Master, Paisley. Clerk, Joint Lines Railway 1885.

John Brown: Secretary, No. 31 (Bridgeton) District, 1884.

Jonathon Burns: Labourer, PM, LOL. No. 344, Greenock, WM LOL No . 97, 'Blythswood's Purple Heroes', 1880s .

W Cadman: Leather merchant, Park Place, Glasgow. Instrumental in setting up Glasgow Working Men's Conservative Association. Chairman 6th Ward Conservative election committee 1874. Appeared on Orange platform, Johnstone 1871.

Archibald Campbell: (Lord Blythswood) Born 22/2/1837. Served in Crimea. 1873-4 represented West Renfrewshire as MP and from 1885-1892. Become a Peer 1892. ADC to Queen Victoria. Presided over various Paisley Orange *soirées*. Obituary, *Glasgow Herald*, 8/7/1908, see also *Prominent Profiles*, J.M. Hamilton (1902), *Bailie* No. 25, 1/9/1873 .

Rev. J K Campbell: Minister of Augustine Established Church Mission, Greenock, and former UP clergyman. Elected Greenock School Board 1873. Active 'convert' to Orangeism from 1879 .

Thomas Caulfield: WM LOL No. 680, Royal True Blues, Glasgow, 1885 .

Rev. H Charleton: Minister in the Irish Presbyterian church. Called to Greenock, Wellpark Church of Scotland (the Irish Protestant 'Orange Church'), 1876. Called later to Stranraer. Active in Orange Public events 1870s and 80s.

Robert Chestnut: Wine and Spirit Merchant. Treasurer, LOL No. 336, Greenock . Candidate in School Board elections.

Robert Clements: First Deputy Grand Master of Scotland, in effective control 1835-1860s. Surgeon, residing at Gallowgate, Glasgow.

Hamilton Coats: Prominent in Paisley Orangeism 1880s. Church Officer.

Rev. G M College: Wesleyan Methodist Greenock. Orange supporter, on 1874 *soirée* platform.

Laurence Craigie: Lawyer. Secretary of Royal Gordon Lodge, Glasgow. Died 1834.

J N Cuthbertson: Merchant in chemical products. Conservative politician, contested St. Rollox Glasgow unsuccessfully 1885 and 1886. Orange sympathies though remained outside the Institution. See *Bailie* 18/2/80 for portrait.

Rev. R H Dignum: Chaplain to Greenock Orangemen 1870s. Ulsterman. Minister of Wellpark Church of Scotland, called to Partick Congregation, 1876 .

James Dudgeon:. Eating-house keeper. Officebearer LOL No. 44, 'No Surrender', Glasgow.

W Ellis: Boot and shoe manufacturer, Bridgeton. Grand Treasurer 1896.

Earl of Enniskillen: William Willoughby Cole, 1807-86, Grand Master of Scotland, 1835-1860s.

J E Fairlie: Surgeon, HDGM, Glasgow. Tory, Chairman of 2nd ward committee.

Robert Farmer: Coal merchant, District Master Paisley 1880s.

Rev. W Fraser: Strong Tory and Orange partisan, though not an LOI member. Minister, Free Middle Church, Paisley. 'Thorough constitutionalist' in his political opinions he was opposed to disestablishment and an ardent pamphleteer. Member of Paisley Philosophical Society and addressed 'Social Science' meeting in 1861. *Paisley Express* 23/9/79, 29/9/79 for obituary and funeral.

Rev. A Fullerton: Minister, Cartsburn Church of Scotland, Greenock, 'his catholicy of spirit [was] so remarkably extreme as to make him equally at home on papal and Orange platforms'. *Greenock Telegraph*, 16/11/78.

J Galloway: Labourer, Secretary of No. 38 Cowcaddens (Glasgow) District, 1884.

Rev. Robert Gault: Ulsterman, one of the first ministers in Scotland to embrace Orangeism. Grand Chaplain to the Order in the 1860s. Minister of Kingston Free Church, 'moderate Conservative' active in GCA and on A Whitelaw's (q.v.) election committee 1874. Author of prize-winning essay 'Popery, Man of Sin and Son of Perdition' (1853). Superintendent of Free Church Anti-Popish Mission.

Samuel Geddes: Traveller. Master of LOL No. 690 Partick, 1881. HDGM, 1883.

Allan Gilmour of Eaglesham: Tory landowner, increasingly noted on Orange platforms 1880s. HDGM 1883. Cambridge-educated Barrister-at-Law. *Burkes Peerage*, 1879.

T H Gilmour: Agent, Royal Liver Friendly Society, SGM 1894. Prominent Conservative, vice chairman Camlachie Conservative Association

1884. Paid Tory organiser in Camlachie District 1900.

Duke of Gordon: George Gordon, 5th Duke, kinsman of Lord George Gordon the anti-Roman Catholic agitator, but forebears 1st and 2nd Dukes were leading Roman Catholic magnates. Distinguished military career raised 100th (later 92nd) Gordon Highlanders from his estates, regiment saw service in '98 rebellion at Wexford. 1806 became MP for Eye, entered House of Lords 1807. Ultra-Tory figurehead of Scottish Orange Lodges 1830s but confined activities to meetings of Grand Lodge in London. Died 28th May 1836.

See Sir George Bell's *Rough Notes of Old Soldier*, ii.39. Anderson's *Scottish Nation* ii319-20, Cannon's *Historical Record of the 92nd Highlanders*, pp.1-20, 127-8.

J Griffen: Fishmonger, Glasgow. Grand Lodge official 1875.

J Haddock: Spirit dealer, Gallowgate. Officebearer, LOL No. 5 'Victoria', Glasgow.

W J Hamilton: Labourer, WM LOL No. 442 (Maryhill).

Rev. J C Halliday: Evangelist in charge of Emmanual Episcopal Church, Glasgow. Grand Chaplain to Orangemen, 1899.

Z C Hawkes: Leading GCA member. Tea and wine merchant. On Orange platforms from 1881. Obituary, *Glasgow News*, 21/1/83.

F Y Henderson: Accountant. Treasurer Grand Lodge, 1881 on. Secretary of Glasgow General Building Society. Active in Scottish Protestant Alliance.

Rev. J C Hodgekinson: Minister, Emmanuel Church, Glasgow. Grand Chaplain to the Orangemen, 1892.

H Houston: Clothing manufacturer, Bridgeton, Glasgow. WM, LOL. No. 5 'Victoria'.

W Hunter: Tobacconist. DM Parkhead No. 21 District, 1878. ASGM 1892.

P Hutcheson: Steamship Agent. GSB Grand Lodge, 1875, but little subsequent involvement. Director, West of Scotland Protestant Association. Chairman of Central Conservative Association, Glasgow, 1885-99. Councillor 1896. Died 1899.

Rev. Quintin Johnstone: Minister, Whiteinch Parish Church. Keen Orange partisan and active in anti-Home Rule cause from 1880.

William Kerr: Prudential Insurance agent. Secretary of No. 15. Partick District LOI 1884. GBB 1884. Secretary of Partick Conservative Association.

Dr. John Leech: Grand Master of Orange Association, 1862-June 1869. Physician, 5th Portland Street, Glasgow.

H A Long: Early experience as cavalry soldier, later 'a champion of the Protestant cause and an educationalist'. Working man's missionary in the Saltmarket, Glasgow. A frequent debator on Glasgow Green, he was attended by a bodyguard of Orangemen as personal protection, 'his bigoted and uncompromising Calvinism was not of the soorfaced variety for it did not cloud his happy optimism'. See S. Mavor, Memories of People and Places, *Bailie* 9/7/1873, 29/4/85.

Isaac Low: Plumber and gasfitter. Grand Lodge official 1975.

R G Lowndes: Partner in power loom muslin manufacturers. Official LOI Thornliebank.

Thomas Macklin: Professor of Classics, Andersonian University, Glasgow. Free Churchman. Ulsterman. Grand Secretary LOI Scotland 1864-91. Conservative election committee 1874.

W C Maugham: Accountant. Honorary treasurer, GCA. 'True blue' Tory. Prominent SPA. Unsuccessfully contested Blackfriars and Hutchesonstown and Bridgeton constituencies 1885, 92 and 95. 'Orange' candidate 1892 School Board elections. Obituary GCAAR, 1915.

Rev. J U Mitchell: Ulsterman. Minister of New Congregational Church, 1885. Grand Chaplain, LOI. 1896-1900.

D S Mitchell: Shipping insurance agent. DM No. 41, Anderston District.

Robert Mitchell: Shipping Master and emigration agent, 1865-70. Agent for Anchor Line steamers 1870-80. Member of Orange Institution of Great Britain, and their candidate in 1876 School Board elections.

P Morrison: Jeweller, Argyle Arcade, Glasgow. Prominent Orangeman and active in Tradeston Conservative Association. GCA representative 1888.

William Motherwell: 1797-1835, poet and journalist. Son of an ironmonger, descended from an old Stirlingshire family. As a youth had radical opinions but relations with reformers turned him into zealous Tory. Trooper in Renfrewshire Yeomanry. Works: 1819 'Harp of Renfrewshire', 1824 'Renfrewshire Characters and Scenery', 1827 'Minstrelsy Ancient and Modern'. A collaborator with James Hogg in an edition of Burns' poems. Editor of *Glasgow Courier* 1832. Identified himself actively with Orangeism, examined by Parliamentary committee, completely broke down and died of apoplexy Glasgow, 1st November 1835. *Blackwood's Magazine* xxxiii 670; portrait and busts in National Portrait Gallery, Edinburgh.

W Mullen: Boilermaker. Secretary of No. 41 (Anderston) District.

Gilbert R Murray: DM, Galloway; DPGM, Scotland 1875.

A McAllister: Engineer, DM, Partick District LOI.

Hugh McGuire: Plasterer. GS, Grand Lodge, 1875.

W McHaffie: WPGM, Black Chapter 1876. Committee 1877, GCA Representative from Tradeston to GCA 1887.

Dr. T MacKnight: Physician. County DGM Ayrshire. Active Tory and anti-Voluntaryist.

George McLeod: Wincey and tartan manufacturer, Glasgow. MWGM of Orange Institution 1869-74. Active in GCA and Scottish Reformation Society. Founding member of Glasgow Athenaeum (cultural society). Also involved in Commercial Travellers' Society and Sabbath Protection League. See *Glasgow News*, 12/12/74, 16/10/74, for Athenaeum dinner in his honour.

James McManus: Insurance collector. Secretary of No. 44 Bridgeton/Dalmarnock District. Later Deputy Grand Master of Scotland and very active in the Grand Lodge in the late 1880s. Vice President of Bridgeton Conservative Association 1885-1907. Representative to Western Divisional Council, 1898.

R McNish: Local gentry Glasgow area. Joined LOI in 1880s but not active.

W McWilliams: Printer. DM, LOL No. 680 Gallowgate, Glasgow.

Rev. David Ness: Minister, Whiteinch Parish Church. MWGM, Orange Institution 1900 on. Also prominent Freemason. See *Partick Star*, 6/7/ 1895.

Chalmers Izatt Paton: Head of Hugh Paton and Sons, Carvers and Gilders, Edinburgh, 'held no insignificant place in art circles'. MWGM, 1874-94, Orange Institution. Died 7th October 1889. Obituary, *Glasgow Herald*, 9/10/89.

Rev. T W Patrick: Congregationalist Minister, Rutherglen. Ulsterman and active Orangeman. See *Glasgow News*, 12/9/81.

George Phair: Railway signal maker. Master No. 38 (Cowcaddens) District. Vice Chairman 10th Conservative Ward Committee.

A R Pollock: Partner of Jas. Pollock and Co., Drysalters Paisley. District Master, Paisley LOI 1870s Convenor of Antiquities, Paisley Philosophical Society. Instrumental in setting up Paisley Conservative Association.

T Richard: Accounts clerk. Master, No. 31 (Bridgeton) District.

James Rattray: Boilermaker, later full time missionary for the Protestant Missionary Society. Prominent Greenock Orangeman, 1860s, 70s.

W Richmond: Confectioner and fruiterer, Glasgow. First Grand Secretary of the Orange Association in Scotland, 1835-59.

James Rice: House painter, Glasgow. Grand Secretary of Orange Institution in Scotland 1891.

Rev. William Robinson: Primitive Methodist, Paisley. Member of LOI 1837-1906.

Edward J Saunderson: Irish politician, ardent Protestant and Orangeman, with absolute faith in divine guidance. Commander of Cavan militia 1891-3. Landowner and Whig admirer of Lord Palmerston, he became the most conspicuous opponent of Home Rule in the House of Commons as MP for North Armagh. County Grand Master of Belfast Orange Lodges, MWGM Scotland 1889-95, resigning due to pressure of parliamentary duties. See R. Lucas, *Memoir of Col. Saunderson MP* (1906).

Jas Somervell of Sorn: Ayrshire landowner, born 1845, education Loretto, Harrow, Oxford. Conservative candidate for Glasgow, adopted 1883. See *Glasgow News* 7/3/84, *Bailie* Nos. 684, 909.

Dugald Stewart: Wright and builder. Grand Lodge Official, Glasgow 1875.

W Stewart of Gearholm: Landowner. MWGM, County Grand Lodge, Ayrshire, 1870s.

A Thomson: Moneylender, Calton, Glasgow. DGM, Orange Institution of Great Britain, 1874.

Rev. Robert Thompson: 'Rubbart', eccentric Minister of Ladywell Church of Scotland, Glasgow. See *Bailie*, 18/7/77, 31/10/83, 14/5/84.

W H Webster: Grocer, South Side, Glasgow. Procession Marshal, LOI, 1880.

Thomas Wetherall: Born Waterford 1809. Came to Glasgow 1860, acted as manager to a cutler and surgical instrument maker and eventually purchased a share in the business. Deputy GM, LOI Scotland, 1874 and active in GCA. Treasurer, Glasgow Debating Society and chairman of the Working Men's Evangelical Mission. Died April 3rd, 1883. For obituary, *Glasgow News*, 5/4/83.

Alex Whitelaw: Partner in W. Baird and Co., Ironmasters. Conservative MP for Glasgow, 1874. Chairman of first Glasgow School Board. Strongly committed to Church of Scotland. Died 1st July, 1879. See *Illustrated London News*, ixvi 146 (1875); *The Graphic*, xi 174 (1875) for portrait.

William Whitelaw: Third son of the above, born 1868, educated Eton, Harrow, Trinity College, Cambridge. Member LOI. 1892, aged 24, won Perth for the Conservatives after a split in the Liberal vote. Defeated 1895 and 1900. Became director of Highland Railway Company. Contested Banff unsuccessfully in 1907 and Stirling Burghs, also unsuccessfully, 1907. See *Bailie*, 27/5/1907, for portrait.

Rev. W. Winter: Episcopal Clergyman, Glasgow. GC of Orangemen, 1896.

James Wyllie: Ulster Protestant. School teacher Free St. George's School. Orange SGM 1874, also active in GCA. See Annual Reports 1874, 5 etc. For speech to GCA, *Glasgow News* 21/3/74. Vice Chairman 11th Ward Committee (Conservative), 1884.

Samuel Young: Slater. Officebearer in Cowcaddens LOI, 1892; DGM, 1900.

William Young: Tailor, Bridgeton, Glasgow. Secretary of No. 44 (Baltic Street) District, LOI, but climbed ladder rapidly reaching Deputy Grand Master for Col. Saunderson (q.v.) and MWGM in 1895 after his resignation. Also active Tory, Vice President Bridgeton division 1885-1904, representative to Western Divisional Committee 1898.

William Yuille: Storeman Member of OA of S Grand Lodge, early 1870s, but in 1875 began to publicly criticise this body for its lack of independent action in pursuit of 'Protestant Issues'. Subsequently drops out of reported Grand Lodge activity.

Appendix F
Clergymen with Orange Links 1865-1900

Name	*Denomination*	*Location*
*Hugh Park	Church of Scotland	Cumbernauld
W B Turnbull	"	Townhead, Glasgow
James Dodds	"	St George's, Glasgow
*†R H Dignum	"	Greenock
*A Walker	"	Airdrie
*Robert Thompson	"	Ladywell, Glasgow
A Leiper	"	Gorbals
Rev. J McNaught	"	Glasgow
P McLaughlin	"	Abbotsford, Glasgow
R. Pryde	"	Not known
J Hay	"	Not known
*Quintin Johnstone	"	Whiteinch, Glasgow
James Bryce	"	Crown St., Glasgow
W Hutcheson	"	Not known
*J K Campbell	"	Port Glasgow
T Kay	"	Greenock
*†W Wilson	"	Greenock
*†H, Charleton	"	Greenock
A Fullerton	"	Greenock
J. McPherson	"	Gaelic Church, Greenock
J. Potter	"	Not known
Rev. Douglas	"	Stranraer
H Ramsay	"	Baillieston
J Wilson	"	Renfrew
William McDermott	"	Johnstone
*Rev. Lorraine	"	Dalry
Rev. J Gunson	"	Greenock
†J McCann	Episopalian	Glasgow
W Williams	"	St. Jude's, Glasgow
*J. Hodgekinson	"	Emmanual Church, Glasgow
*Wr Winter	"	Glasgow
W E Bradshaw	"	Glasgow
*J C Halliday	"	Glasgow
*William Robinson	Primitive Methodist	Paisley
Rev. Jenkinson	"	Townhead, Glasgow

Rev. Havers	"	Tollcross, Glasgow
Emerson Phillipson	"	Suffolk St. Glasgow
Rev. Boulton	Methodist	Greenock
G M College	"	Greenock
*†Robert Gault	Free Church	Kingston, Glasgow
Rev. Dr. Fraser	"	Paisley
*†J U Mitchell	Independent	Partick
	Congregationalist	
*†T W Patrick	"	Rutherglen

* Denotes a member of the LOI.
† Denotes of known Irish, or more commonly, Ulster origin.

Bibliography

By way of introduction to this biographical account, two general observations should be made. First, one should be aware that as befits the contentious subject of Orangeism, the primary sources available are soundly partisan and should therefore be approached with caution. This is very much the case with contemporary histories of the 19th century movement which as a rule are the work of Orange supporters or their opponents and which, although containing important 'raw material', have as their main concern the simple assertion or denial of charges against Orangemen, rather than any real analysis of their influence and development. Secondly, it seems rather a paradox that despite the LOI's often high public profile in the West of Scotland, there has been a dearth of secondary material on the Order. Probably since much of Orange history appears rather too peripheral or 'obscure' to be investigated by commentators whose primary object is other aspects of Scottish or British history, one is often left with a series of isolated – though sometimes illuminating – references but little in the way of analysis or explanation.

As regards the primary sources, it is unfortunate that most of the leading Scottish Orangemen of the 19th century, McLeod, Paton, and Young, left no personal papers, or none of any significance. (A marriage trust for Peter Hutcheson's daughter survives and H A Long characteristically bequeathed his press cuttings and a marble bust of himself, now in Glasgow People's Palace Museum.) Similarly, the poet Motherwell left a fairly large amount of correspondence in the Robertson Mss. Collection of Glasgow University, but mostly on literary subjects, for it is likely that the most sensitive documents pertaining to Orangeism were destroyed in the wake of the 1835 debacle. The honorific MWGM of the movement from 1889-95, the Irish landowner Col. Saunderson, has also left voluminous papers and correspondence but again these reflect his overwhelming concern with wider political issues and parliamentary business which eventually prompted him to resign his Orange office in Scotland.

Conservative and Liberal Unionist politicians whose names were linked with Orangeism provide another potential line of research. J. Parker Smith's correspondence in the *Smith of Jordanhill Collection* Strathclyde Regional Archives is most useful on the practical conduct of a by-election campaign in the late 19th century, and Alex Whitelaw's extant papers are further instructive on the Scottish Disestablishment issue. Apart from this, Allan Gilmour and J Stirling Maxwell left only estate and business archives, while James Bain, W C Maugham, Lord Blythswood, C B Renshaw and Alex Stuart left no personal papers. Indeed, on the whole leading Tories seem to have been much less conscientious in this respect than their Liberal counterparts.

The second major body of manuscript material is formed by institutional records. The reports of proceedings May-December 1864 and December 1867 of the Grand Lodge of the Orange Institution of Ireland are deposited in the Linen Hall Library, Belfast. In Ireland a special 'Lodge of Research' LOL. No. 1020 has been established for the specific purpose of collecting historical materials.

It soon became apparent that in Scotland, however, there were problems not only of access but of basic availability. I was informed that the Grand Lodge here has only begun comparatively recently to take a serious interest in the movement's history, and that in the past records of membership, minute books etc., seem to have been retained by local lodges. In these circumstances material has often not survived. Most of the records of Glengarnock LOL No. 100 were used to stoke a boiler in the Orange Hall during fuel shortages in 1974, though I was permitted to examine the remaining ephemera such as membership certificates for the LOI (and a local Black Preceptory, No. 795), Lodge Masters' credentials and transfer certificates, some of these dating from the 1870s.

Yet this want of internal records was not a serious obstacle – it is doubtful whether questions of class affiliation, motivation and political practice could have been satisfactorily answered from such official sources. In fact, on such topics the manuscript material from other institutions relevant to the progress of 19th century Orangeism proved an extremely effective alternative. The archives of the Conservative and Liberal Unionist parties in Scotland are one such resource; in particular the *Glasgow Conservative Operative Association Annual Reports and Minute Books 1839-41*, the *1893 Annual Report of the National Union of Conservative Associations of Scotland*

and Minute Books 1893-1902. The detailed membership records contained here permitted an account of Orange involvement in Conservative and Unionist politics from local ward committees to constituency associations and executive bodies.

Also as a useful point of reference for the LOI's more general standing in Scottish society the annual reports of other militant Protestant bodies in Glasgow and the West can be examined. These include *Glasgow Protestant Laymen's Association Annual Report 1879,* the *Glasgow Protestant Missionary Society Annual Reports 1879-80* and the *Glasgow Working Men's Evangelistic Society 1879-83.*

Other institutional records consulted were those of friendly societies such as the 'Patna Loyal Orange and Protestant Friendly Society', deposited under the various Friendly Society Acts and now held at the SRO. These are important in grasping the extent of material provisions offered by Orangeism.

A final source of manuscript material which should be noted is the collection of Lord Advocates' papers also in the SRO. Notably this includes witnesses' precognitions and the reports of local sheriffs relating to Orange disturbances and riots in the 1840s and 50s.

Further compensating the lack of official Orange records, however, is the wealth of primary printed material produced by the Lodges. This includes, for example, a printed ritual of introduction as copies of Orange *Laws and Ordinances* from 1800, 1820, 1828, 1830, 1846, 1849, 1860, 1886 and 1899. (These pertain directly to the Irish body but, as suggested, practices in Scotland were very similar.)

Also important here though were the many ballads, polemical pamphlets and recorded lectures which were provided for internal consumption by the Scottish and British organisations. Of special interest is one of the earliest pamphlets *The Orange Institution a Slight Sketch* (1813) which actually contains recruitment advertisements for the Lodges as well as reproducing rules and regulations, and also *A Report of the Protestant and Orange Soirée Held in Paisley on 5th November* (1856) which offers a detailed account of probably the first Orange *soirée* held in Scotland. As for the later period from the 1860s various leading Orangemen such as Gault, Macklin and Paton, as noted in Chapter One, produced 'educational' material – knowledge of Paton's *Catechism of the Principles of Protestantism* (1879) was a prerequisite for passing to the Purple Degree. Particularly prolific was H A Long who wrote tracts, for example, on *Transubstantiation* 1864, *In partibus Infidelum or three evenings among the Glasgow Eclectics* (nd), *The Glasgow School Board Elections* (nd) as well as *The Orangeman's Anti-Papal Tract* (nd).

Of course, there are also pamphlets from hostile sources such as *The Orange Bogey* (1886) produced by the Irish National League. And, popular broadsides, one of which, in Wyllie Collection GUL, *An Account of the Proceedings of Orange Procession...* describes the first public 12th July celebration in Glasgow in 1822.

The most vital printed sources for the early part of Orange history, though, are the UK parliamentary debates and reports of the parliamentary select committee on Orange lodges, established in 1835 under pressure from radical and Irish MPs. The former provide an excellent record of the speeches of leading Irish Orangemen like Verner and Gowan and act as a useful index of the prominence of Orangeism from 1800-35. Consultation of the four huge Select Committee reports of over 4,500 pages is even more profitable, containing appendices with details of financial statements, minutes, membership lists, and correspondence of officers of the movement. The first three reports deal only with the Irish institution and contain no conclusion or summary of evidence. The fourth, though, concerns the British and military Lodges and contains an abundance of Scottish material, including proceedings of the Royal Gordon Lodge. A summary is provided designed to suggest that there was a dangerous conspiracy.

This parliamentary material should also be supplemented by consideration of autobiographies and contemporary Orange Histories, *Some Account My Life and Writings* (1888) by Archibald Alison, Sheriff of Lanarkshire in the 1830s, is useful though the histories tend to centre mainly on the Irish Movement. Of these, O R Gowan's *Annals and Defence of the Loyal Orange Institution of Ireland* (1825) and *Orangeism: its Origin and History* (1859) are most worthy of note as 'official' histories (Gowan fostered the Canadian Movement) and as bases on which accounts such as Sibbet's have drawn. Similarly important in this respect is Cusack's *Orangeism: its Principles, its Purposes, its Relation to Society Defended* (1875) and Rodgers *The Revolution of 1688 and the History of the Orange Association of England and Ireland* (1881). Useful to balance these is Fr Cleary's *The Orange Society* (1897), published by the Catholic Truth Society.

The final set of primary sources are newspapers and periodicals. The most interesting early paper is the *Glasgow Courier* aimed at a Glasgow and West of Scotland working class readership and cast by its opponents as an 'Orange' paper. Motherwell was its editor in the early 1830s and it displays some spirited defences of the Movement.

Even more central to research on 19th century Orangeism though, is the *Glasgow News* 1873-86 (thereafter the *Scottish News*). Again it was sponsored by leading Conservatives but was not at all warmly disposed towards the Scottish Orangemen. Its standard of reports was, however, excellent and it carries lengthy verbatim reports of speeches at 12th celebrations, Orange *soirées*, and Grand Lodge biennial meetings. It also has much incidental material on ordinary lodge meetings, Orange funerals, Grand Lodge memorials and resolutions, and for this reason a day by day examination of the *News* was essential – a strategy which also provided much detailed background on social, religious and political developments in late 19th century Glasgow.

For a fully rounded analysis of how Orangeism was received in Scotland also consulted for 12th and *soirée* reports and election coverage were the Radical Liberal *North British Daily Mail* and Whiggish Liberal (later Liberal Unionist) *Glasgow Herald*. Local newspapers, too, notably the *Greenock Telegraph* and *Paisley Express* were also examined.

As for the periodicals, the 19th century Grand Lodge does not seem to have had its own journal like the current 'Orange Torch' (*The Scottish Patriot may* have had this role but no surviving copies could be located). *The Protestant*, edited by H A Long, is strongly representative of the Orange world view though, and again for the sake of comparison there are various other Protestant magazines, *The Scottish Protestant*, *The Glasgow Protestant Watchman*, for example. Some biographical insights can also be gained from *The Bailie* an illustrated Tory publication specialising in laborious satire.

In the case of the secondary material three more modern studies merit attention. First, R M Sibbet's *Orangeism in Ireland and Throughout the Empire* is again an official history, written by an Orangeman with Grand Lodge approval. It first appeared in serial form in *Belfast Weekly News* during the Home Rule agitation to wwi and was first published in book form in 1915. The first edition of the two volume work carries the history of the Movement to 1830 while the second edition is revised by 'an anonymous member of the Order' and includes the latter period of Orangeism with more relevant Scottish material. Sibbet's narrative, however, is extremely turgid and rambling, with a peculiar mixture of folklore and original documents to the exclusion of any inconvenient evidence. From a similar official viewpoint is Clougley's very sketchy 'history' of Orangeism in Scotland, again serialised in the *Belfast Weekly News* in 1929. Such vices are by no means reproduced in H Senior's *Orangeism in Ireland and Britain 1795-1835*, but this solid factual narrative contains only a few Scottish references.

Most other recent works have done little to build on Sibbet and Senior's contributions. *Orangeism: A New Historical Approach* (1967) by Dewer *et al*, for example, is basically a very partisan rehash of earlier histories for popular consumption; while T Gray's *The Orange Order* (1972) is journalistic and anecdotal in style. In strong contrast though is H Patterson's work on dissident Orangeism and the Independent Orange Order in Belfast – *Independent Orangeism and Class Conflict in Edwardian Belfast* (1980) and *Class Conflict and Sectarianism: The Protestant Working Class and the Belfast Labour Movement 1868-1920* (1981) which employ original research and a modern Marxist approach for a class analysis of Orange activity.

Beyond this, information on Orangeism in secondary sources has been limited to brief and tangential references. A Campbell's *The Lanarkshire Miners: A social history of their Trade Unions 1775-1974* and A McDonagh's *Irish Immigrants and Labour Movements in Coatbridge and Airdrie 1881-1931* (BA dissertation 1970s) are useful here, as is D Urwin's *The Development of the Conservative Party in Scotland till 1912* (SHR, No. 138, 1965), and I Hutchinson's thesis *Society and Politics in Mid Victorian Glasgow 1846-86* (1975).

Written from a different perspective, J E Handley's work is also an important source of reference. *The Irish in Scotland* (1945) and *The Irish in Modern Scotland* (1947) contain descriptions of Orange disturbances which are not found in other secondary works, and also stress the importance of Orangeism as a manifestation of splits between Irish immigrants.

There are in addition, occasional mentions of Orangeism in local histories such as J Strawthorn's *Ayrshire;Story of a County* (1976) and *The New History of Cumnock* (1966); but other local authors like J McLellan, *Larkhall* (1979), are anxious to present their subject in its best light and apparently this does not include drawing attention to its Orange Lodges. Finally and most encouragingly, however, a body of work is now developing on sectarianism, militant Protestantism and Roman Catholics in Scotland.

See T Gallagher, *A City Divided* (1988), *Glasgow, The Uneasy Peace* (1987), S Bruce, *No Pope of Rome! Militant Protestantism in Modern Scotland* (1985) and B Murray *The Old Firm, Sectarianism, Sport and Society in Scotland,* (1985). This material has a fairly broad focus and concentrates on the twentieth century period, but it is the source of many valuable insights, and has been used extensively in considering the further development of the LOI in modern Scotland.

I. MANUSCRIPT AND ARCHIVAL MATERIAL

i) *Personal Papers*

J M Airlie, Collected Papers, National Library of Scotland.

Robertson Mss., Glasgow University Library, Special Collections (for Motherwell material).

E J Saunderson Papers, Northern Ireland Public Record Office (T.2996).

Smith of Jordanhill Collection, Strathclyde Regional Archives.

Whitelaw Correspondence, Glasgow University Business Archives.

ii) *Institutional Records*

Conservative Party Miscellaneous Papers 1885-1912, Conservative Offices, Edinburgh.

Glasgow Church of Scotland Presbytery Minute Books, SRO.

Glasgow Conservative Association (Formerly GWMCA) Annual Reports, 1870-1900.

Glasgow Conservative Operatives Association, Minute Book, 1837-43

Glasgow Orange Union Funeral Society, Rules and Regulations, FSI 16/108, 1835, SRO.

Glasgow Protestant Laymen's Association, Annual Report 1879.

Glasgow Protestant Missionary Society, Annual Reports, 1879-1880.

Glasgow Working Men's Evangelistic Association, Annual Reports 1879-83.

Maryhill Conservative Association, Letterbooks and Minute Books 1884-1900.

National Union Conservative Associations for Scotland, Minute Books 1882-1902, Rules, Annual Report 1882-93.

Orange Institution of Ireland, Reports of Proceedings of Grand Lodge May-December 1864, December 1867, Linen Hall Library, Belfast.

Patna Loyal Orange Permanent Friendly Society, Rules and Regulations, c1872, FS4 101, SRO.

Scottish Conservative Club Miscellaneous Papers, 1878-1900.

Scottish Protestant Alliance, Annual Reports, 1883-1900.

Scottish Unionist Association, Annual Reports, 1913-1930.

West of Scotland Branch of the Liberal Committee for Maintenance of the Legislative Union between Great Britain and Ireland, Minute Book, 1886.

West of Scotland Liberal Unionist Association, Minute Books, 1894-1912.

West of Scotland Protestant Alliance, Annual Reports 1874-1883.

iii) *Legal Material*

Lord Advocate's Papers, SRO, including AD 58-70 a Proclamation by the Sheriff of Ayrshire and Report on Orange disturbances.

II. PRIMARY PRINTED SOURCES

1) *Pamphlets, Broadsheets*

An Account of the Proceedings at the Orange Processions which took place at Glasgow on 12th July 1822 when the whole of the Orangemen were apprehended by the Magistrates and a Strong Body of the Military and Marched to Jail, Wyllie Collection, University of Glasgow.

Anderson, J, *Protestantism and Orangeism,* Belfast. n.d.

Association for Promoting the Social and Religious Improvement of the City, *Report on the Religious Condition of Glasgow,* Glasgow, n.d.

Banks, W, *A History of the Orange Order,* Belfast, n.d.

British Anti-State Church Association, *Scotland and its Kirk,* London, 1850.

Clancy, J J , *The Orange Bogey,* Irish National League, Belfast, 1886.

Commins, A, *Orangeism: What is it? and What Will You Do With It?,* National Press Agency, London, 1886.

Cusack, T, *Orangeism, its Principles, Purpose and Relation to Society,* Belfast, 1875.

Glasgow Protestant Association, *Lectures on Popery delivered in Glasgow at the Request of the GPA and Afterwards Published* (series of 12), 1836.

Kidson, W, *The Captious and Ensnaring Question: An Address,* Glasgow, 1870.

Laws and Ordinances of the Loyal Orange Institution of Ireland, 1826, 1846, 1849, 1860, 1886, 1896, 1916, Dublin.

Lilburn, R, *Orangeism, its Origin, Constitution and Objects,* Guardian Steam Printing Office, Armagh, 1866.

Long, H A, *Digest of the Debate Held on the Evenings of the 6th, 10th, 13th, 17th, 20th, 23rd May 1867 in Nelson Street Chapel, Trongate, upon Toleration and Persecution,* Glasgow,

Long, H A, *The Glasgow School Board Elections,* Glasgow, n.d.

Long, H A , *In Partibus Infidelum or Three Evenings Among the Glasgow Eclectics,* Glasgow, n.d.

Long, H A, *Mene: The Numeration of Babylon Mystical. A tract for the Times and the Coming Fate of the Papacy,* Glasgow, 1865.

Long, H A, *The Orangeman's anti-Papal Tract,* Glasgow, n.d.

Long, H A, *To the Three Clergymen of Edinburgh and Two of Glasgow who sent letters of apology to the Chairman of Mr. Bradlaugh's meetings,* Glasgow, 1881.

Long, H A, *Transubstantiation,* Glasgow, 1864.

Macklin, T, *The Burning of Santiago, but an Accident in the Mariolatry of the Church of Rome,* Glasgow, 1864.

Macklin, T, *Reasons of Protest Against the Endowment of Maynooth,* n.d.

Minutes of a Conference of the Protestants of Scotland, Edinburgh, 1854.

MP, *The History of Orangeism: Its Origin, Rise and Decline* Dublin, 1825.

MacKenzie, P, *Letters of the Tory Conspirators in Glasgow to Fairman,* Glasgow, n.d.

National Education, The Bible in the School, Authorised Report of the Public Meeting held at the City Hall, Glasgow, Monday 25th April 1870, Glasgow, 1870

Niven, R , *Orangeism as it was and is.* W J Baird, Belfast,

The Orange Institution: A Slight Sketch, J J Stockdale, London, 1813.

Orange Lodges A Supplemental Review (to 1835 Report), Roake and Varty, London, 1836.

An Orangeman, *The Ass and the Orangeman's Daughter – a Slip*, 1840, British Library.

Orange Songs, (compiled by W Peake, Belfast), W Bridgett & Sons, Belfast, n.d.

Paton, C I, *A Catechism of the Principles of Protestantism*, n.d.

Phillips, E, *The Loyal Orange Institution: Its History, Triumphs and Bases*, LOI Belfast, 1924.

A Report of the Protestant and Orange Soirée held in Paisley on 5th November, 1856, J R Parlane, Paisley, 1856.

Rise of Orangeism: An Address given to the Orangemen of Greenock in 1864 by a Christian Orangeman, Christian Irishman Office, Belfast, n.d.

Rodgers, E, *The Revolution of 1688 and a History of the Orange Association of England and Ireland*, W J Baird, Belfast, 1881.

Rules and Regulations for the Use of All Orange Societies, Grand Lodge of Ireland, Dublin, 1800, 1820.

Wagtale, Bro., *Story of an Orange Lodge*, 1864.

2) *Parliamentary Reports*

Minutes of Evidence from the Select Committee on Emigration and Immigration (Foreigners), 311, 1889.

Report from the Select Committee Appointed to consider the Laws Related to the Passing of Irish and Scots Vagrants to Their own Country, 1828 (513), IV.

Report from the Select Committee Enquiring into the Condition of the Poorer Classes in Ireland. Appendix G Report on the State of the Irish Poor in Great Britain, 1836 (40), XXXIV, 427.

Report from the Select Committee Appointed to Enquire into the Nature, Character, Extent and Tendencies of Orange Lodges, Associations or Societies in Ireland, HC 1835 (377), xv .

Second Report... HC 1835 (475), xvi.

Third Report... HC 1835 (476), xvi.

Report from the Select Committee Appointed to Enquire into the Origin, Nature, Extent and Tendency of Orange Institutions in Great Britain and the Colonies, HC 1835 (605), xvii, 1.

3) *Books and Articles (Including Orange Histories)*

Alison, A, *Some Account of My Life and Writings*, Blackwood, Edinburgh, 1888.

Chalmers. A K , *Census 1901 A Report on Glasgow and its Municipal Wards*, Glasgow, 1901.

Cleary, H W , *The Orange Society*, Catholic Truth Society, Melbourne, 1897.

Cloughley, J, *Orangeism in Scotland its Rise and Progress*, Serialised in Belfast Weekly News, November 1929.

Denvir, J, *The Irish in Britain*, Kegan Paul, London, 1892.

Gaskell, K, *Lanarkshire Leaders Social and Political*, Glasgow, 1908.

Gault, R, *Popery the Man of Sin and the Son of Perdition*, W R McPhun, Glasgow, 1853.

Gowan, O R, *Annals and Defense of the Loyal Orange Institution of Ireland*, Dublin, 1825.

Gowan, O R, *Orangeism: Its Origin and History,* Toronto,

Graham, N, *The Orange Songster,* J Kerr, Glasgow, n.d.

Guthrie, W, 'Recollections of Bridgeton', *Transactions of the Old Glasgow Club* 1900-8, pp. 215-23.

Hamilton Muir, J, *Glasgow in 1901,* Hodge, Edinburgh, 1901.

Hodgeson, W E, Why Conservatism Fails in Scotland, *National Review* 2, 1883-4.

Howie, R, *Churches and Churchless in Scotland,* Glasgow, 1893.

Knox, J., *Airdrie,* Baird and Hamilton, Airdrie, 1921.

Lucas, R, *Colonel Saunderson M.P.: A Memoir,* Murray, London, 1908.

Madsen, A, *The Loyal Orange Association – Facts and Fables,* Melbourne, 1898.

McCrie, T, *Life of Andrew Melville,* Edinburgh, 1824.

Rankine, J, *Handbook of the Church of Scotland,* Edinburgh, 1888.

Ravenstein, E, 'The Laws of Migration', *Journal of the Statistical Society,* 48, 1885.

Strong, J, *Glasgow and its Clubs,* Glasgow, 1883.

4) *Newspapers and Periodicals*

Ayr Correspondent (1824-5).

Ayrshire Democrat (1839-40).

Ayrshire Inspirer (October, December 1839).

Ayrshire Mirror (November 1820 – June 1821).

Ayrshire Miscellany (August 1817-1822 imp.).

The Bailie (1872-86).

Dumfries Weekly Journal (1814-16).

Dumfries and Galloway Courier and Herald (1811-14, 1817-19).

Forward (1906-8).

Glasgow Courier (1832-59).

Glasgow Free Press, (1823-6, 1832-5).

Glasgow Herald, (September 1805 – 1900).

Glasgow News (1873-86, Becomes *Scottish News* 1886-8).

Glasgow Observer (1885-1900).

Glasgow Protestant Watchman (1854).

Glasgow Saturday Post (1846-75).

Glasgow Sentinel (1850-75).

Govan Chronicle (1878 April-June).

Govan Press (1885).

The Graphic (1878-90 imp.).

Greenock Telegraph (1864-1900).

North British Daily Mail (1847-1900).

Paisley Ephemera (November 1855 – June 1858).

Paisley Express (1873-1900).

Paisley and Renfrewshire Standard (1869-71).

Partick Observer (May 1877 – March 1878).

Partick Star (1892 – June 1901).

Pollokshaws News (August 1885).

The Protestant (1818-22).

The Protestant (H A Long) (1874).

The Scotsman (1817-1900).

The Scottish Protestant (1851-2).

III. SECONDARY SOURCES

1. *Modern Orange Histories*

Dewar, M W, Brown, J, Long, S E, *Orangeism: A New Historical Appreciation*, The Grand Lodge of Ireland, Belfast,

McClelland, A, 'The Origin of the Imperial Grand Black Chapter of the British Commonwealth', *Journal of the Royal Society of Antiquaries of Ireland*, Vol. 98, Pt. 2, 1968.

McClelland, A, *The Formation of the Orange Order*. Belfast, 1970.

Senior, H, *Orangeism in Ireland and Britain 1795-1835*, Routledge & Kegan Paul, London, 1966.

Senior, H, 'The Early Orange Order 1795-1820', in *Secret Societies in Ireland*, T D Williams (ed), Dublin, 1973.

Senior, H, *Orangeism, the Canadian Phase*, Toronto, n.d.

Sibbet, R M, *Orangeism in Ireland and Throughout the Empire*, Thynne & Co, London, 1939.

2. *General Material*

Arnstein, W L, *Protestant versus Catholic in Mid-Victorian England : Mr Newdegate and the Nuns*, Columbia and London, 1982.

Aunger, E A, Religion and Occupational Class in Northern Ireland, *Economic and Social Review*, Vol. 7, No. 1, 1975.

Barkley, J M, *A Short History of the Presbyterian Church in Ireland*, Belfast, 1959.

Bell, G, *The Protestants of Ulster*, Pluto, London, 1976.

Belton, N, 'Ireland: Unravelling the Knot', *Bulletin of Scottish Politics*, No. 2, Spring 1981.

Best, G F A, 'The Protestant Constitution and its Supporters 1800-29', *Transactions of the Royal Historical Society*, 5th Series, Vol. III., 1958, pp. 105-24.

Best, G FA, 'Popular Protestantism', in *Ideas and Institutions of Victorian Britain*, R Robson (ed), Bell, London, 1967.

Best, G F A, 'The Scottish Victorian City', *Victorian Studies* II, 1867-1968, pp. 329-58.

Billington, R, *The Protestant Crusade*, New York, 1938.

Black, E, 'The Tumultuous Petitioners, The Protestant Association in Scotland', *Review of Politics*, 25, 1963, pp. 183-211.

Blake, R, *The Conservative Party from Peel to Churchill*, Eyre, London, 1970.

The Book of Airdrie: Being a Composite Picture of the Life of a Scottish Burgh, Jackson & Sons, Glasgow, 1964.

Boyce, D G, British Conservative Opinion, the Ulster Question and the Partition of Ireland, *Irish Historical Studies* LXVII, 1970-1.

Boyle, J, 'The Belfast Protestant Association and the Independent Orange Order, *Irish Historical Studies* XIII, 1962.

British and Irish Communist Organisation, *The Birth of Ulster Unionism*, Belfast, 1973.

British and Irish Communist Organisation, *The Economics of Partition*, Belfast, 1972.

Bruce, S, *No Pope of Rome! Militant Protestantism in Modern Scotland*, Mainstream, Edinburgh, 1985..

Buckland, P, 'The Unity of Ulster Unionism', *History* 60, 1972.

Bugler, J, 'The House of Orange', *New Society* 19/12/68, Vol. 12, pp. 905-6.

Bullock, J, and Drummond, A L, *The Scottish Church 1688-43*, St Andrews Press, Edinburgh, 1973.

Bullock, J, and Drummond, A L, *The Church in Victorian Scotland 1843-74*, St Andrews Press, Edinburgh, 1975.

Bullock, J, and Drummond A L, *The Church in Late Victorian Society 1874-1906*, St Andrews Press, Edinburgh, 1978.

Burleigh, J H S, *A Church History of Scotland*, Oxford University Press, London, 1960.

Burrell, S A, 'The Apocalyptic Vision of the Early Covenanters', *Scottish Historical Review*, Vol. XLIII, 1964.

Butt, J, *Scottish Themes: Essays in Honour of Prof. S G E Lythe*, Scottish Academic Press, Edinburgh, 1976.

Cahill, G A, 'Irish Catholicism and English Toryism', *Review of Politics*, 1957, pp. 62-76.

Campbell, A B, *The Lanarkshire Miners: A Social History of Their Trade Unions 1775-1974*, John Donald, Edinburgh, 1979.

Campbell, R H, Dow, J B S, *Source Book of Scottish Social and Economic History*, Oxford, 1968.

Cassirer, R, *The Irish Influence on the Liberal Movement in England 1798-1832*, Ph.D., London, 1938.

Checkland, S and O, *Industry and Ethos: Scotland 1832-1914*, Edinburgh University Press, 1989.

Clarke, J, *Working Class Culture*, Hutchison & Co., London 1979.

Collins, B E A, *Aspects of Irish Immigration into Scottish Towns (Dundee, Paisley), during the mid 19th century*, M.Phil, Edinburgh, 1979.

Corrins, R D, *William Baird and Company, Coal and Iron Masters 183–1914*, Ph.D., Strathclyde, 1974.

Crapster, B, 'Scotland and the Conservative Party in 1876', *Journal of Modern History*, xxix, 1957, p. 357.

Cornford, J, 'The Transformation of Conservatism in the late 19th Century', *Victorian Studies* 7, 1963-4, pp. 35-66.

Cowan, I B, *The Scottish Covenanters 1660-1688*, Gollancz, London, 1976.

Cunningham, H, 'The Language of Patriotism 1790-1914', *History Workshop Journal*, No. 12, Autumn 1981

Cullen, L M and Smout, T C, *Comparative Asects of Scottish and Irish Social and Economic History 1600-1900*, John Donald, Edinburgh, 1977.

Curtis, L P, *Anglo Saxons and Celts*, University of Bridgeport Press, Connecticut, 1968.

Curtis, L P, *Apes and Angels: the Irishman in Victorian Caricature*, Smithstonian Institute Press, Washington, 1971.

De Paor, L, *Divided Ulster*, Pelican, Harmondsworth, 1973.

Dickson, T, (ed), *Scottish Capitalism, Class State and Nation From Before the Union to the Present*, Lawrence & Wishart, London, 1976.

Dickson, T (ed), *Capital and Class in Scotland*, John Donald, Edinburgh, 1982.

Donaldson, G, *The Scottish Reformation*, Cambridge University Press, 1960.

Donaldson, G, *Scotland: Church and Nation Through Sixteen Centuries*, Scottish Academic Press, Edinburgh, 1972.

Farrell, M, *Northern Ireland: The Orange State*, Pluto, London, 1976.

Feuchtwanger, E J, 'The Conservative Party Under the Impact of the Second Reform Act', *Victorian Studies*, 2, (195809), pp. 289-304.

Fleming, J R, *A History of the Church in Scotland 1843-74*, T T Clarke, Edinburgh, 1927.

Foster, J, *Class Struggle and the Industrial Revolution*, Methuen & Co., London, 1974.

Foster, J, and Woolfson, C, *The Politics of the UCS Work-in*, Lawrence and Wishart, London, 1986.

Gallagher, T, 'Catholics in Scottish Politics', *Bulletin of Scottish Politics*, No. 2, Spring 1981.

Gallagher, T, *Glasgow, The Uneasy Peace*, Manchester University Press, 1987.

Gallagher, T, *Edinburgh Divided*, Mainstream, Edinburgh, 1988.

Gibbon, P, 'The Dialectic of Religion and Class in Ulster', *New Left Review*, 56, 1969.

Gibbon, P, *The Origins of Ulster Unionism*, Manchester University Press, Manchester, 1975.

Gilley, S, and Swift, R, *The Irish in the Victorian City*, Croom Helm, London, 1985.

Gilley, S, 'English Attitudes to the Irish in England 1789-1900, *Immigrants and Minorities in British Society*, Gt Holmes (ed), Allen & Unwin, London, 1978.

Gray, R, *The Aristocracy of Labour in 19th Century Britain c.1850-1914*, Oxford University Press, 1973.

Gray, R, 'Bourgeois Hegemony in Victorian Britain', in *Class Hegemony and Party*, J Bloomfield (ed), Lawrence & Wishart, London, 1977.

Gray, T, *The Orange Order*, Bodley Head, London, 1972.

Handley, J E, *The Irish in Scotland 1789-1845*, Cork University Press, 1943.

Handley, J E, *The Irish in Modern Scotland*, Cork University Press, 1947.

Handley, J E, *The Navvy in Scotland*, A Blond, London, 1970.

Hanham, H J and Thayer, G, *The British Political Fringe*, 1965.

Hardcastle, A W, *Glasgow Conservative Association 1869-86*, B.A. Thesis, Department of History, Strathclyde University, No. 143, 1973.

Harvie, C, *No Gods and Previous Few Heroes: Scotland 1914-80*, Edward Arnold, London, 1981.

Hill, R, *Toryism and the People 1832-46*, London, 1929.

Hutchinson, I G C, *Politics and Society in Mid Victorian Glasgow 1846-86*, Ph.D., University of Edinburgh, 1975.

Jackson, J., *The Irish in Britain*, Routledge & Kegan Paul, London, 1965.

Johnston, C I, *Developments in the Roman Catholic Church in Scotland 1784-1829*, Ph.D., Edinburgh, 1980.

Joyce, P, Work, *Society and Politics, the culture of the Factory in Later Victorian England*, Harvester, Brighton, 1980.

Kellas, J G, 'The Liberal Party and the Scottish Church Disestablishment Crisis', *English Historical Review*, 79, 1964, pp. 318-29.

Kellas, J G, 'The Liberal Party in Scotland 1876-1895', *Scottish Historical Review*, 44, 1965, pp. 1-16.

Kerr, B, *Irish Immigration to Great Britain*, B.Phil., Oxford, 1939.

King, E, *Scotland, Sober and Free: The Temperance Movement 1829-79*, Glasgow Museums and Art Galleries, 1979.

Knoop, D, and Jones, G, *A Short History of Freemasonry*, Manchester, 1940.

Larrain, J, *The Concept of Ideology*, Hutchinson, London, 1977.

Lenman, B, *An Economic History of Modern Scotland*, Batsford, London, 1977.

Levitt, I, and Smout, T C, *The State of the Scottish Working Class in 1843*, Scottish Academic Press, Edinburgh, 1979.

Levy, C, *Conservatism and Liberal Unionism in Glasgow 1874-1912*, Ph.D., Dundee, 1983.

Lobban, R D, 'The Irish Community in Greenock in the 19th Century', *Irish Geography*, Vol. 6, No. 3, 1971.

Lunn, K (ed)., *Hosts, Immigrants and Minorities*, Dawson, Folkstone, 1980.

Machin, C I T, *The Catholic Question in English Politics 1820-30*, Clarendon Press, Oxford, 1964.

Marwick, W, *A Short History of Labour in Scotland*, Chambers, Edinburgh, 1967.

Middlemass, K, *The Clydesiders*, Hutchinson, London, 1965.

Miles, R, *Racism and Migrant Labour*, Routledge & Kegan Paul, London, 1982.

Moorhouse, H F, 'The Political Incorporation of the British Working Class', *Sociology*, 1973.

Moorhouse, H F, 'The Marxist Theory of the Labour Aristocracy', *Social History*, Vol. 3, 1978.

Montgomery, F A, *Glasgow Radicalism 1830-48*, Ph.D., University of Glasgow, 1976.

Morris, R J, 'Bargaining with Hegemony', *Bulletin of the Scottish Society for the Study of Labour History*, No. 35, 1977.

Morris, R.J, 'Skilled Workers and the Politics of the 'Red Clyde ', *Journal of the Scottish Labour History Society*, No. 18, 1973.

Murdoch, J L, 'Policing Public Processions in Scotland, *Journal of the Law Society*, March 1983.

Murray, D M, *Scottish Church Society 1892-14: A Study of the High Church Movement in the Church of Scotland*, D.Phil., Cambridge, 1976.

Murray, B, *The Old Firm: Sectarianism, Sport and Society in Scotland*, John Donald, Edinburgh, 1984

McCaffrey, J F, *Political Reactions in Glasgow Constituencies at the General Elections of 1885 and 1886*, Ph.D., University of Glasgow, 1970.

McCaffrey, J F, 'The Origins of Liberal Unionism in the West of Scotland', *Scottish Historical Review*, 50, 1971.

McCaffrey, J F, 'The Irish Vote in Glasgow in the Later 19th Century', *Innes Review*, XXI, 1970.

McCarthy, M, *A Social Geography of Paisley*, Paisley Corporation, 1969.

McClelland, 'The Occupational Composition of Two Orange Lodges 1853', *Ulster Folklife*, Vol. 14, 1968.

McDonagh, A M, *Irish Immigrants and Labour Movements in Coatbridge and Airdrie 1891-1931*, B.A. Dissertation, University of Strathclyde, History Department (197?).

McDowell, R B, *British Conservatism 1832-1914*, Faber and Faber, London, 1957.

McLellan, J, *Larkhall,* Mathew, Larkhall, 1979.

Niebuhr, H R, *The Social Sources of Denominationalism,* Living Age Books, New York, 1960.

Patterson, B, *The Social and Working Conditions of the Ayrshire Mining Population 1840-1875,* Ayrshire Archaeology, Natural History Society, Ayr, 1972.

Patterson, H, 'Independent Orangeism and Class Conflict in Edwardian Belfast', *Proceedings of the Royal Irish Academy,* Vol. 80, Section C, No. 4, 1980.

Patterson, H, *Class Conflict and Sectarianism: The Protestant Working Class and the Belfast Labour Movement 1868-1920,* Blackstaff, Belfast, 1981.

Pelling, H, *Popular Politics and Society in Late Victorian Britain,* Macmillan, London, 1968.

Penn, R, *Skilled Workers in the Class Struggle,* Cambridge University Press, 1985.

Pollard, S, *The Economic History of British Shipbuilding 1870-1914,* Ph.D., University of London, 1951.

Poulantzas, N, *Political Power and Social Classes,* New Left Books, London, 1965.

Price, N D, *Aspects of the Scottish Liberal Party in the Central Lowland Belt 1868-1880,* Ph.D., University of Strathclyde.

Probert, B, *Beyond Orange and Green: The Political Economy of the Northern Ireland Crisis,* Zed, London, 1978.

Redford, A, *Labour Migration in England 1800-50,* Manchester University, 1976.

Reid, J M, *Kirk and Nation,* Skeffington, London, 1960.

Roberts, D, The Orange Order in Ireland: A Religious Institution?, *British Journal of Sociology* XXII, 1971,

Roxburgh, J M, *The Glasgow School Board 1873-1919,* B. Litt. University of Glasgow, 1968.

Sayer, D, 'Method and Dogma in Historical Materialism', *Sociological Review,* 1975.

Sayer, D, *Marx's Method,* Harvester, Folkstone, 1979.

Shaw, J E, *Ayrshire 1745-1950: A Social and Industrial History of the County,* Oliver & Boyd, Edinburgh, 1953.

Simms, S, 'The Orange Society, a Select Bibliography', *Irish Book Lover* Vol. 25, 1937.

Smout, T C, *A History of the Scottish People 1500-1830* Collins, London, 1969.

Smith, J, *Commonsense and Working Class Consciousness. Some Aspects of Glasgow and Liverpool Labour Movements in the Early Years of the 20th Century,* Ph.D., Edinburgh, 1984.

Smyth, W M, *The Message of the Banners,* Evangelical Protestant Society, Belfast, n.d.

Strawthorn, J, *The New History of Cumnock,* SCWS, Glasgow,

Strawthorn, J, *Ayrshire – Story of a County,* Ayrshire Archaeological and Natural History Society, Ayr, 1975.

Taylor, H A, *The Strange Case of Andrew Bonar Law,* London,

Thompson, E P, *The Making of the English Working Class,* Pelican, Harmondsworth, 1979.

Treble, J H, 'The Navvies', *Journal of the Scottish Labour History Society*, 1972, pp. 227-47.

Urwin, D W, 'The Development of the Conservative Party in Scotland till 1912', *Scottish Historical Review*, Vol. 44, 1965.

Walker, W M, 'Irish Immigrants in Scotland: Their Priests, Politics and Parochial Life', *The Historical Journal* XV, 4 1972.

Walker, W ., *Juteopolis, Dundee and its Textile Workers*, Scottish Academic Press, Edinburgh, 1979.

Waller, P J, *Democracy and Sectarianism: A Political and Social History of Liverpool 1868-1939*, Liverpool University Press, 1981.

Weber, M, *The Protestant Ethic and the Spirit of Capitalism* Allen & Unwin, London, 1976.

Wilson, A, *The Chartist Movement in Scotland*. Manchester University Press, 1970.

Wilson, B., *Sects and Society*, Heinemann, London, 1961.

Wilson, B, *Patterns of Sectarianism*, Heinemann, London, 1967.

Wolff, K H (ed), *The Sociology of George Simmel*, The Free Press, New York, 1950.

Wood, L S, 'Irish Nationalism and Radical Politics in Scotland 1800-1900', *Journal of Scottish Labour History Society*, No. 9, June, 1975.

White, R J, *The Conservative Tradition*, Black, London, 1950.

Wright, F, Protestant Ideology and Politics in Ulster, *European Journal of Sociology*, 14, 1973.

Young, J D, *The Rousing of the Scottish Working Class*, Croom Helm, London, 1979.

Zimmerman, G D, *Irish Political Street Ballads and Rebel Songs 1780-1900*, Ph.D., Geneva (No. 180), 1966.

Index

Adam, J., Orange Official, 92
Adamson, J., Orange Official, 227
Airdrie, 50, 54, 56-7, 62-3, 71, 86, 94n
222, 233
Albigensians, 6-8
Aldermen of Skinners Alley, 31
Allison, Sheriff A., 54-5, 227
America, (USA), 39, 68, 99
Angus, W., Orange Official, 227
Anti-Catholicism, 5-12, 60-1, 96-101,
130-2, See also, No popery
Apprentice Boys, 48
Ardrossan, 50, 88
Argyle Fencibles, 49
Armagh, 31-3, 37
Ashley, E., Conservative candidate,
191-2
Australia, 39, 46n
Ayrshire, 49-50, 55-7, 63-4, 71-3, 84-
5, 95, 126, 153, 175, 212, 214,
220, 230-1

Bailie, The, 108, 124, 141
Bain, J., Provost, 148, 166-7, 187n, 227
Balfour. A.J., 198
Beaconsfield's Purple Guards, 144,
169
Beith, 50, 68, 85
Belfast, 20, 40-2, 83, 86, 88, 121, 141
Biblical Criticism, 8
'Billy Bands', 1 41
Blackfriars, 74, 171, 176, 193, 198,
214
Bonar Law, A., 198
Bridgeton, 74, 84, 133, 190-4, 197,
214
British Lodges, [1795-1836], 36-39,
60-1
British Movement, 217
Browne, J., Orange Official, 225, 227.
Brunswick Clubs, 30, 37
Bryce, D., Orange Official, 217
Burgh Police Act, (Scotland), [1892],
54

Cadman, W., Conservative Activist,
165, 227
Calton, 50, 74, 84, 220
Camlachie, 74, 84, 168-9, 171, 177,
190, 217
Campbell, A., (Lord Blythswood),
144-5, 227
Canada, see Orangeism in Canada
Catholics, see Roman Catholic Church
Catholic University, 198, 207
Charleton, Rev. H., Orange Clergy-
man, 127, 227, 233
Chestnut, R., Orange Official, 221,
228
Church Discipline Bill, [1897], 200
Church of Ireland, 132-3, 135;
Disestablishment of, 10. 96, 180-1;
links with Orangeism, 121-2;
Scottish Orangemen Communicants
of, 132; 181
Church of Scotland, 129, 215:
anti-catholicism, 130-2;
competition with Free Church, 119-
20, 127-9;
Disestablishment agitation, 10, 119-
20, 125, 182;
Disruption. [1843], 117-8, 130-2;
links with Orangeism, 120-5;
1923 General Assembly, 132
Churchill, R., 42, 176
Cleary, Fr., 15, 32, 39, 46n
Clements, R., Orange Official, 62, 228
Cloughley, J., Orange historian, 67-8,
91, 95, 103
Coatbridge, 123, 130
Conditional Loyalty, 5
Connolly, J., 18, 34, 70
Conservatives, 58, 152, 161, 172-8,
196-8, 217:
bourgeois involvement in, 173-4;
conflict with LOI, 59-61, 173-4, 186,
200-2, 209, 212-3, 217;
electoral cul de sac, 162, 174-8;
Glasgow Conservative Assocation